THREE KINGDOMS
AND CHINESE CULTURE

SUNY Series in Chinese Philosophy and Culture

Roger T. Ames, *editor*

THREE KINGDOMS AND CHINESE CULTURE

Edited by

KIMBERLY BESIO
and
CONSTANTINE TUNG

STATE UNIVERSITY OF NEW YORK PRESS

Published by
STATE UNIVERSITY OF NEW YORK PRESS
Albany

Cover art: "Returning to Jingzhou" courtesy of The Hermitage, St. Petersburg

For information, address
State University of New York Press
194 Washington Avenue, Suite 305, Albany, NY 12210-2384

Production, Diane Ganeles
Marketing, Michael Campochiaro

Library of Congress Cataloging-in-Publication Data

Three kingdoms and Chinese culture / edited by Kimberly Besio, Constantine Tung.
   p. cm. — (SUNY series in chinese philosophy and culture)
Includes bibliographical references and index.
ISBN-13: 978-0-7914-7011-4 (hbk. : alk. paper)
ISBN-13: 978-0-7914-7012-1 (pbk. : alk. paper)
   1. Luo, Guanzhong, ca. 1330–ca. 1400. San guo zhi yan yi.   I. Besio, Kimberly Ann.
II. Tung, Constantine.   III. Series.
PL2690.S33T47 2007
895.1'346—dc22   2006013802

10   9   8   7   6   5   4   3   2   1

Contents

Foreword

The Language of Values in the Ming Novel *Three Kingdoms*

Moss Roberts

Three Kingdoms (Sanguo yanyi) can be read as a study of values in conflict, such as righteousness (*yi*) against loyalty (*zhong*), and filial piety (*xiao*) against brotherhood (*xiongdi*). In a time of peace and stability, these ideals should coexist and enhance one another; in a time of crisis they may become incompatible. The word *yi*, a key term in the novel, can be rendered widely in English by any of the following: responsibility, obligation, duty, the Code, commitment, service, cause, self-sacrifice, honor. In his essay in this volume Jiyuan Yu translates the term as "appropriateness." At the "conventional" end *yi* refers to the duties required of a particular role. In the "Liyun" chapter of the *Liji* the phrase "duties of men" (*zhongcheng*) covers a wide range of social and political obligations including "the father's kindness, the son's filiality . . . the ruler's benevolence, the vassal's loyalty," and so on. At the "extreme" end, however, *yi* involves sacrifice, as in the common phrases *jiuyi* (to die for the mission) or *dayi mieqin* (for the sake of the greater cause to destroy family bonds). The phrase *yanyi* in the novel's title, really a genre title, probably signifies "elaborating on the moral significances of." Thus *yi* in its semantic richness and versatility forms a contrast with the more restricted term *zhong*. In early and mid Warring States texts *zhong* typically meant "single-minded sincerity"; by the end of the period, in the *Xunzi*, for example, it means a vassal's loyalty to the state or the emperor, as in the "Liyun" phrase cited above, *zhongcheng*. Thereafter, the word *zhong* stabilized in that sense, and *cheng* roughly meant "sincerity." The common compound *zhongcheng* probably is a synonym compound, "true-hearted sincerity."

Ideally, *zhong* and *yi*, loyalty and honor, should reinforce each other. In chapter 1 of *Three Kingdoms*, when the three brothers take an oath *jieyi* (binding their honor) to die for one another and to aid the Han royal house, *zhong* and *yi* are aligned. The brothers' mutual commitment (*yi*) supports their loyal service to the Han throne. At a later point in the narrative, however, the two values become opposed. When Cao Cao captures Lord Guan (Guan Yu), Lord Guan chooses not to die honorably for his lord, Liu Bei (Xuande), who has disappeared in the chaos of battle; instead Lord Guan surrenders to Cao Cao, stipulating that his surrender is to the Han throne and not to Cao Cao, who is virtually the shogun of the Han dynasty. In this way Lord Guan turns his submission to Cao Cao into an act of loyalty to the Han emperor, a virtual puppet of Cao Cao. Soon after, upon discovering that Liu Bei still lives, Lord Guan chooses to honor his commitment to his elder brother Liu Bei: he leaves Cao Cao's service to rejoin Liu Bei. At this point *yi* again takes precedence over *zhong*. The ambiguity of values here is reflected in Zhang Fei's behavior. The third brother has become suspicious of Lord Guan's sojourn with Cao Cao, and attacks Lord Guan for betraying Liu Bei (chapter 28). It falls to Liu Bei's wives to defend Lord Guan's conduct and avert a showdown between the two brothers.

Two decades later, in the final crisis brought on by Shu's ill-fated invasion of Wu, it is Liu Bei's turn to repay Lord Guan's devotion. The Southland leader Sun Quan has captured Lord Guan and put him to death; Liu Bei decides to avenge his brother (to satisfy the demands of *yi*) by leading the Riverland (Shu-Han) attack on the Southland (Wu). By launching this invasion, Liu Bei forsakes his quest to overthrow the usurping Wei dynasty and restore the Han (*zhong*). Kongming (Zhuge Liang), who stands for *zhong* and for *xiao*, but not for *yi*, had opposed this campaign, just as he has had his doubts about the brotherhood all along. The novelist, however, means to show that *yi* prevails over *zhong*. It is perhaps for this very reason—namely, the brothers' commitment to one another rather than to Liu Bei's imperial career—that readers have taken the three into their hearts.

If for the brothers *yi* takes precedence over *zhong*, it also takes precedence over family ties and values. The rubric phrase comes from the *Zuozhuan* (Yin 4): *dayi mieqin*. This means "for the sake of the higher cause to sacrifice the bonds of kinship." The principle of *dayi mieqin* is enacted in the opening of chapter 42 of *Three Kingdoms*, when Liu Bei hurls (or pretends to hurl) his newborn son, A Dou, to the ground. Zhao Zilong had found A dou stranded on a battlefield, carried him safely back to camp, and then presented the baby to Liu Bei. (The novelist gives the task of saving A Dou to Zhao Zilong because Zilong belongs to Kongming's camp and is not part of the fraternity.) But instead of gratefully rewarding Zhao Zilong, Liu Bei throws A Dou aside, crying out, "For the sake of an infant I risked losing a commander!" Perhaps Liu Bei intended an homage to the first Han emperor, Liu Bang, who is occasionally invoked in the novel. Fleeing Xiang Yu's cavalry, Liu Bang offers to throw his son from his carriage to lighten it, as recounted in the *Shiji's* "Annals for Xiang Yu." Both leaders, Liu Bang and Liu Bei, have good reasons for publicly rejecting their sons.

Why do Liu Bei and Liu Bang reject their offspring? Why does Agamemnon sacrifice Iphigenia? Why does Abraham offer up Isaac? Each case exemplifies the rejection of *qin* (kin) for the sake of *yi*, as a means both to sustain morale among the followers and to protect a leadership position by a transcendent self-denial. This shows the power of the term *yi* to bind commitment outside as well as inside conventional relationships; *zhong* and *xiao* apply only within established relationships. *Yi* is an outer virtue. The sacrifice of personal interest and affection to the larger mission (*dayi*) enhances a leader's virtue and stature. In the specific circumstances of *Three Kingdoms,* Liu Bei is putting the principle of brotherhood above narrow family interest. An underdog contender, Liu Bei does not want his brothers and comrades to see him give in to a fatherly concern, lest it threaten the solidarity on which the whole military enterprise depends. And yet, the father-son relationship is the bedrock of dynastic government in that it effectively addresses the all-important succession problem. Every king must name an heir or risk losing control of the succession. This is the very reason Kongming values the filial tie above all others. Is it possible, then, to reconcile fraternal comradeship and filial dynasty building? I think that this is the principal problematic of *Three Kingdoms.*

In the *Analects, xiao* (filial piety), is a primary value and generally in harmony with state service and loyalty. "It is rare for someone who is filial and fraternal to defy his superiors" (*Analects* 1.2). The *Analects* advocates the integration of family and state roles in such phrases as *jun jun chen chen, fu fu zi zi,* which means "Let the ruler rule as he should and then the ministers will serve as they should; let the father guide as he should and then the sons will serve as they should" (*Analects* 12.11). Notwithstanding the placement of loyalty first in this formula, we still find an *Analects* passage where political and familial loyalty conflict, and Confucius requires the subordination of *zhong* to *xiao,* state to family. In *Analects* 13.18 Confucius expresses disapproval of a son who reports his father to the authorities for stealing a sheep.

Filial piety is the core value, the cornerstone of the Confucian ethical system. The "Zengzi" chapters of the *Da Dai Liji* are organized around this principle. The bond of father and son supports and integrates all other relationships. For the *Analects* and most other Confucian texts the *junzi* (noble man, man of honor) is the central figure. The *junzi* is an idealized royal son, fit either to rule or to support a ruler. But the *junzi* is also more than that; he is a humanitarian. Perhaps this is why in the *Analects,* we find connected to *xiao* some recognition of the complementary and faintly egalitarian principle of brotherhood (*ti*). The best-known instance is the above-cited *Analects* 1.2. Youzi, perhaps Confucius's leading disciple, combines *xiao* with *ti,* to make of each equally, the foundation of *ren,* the broad humanitarian principle that is the paramount sociopolitical value of the Confucians. Thus, Youzi used the brother-tie to widen the scope of filial

discipline. Despite holding a major place in the *Analects* (Youzi is the text's sec‐
ond speaker, appearing only after Confucius in book 1), Youzi seems less impor‐
tant than other disciples; and *xiao* and *ti* are combined only one other time in the
Analects, whose editors may not have done Youzi justice. We read in the *Mencius*
(MIIIA.4) that after Confucius's death three noted disciples (Zizhang, Zixia, and
Ziyou) had tried to put Youzi in the Master's place, only to be thwarted by Zengzi.
Note that Zixia speaks the famous phrase "within the four seas all are brothers;
need a man of honor fear having no brothers?" (*Analects* 12.5). Zixia spoke these
words to comfort Sima Niu for lacking kinsmen. Perhaps, Zixia and Youzi were
part of a *fraternité* faction close to the Mohists, for whom the principle of *jian ai,*
comprehensive love, was a family‐transcending ideal.

Zengzi, the famed exponent of filial duty, blocked this proposal to anoint
Youzi as Confucius's heir; the "Zengzi" chapters never mention *ti.* (And Confucius,
as Sima Qian tells us—perhaps ironically—in his "Kongzi shijia," died without
naming an heir, *mo neng zong yu.*) Not only did Zengzi emphasize *xiao,* but also
he is the disciple credited with emphasizing the bond between family and state.
Zengzi reinforced the doctrine of *xiao* as state ethic. Zengzi also links *xiao* with
zhong in the Zengzi chapters, but he still used *zhong* in its older sense of "single‐
minded dedication." The compound *zhong‐xiao* occurs as early as the Later Han,
but does not become a keynote value until the neo‐Confucian era. From the Song
period on down, in Japanese (*chû‐kô*) as well as in Chinese, we find the binom is
pervasive, and always in the sequence *zhong‐xiao* (never *xiao‐zhong*), crystallizing
the primacy of state over family.

As a touchstone of the ideology of Chinese civilization, *zhong‐xiao* prevailed.
Youzi's idea of balancing (if not equalizing) filial and fraternal devotion, of widen‐
ing *xiao* to include *ti,* did not develop in the main Confucian tradition. Tied to and
shaped by *xiao,* *ti* was limited to mean obedience to the elder brother. An interest‐
ing instance of *xiao‐ti* is in the Guodian text *Liu de,* where it seems to mean "family
values." In this text, family takes precedence over state: "[S]ever relations with the
ruler before severing relations with the father." In the *Analects,* however, only traces
of *xiao‐ti* survive, as we have seen.

Mencius saved something of Youzi's *xiao‐ti* formula, though in weakened
form, by linking filial piety to *ren* and fraternal love to *yi.* *Ren‐yi* exists in the *Men‐
cius* mainly as a bound term, and sometimes seems equivalent to "civilized values."
Seldom taking up *yi* as an independent value—indeed, opposed to construing *yi*
as an "outer ethic"—Mencius often speaks of *ren* as a gate and *yi* as a road, *ren*
implying an orientation or direction or even a frame of mind, in contrast to *yi,*
the actual course of conduct. Thus, for the most part *yi* was subordinate to *ren.*
Much as *ren‐yi* seems to function as a term that transcends its components, with
a meaning like "civilized values," so *xiao‐ti* probably meant little more than family
values—filial service and fraternal harmony. The two terms lose their individual
force and the first dominates. Perhaps allowing *ti* to have equal status with *xiao*
would have made inheritance patterns too chaotic. Perhaps there was enough to do

to control the sons of multiple wives without the complications that including the claims of brothers (and the nephews) would create. Wasn't this one of the lessons of the round-robin interkingdom wars of the entire Warring States era, wars driven by succession crises?

Thus, *xiao* become the dominant value. The main Confucian interest was supporting aristocratic lineage. The impulse to limit, refine, or reform *xiao* never prevailed, because generational continuity, meaning stability of inheritance of position and property, was all-important to the Confucians, who spoke for the landholder lords and the state bureaucracy that served them. And those interests prevailed over the idealist strains in the tradition. Zhuge Liang's political orthodoxy on this point is underscored by his *hao*: Kongming, "wise as Confucius."

In Chinese culture, brotherhood, as an independent relationship outside the established roles, acquired a quasi-subversive significance. Though not called *ti*, but rather *baixiongdi*, fraternal devotion severed from filiality and family, or in conflict with them, is the crucial relationship in certain major works of Chinese fiction, among them *Three Kingdoms* and of course *Shuihu zhuan* or *Outlaws of the Marsh*. In the latter work, the central figure is Song Jiang. He aids, joins, and eventually leads the outlaw brotherhood, but his filial devotion conflicts with his commitment to his brothers. And this contradiction not only defines his character, but also drives the narrative's dialectical swings between rebellion and capitulation.

Perhaps *fraternité* would be a translation for *jieyi* (strangers taking an oath of brotherhood), distinguishing it from the more limited fraternal devotion (*ti*), which is restricted to blood brothers. Notice particularly the independent use of *yi* and the absence of the more familial *ren* in this brotherhood discourse. The brother-oath has a touch of the "barbarian" as well as the underworld about it, since most Ming readers would remember that before going into battle Mongol warriors took the *anda* or the pact of brothers-in-arms, the band of brothers.

In the first chapter of *Three Kingdoms*, three unrelated warrior-heroes-to-be—Liu Bei, Lord Guan, and Zhang Fei—pledge a fraternal oath in the Peach Garden (the peach symbolizes fidelity in marriage according to *Shijing* ode 6, "Tao yao"). The three loyally place themselves at the service of the Han emperor Ling, and win signal honors in suppressing the Yellow Scarves revolt. In effect, the oath ties loyalty to brotherhood and *xiao* is left out. The brothers' oath supersedes all other family ties, with the exception of the useful claim that Liu Bei is a distant relation of the emperor. This family connection counteracts the barbarian or underworld taint on a brotherhood formed by strangers, and it also endows Liu Bei with a degree of lineage prestige or virtue, for he is a Liu and thus can claim royal blood and a remote right of succession. At the same time, the brotherhood's moral standing is enhanced by contrast with established families in power, both at the imperial court and in the regional capitals. These families are breaking apart due to succession conflicts among sons and brothers—manifest failures of both *xiao* and *ti*. In these ancillary conflicts the junior usually displaces the senior brother—a sign of moral disorder and a harbinger of political disintegration. Dong Zhuo commits the same offense against descent protocol when he deposes Shaodi (age 14) and enthrones his younger brother Xiandi (age 9), who reigns until the end of the Han. With conventional family bonds breaking down at the dynastic and regional governing levels, the Peach Garden brotherhood initially offers a possible new way to organize political rule, a reaching toward something like *fraternité*, even *egalité*. (*Shui hu* further develops this theme in a revolutionary direction.)

But can dynastic government be organized this way? Can the realm be governed on such a principle? The author of the novel raises the question but does not resolve it. He simply shows the conflict between *fraternité* and dynasty (with its dependence on *xiao*) as forms of organization, and he portrays Liu Bei as the liminal figure who must choose between the two. Note, for example, how Liu Bei's adoption of Kou Feng annoys his two brothers, who protest their elder brother's acquisition of a son with the remark, "What do you want with another's young?" Later the other two brothers acquire families, too. These acts and other instances of filial relations and responsibilities weaken their fraternal bond.

Another example of the conflict between family and comrade solidarity concerns Liu Bei's loss of Shan Fu, his first military adviser. Cao Cao manages to lure Shan Fu to his camp by appeals to his filial piety. In order to win Shan Fu over, Cao Cao has taken Shan Fu's mother prisoner and uses her handwriting to forge letters to her son calling him home. Taken in by Cao Cao's ruse, Shan Fu tells Liu Bei he must leave his service to go to his mother. An adviser urges Liu Bei to kill Shan Fu because he knows so much about the brothers' military operations, but Liu Bei magnanimously lets Shan Fu go over to the enemy side. When Shan Fu reaches his mother, however, she condemns him for joining Cao Cao and then hangs herself, both to shame her son and to prevent him from serving Cao Cao. The incident puts filial piety in a negative light on the mother's authority.

The parting of Liu Bei and Shan Fu is a crucial episode forming the bridge to the imminent meeting between Liu Bei and Kongming. Each man tests the other. Liu Bei needs to confirm that Shan Fu will not serve Cao Cao; Shan Fu needs to verify Liu Bei's acclaimed high-mindedness. In their parting scene Shan Fu reassures Liu Bei that he will never use his knowledge to aid Cao Cao. But he remains unconvinced that Liu Bei will actually let him go. It is a defining moment. Only after he has ridden safely beyond reach can Shan Fu confirm to his own satisfaction Liu Bei's legendary virtue. Having done so, he then rides back to Liu Bei and recommends Kongming. Mindful of Liu Bei's need for a substitute adviser, Shan Fu describes Kongming's talents and urges Liu Bei to seek him out. Then he parts with Liu Bei for the second time. In one of the novel's humorous touches, Shan Fu rides by Kongming's dwelling to inform him that Liu Bei may visit. When Shan Fu knocks on the gate, Kongming receives his visitor personally and promptly. (Later Kongming will compel Liu Bei to make three arduous trips before gaining an audience.) In this way the novel prepares the reader for the entry of Zhuge Liang (Kongming) in chapters 36–37.

Kongming represents the traditional values of filiality bonded to loyalty; he proves to be an ideal dutiful son to Liu Bei, a veritable *Analects junzi*. His fidelity to his roles contrasts with Cao Cao, who overreaches as prime minister and becomes a usurper for his clan. Later in the story, Kongming (together with Zhao Zilong) supports Liu Bei's natural son Liu Shan (A Dou) as the rightful successor to the throne of Shu-Han. Liu Bei views Kongming (twenty years his junior) as the ideal prime minister and political counselor. But the brothers see him as a threat to themselves and the brotherhood, and they show their hostility to the young consigliere. For his part, Kongming is determined not to serve under Liu Bei until he has established his authority over Lord Guan and Zhang Fei. Thereafter, he makes a point of humbling them at every opportunity, while seeking to educate Zhang Fei. The ideal vassal, he wants the brothers to show loyalty to Liu Bei, to serve him as subordinates and vassals, not as brothers; he is hostile to the quasi-egalitarian brother-bond even if he recognizes its military usefulness. But Kongming will not win his battle against the brotherhood.

The contradiction between the filial and the fraternal reaches a climax when Liu Bei has to choose between his role as elder brother and his role as father-emperor. After Cao Cao and the Southern leaders capture and execute Lord Guan, the Peach Garden oath is inevitably invoked. Liu Bei yields to Zhang Fei's pleas and decides to avenge his fallen brother. Significantly, Lord Guan has brought defeat on himself by putting his parental interest above Liu Bei's political cause. Lord Guan's refusal to let his daughter marry Sun Quan's son violates Kongming's primary strategic principle: protect the alliance with the south in order to maintain a united front against the Cao-Wei northern kingdom. Kongming tries his best to assure Liu Bei that after Wei is defeated, the South will fall, but Liu Bei remains determined to attack the South at once, sacrificing his imperial hopes to honor the brother-oath. Thus *yi* prevails over *zhong*, brother-bond over *jun-chen*, and military solidarity over dynastic politics. Lord Guan's death has forced on Liu Bei a fateful choice: to attack the South at once rather than follow Kongming's long-range war plan. Kongming's bitterness over Liu Bei's choice is immortalized in the last line of Du Fu's poem "Bazhentu" (The Maze of Eight Ramparts): "A legacy of rue / that his king had choked on Wu"(end of chapter 84).

The failure of the attack on the Southland does not mean that the novelist finally rejects the brotherhood principle. The novel does not validate either the succession of Liu Shan or the brotherhood; both lead to failure. Dynastic politics are criticized, but no cure is proposed. *Three Kingdoms* is a problem novel. To Ming readers some twelve centuries later, the failure of Kongming's plan to save the Han dynasty sounds the tragic doom of Chinese civilization as a unified imperium. The grandeur and the glory of Han were rapidly fading. And Kongming, not the brotherhood, represents an idealized Han dynasty that might have been restored. The historical reunification under the Jin dynasty (with which the novel ends) was a weak stay against the northern foes. The Jin lasted one generation, from 280 to 317. Thus, the fall of the Han meant that invading powers were to play a large role in a China that remained divided for almost four hundred years, until the Sui-Tang reunification at the beginning of the seventh century.

The interim was marked by short dynasties, with no magnificent lineage like that of the Han, and no vast integrated territory governed by a unified bureaucracy; and Buddhism became more ideologically powerful than Confucianism. The Han became the archetype of dynastic achievement, perhaps never again to be equaled, but always alive in the collective imagination. If the author of *Three Kingdoms* had any contemporary agenda, perhaps it was to warn whichever Ming emperor(s) reigned during his lifetime about the fragility of political power. For the Ming began with an emperor who imagined himself as following the model of the first Han emperor, Liu Bang, thus creating a standard of self-evaluation for his successors. The novel, however, dwells not on the first Han reign but on the last. Did the novelist perversely portray the fall of the Han to a dynasty that took the Han as its model?

Perhaps China's only tragic hero in the Shakespearean sense, Kongming is immortalized in Du Fu's "Lines written in memory of Zhuge Liang, Prime Minister of Shu-Han," a poem included in chapter 105 of the novel. In the poem Du Fu freezes Kongming in time. Like the figures on Keats's Grecian urn, fixed in their poses of eternal expectation, Kongming is imagined dying with his men at the front, ever-awaiting word of victory over the Wei, a victory that history never delivered.

> "His Excellency's shrine, where would it be found?"
> "Past Damask Town, where cypresses grow dense."
> Its sunlit court, gem-bright greens—a spring unto themselves.
> Leaf-veiled, the orioles—sweet notes to empty air.
> Thrice to him Liu Bei sued, keen to rule the realm:
> Two reigns Kongming served—steady old heart—
> To die, his host afield, the victory herald yet to come—
> Weep, O heroes! Drench your fronts, now and evermore.

Acknowledgments

The essays collected in this volume are the output of the conference "The Historical, Fictional, Theatrical, and Artistic Three Kingdoms: A Sino-American Colloquium." Held in Chengdu and Nanchong (both in Sichuan Province, PRC) from May 28 to June 1, 2001, the colloquium was followed by a three-day excursion to Langzhong, a beautiful city over which Zhang Fei once presided as magistrate, and where he was eventually assassinated, and to Jian'ge, which, amid majestic mountains, was the last defensive position of the Shu-Han Kingdom. Sichuan University (Sichuan daxue, Chengdu), Sichuan Normal College (Sichuan shifan xueyuan, Nanchong), Southwest Petroleum Institute (Xinan shiyou xueyuan, Nanchong), and the State University of New York at Buffalo jointly sponsored the conference.

Our deep appreciation goes first to the Chiang Ching-Kuo Foundation for International Scholarly Exchanges (U.S.A.), which provided a generous grant to enable participants from the United States to attend this conference on "Three Kingdoms Culture" (*Sanguo wenhua*). The grant ensured the initial success of the Colloquium on this important and colorful subject, which holds such a special place within the Chinese imagination.

We are also grateful to Baozhen Dong, Party Secretary of the Southwest Petroleum Institute (SWPI, now Southwest Petroleum University). Secretary Dong served as the liaison between the American and Chinese conference organizers throughout the entire process of the preparation. Secretary Dong and Dr. Zhimin Du, Vice-President of the SWPI, and their colleagues were responsible for the logistics of the conference. We are much obliged to the noted historian, President Zhengsong She, of Sichuan Normal College at Nanchong and his colleagues; to Professor Beichen Fang, Director of the Three Kingdoms Culture Research Center of Sichuan University; and to Professor Tingzhi Wang, Dean of Sichuan University's College of History and Culture for their contributions to the success of the conference.

During the conference and the excursion, the Party Secretaries, Mayors, and other community leaders of Nanchong, Langzhong, and Jian'ge County graciously extended their hospitality to us. The three cities supplied police escorts, hosted exquisite banquets, and provided specialists to accompany us to various historical landmarks, marvelous temples, and other cultural sites. We will always remember the warm welcome we received.

We express our sincere gratitude to Southwest Petroleum Institute's Messrs. Xinghong Yang, Yiping Sun, Shuguang Mu, and Hong Wang who accompanied us on the excursion. We warmly remember Director Qijun Kang of the SWPI's Chengdu guesthouse, and his staff members who ensured the comfort of each conference participant. The chauffeurs of the SWPI guesthouse deserve special thanks for navigating us through winding and treacherous, but gorgeous, back-country roads.

On the American side, our thanks go to Stephen Dunnett, Vice Provost of International Education, SUNY Buffalo, who was most kind to render his support to the conference on behalf of his university, and Leah Doherty, assistant to the Chair of the then Department of Modern Languages and Literatures, who offered her generous help with the preparation of the colloquium. Catherine Pagani, who arrived at Chengdu a few days before the commencement of the colloquium, helped finalize several conference panels with her quick wit and enthusiastic efficiency.

The coeditors gratefully acknowledge Colby College's Information Technology Services for much needed technical support during the preparation of this manuscript for publication. Ankeney Weitz supplied vital encouragement and professional advice. Catherine Fillebrown contributed in many ways, both large and small, during the final stages of editing; we appreciate both her careful attention to detail and her infectious enthusiasm.

We express our gratitude to the State University of New York Press for choosing to include this volume in their SUNY Series in Chinese Philosophy and Culture under the editorship of Roger T. Ames. We particularly want to thank Nancy Ellegate, Senior Acquisitions Editor of SUNY Press. Her many thoughtful and professional comments and suggestions guided us through the final process of preparing this volume of essays for press.

Finally, we acknowledge the valuable contributions made to the colloquium by Michael J. Farmer of Brigham Young University, John W. Killigrew of SUNY Brockport, David Rolston of the University of Michigan, Roger DesForges of SUNY Buffalo, and our Chinese colleagues on the other shore of the Pacific. We hope that this volume on *Three Kingdoms* will spur further scholarship—both individual and collaborative—on this vital and fascinating element of Chinese culture.

Introduction

The title of the colloquium for which the essays in this volume were first produced was "The Historical, Fictional, Theatrical, and Artistic Three Kingdoms: A Sino-American Colloquium." The Chinese equivalent for this title was simply "Three Kingdoms Culture" (*Sanguo wenhua*), a phrase that encompasses a wide range of meanings requiring more elucidation for a Western audience. The quintessential expression of "Three Kingdoms Culture" is the novel *Three Kingdoms* (*Sanguo yanyi*) one of the "four masterworks of the Ming novel" (*Mingdai si da qishu*).[1] This novel has been made more accessible to English speakers in recent years through Moss Roberts's superb translation.[2] Set in the historical era of disunion (AD 220–280), *Three Kingdoms* depicts pitched battles and Machiavellian schemes; alliances are formed, broken, and reformed as various claimants jockey to attain "the Mandate of Heaven" (*Tian Ming*), and military men and civil advisers alike attempt to identify and back the most likely victor. The novel is vast and sprawling, covering a span of over a hundred years and with over 1000 named characters appearing within its pages; at the same time, it lays claim to some of the most memorable episodes and figures in Chinese literature, including Liu Bei, Guan Yu, Zhang Fei, Cao Cao, and Zhuge Liang.

The most prominent strand within the narrative features Liu Bei and his men. Liu is introduced in chapter 1 as a distant scion of the ruling family, whose own imperial aspirations had been apparent from his childhood. At the time the narrative begins he is twenty-eight. In the first chapter he swears an oath of brotherhood with the two other heroes, Guan Yu and Zhang Fei. The three men swear to uphold the Han dynasty mandate, and to support each other to the death in a solemn ceremony. The consequences of this oath are momentous, and are discussed in more detail in Moss Roberts's foreword and in several of the essays in this volume.

In chapter 1 and throughout the novel, the valiant ideals of Liu and his sworn brothers form a contrast with the treacherous villain (*jian xiong*) Cao Cao. Cao, too has imperial aspirations, and his attitude toward achieving his goals is famously summarized by his own words in chapter 4: "Better to wrong the world, than have it wrong me" (38.) In the early chapters of the novel Liu and Cao team up to support the Han emperor against, first, the rebellious Yellow Scarves, and then against the traitorous minister Dong Zhuo and his general, Lü Bu. However, Cao, who has a genius for recognizing the value of men, soon realizes that Liu and his sworn brothers pose a serious threat to his ambitions to supplant the Han, and they part ways. Cao Cao is a complex figure that generations have loved to hate. In chapter 8 of this collection Elizabeth Wichmann-Walczak discusses a contemporary drama that draws on the complexities of Cao's character to create an antihero with human flaws of universal significance.

After the alliance between Cao Cao and Liu Bei dissolves, Liu is in a difficult position. He has the allegiance of great warriors, among them his sworn brothers, Guan Yu and Zhang Fei, but he has no territory in which to establish himself and he lacks a strategist to help him attain a base of operations. At this point in the novel Liu learns of the genius Zhuge Liang, called Kongming, who is living in seclusion. If any single figure can be said to dominate the novel it is Kongming, even though he appears much later in the narrative than Liu Bei or Cao Cao. The novel combines aspects of history and popular legend to create a character with enduring appeal. In this volume of essays chapters 5 and 6 both explore some of the precedents for the novel's depiction of Kongming, and the connections between changing ideology and Zhuge Liang's evolving characterization.

Determined to gain Zhuge's assistance, Liu visits Zhuge Liang's thatched hut three times before finally meeting with him. Zhuge Liang is so moved by Liu Bei's appreciation of his talent that he agrees to assist Liu, and immediately lays out a plan that will result in the tripartite division of the empire, with Liu occupying the Riverlands (later the Kingdom of Shu, roughly equivalent to modern Sichuan), one of the three parts. Because Zhuge views Cao Cao as the most dangerous enemy, he proposes that Liu ally himself with Sun Quan, the leader of the Southlands (later the kingdom of Wu), the area that makes up the third leg of the "tripod" that Zhuge envisions.

This strategy succeeds wonderfully at first, and results in a stunning defeat of Cao Cao in the Battle of Red Cliff (Chibi). However, from the first, tensions exist between the Sun and Liu camps. Zhuge himself contributes to these tensions by his baiting of Sun Quan's military adviser, Zhou Yu, who eventually dies of apoplexy and chagrin after being bested multiple times by Zhuge Liang. The death of Guan Yu at the hands of one of Sun Quan's generals seals the doom of the alliance between Liu and Sun. Against Zhuge's advice, Liu launches an unsuccessful campaign against Sun's Southlands (Wu), and dies sick and defeated. Liu Bei's son, Liu Shan (called in childhood A Dou), succeeds him, and Zhuge Liang devotes the rest of his life to fulfilling Liu Bei's ambition of reuniting China and reestablishing the Liu family as rulers of the Han. After repeated attempts to retake the North by conquering Wei, Zhuge Liang himself dies. His opponent at the time of his death is the Wei general Sima Yi, whose descendants will eventually depose the Caos and reunite China under the Jin dynasty. The novel ends with the fall of Wu, and concludes with a long poem recapping the events and remarking on the evanescence of human life.

The novel is the first thing that comes to mind upon hearing the term "Three Kingdoms," but there actually exists a vast complex of Three Kingdoms materials in a wide variety of mediums directed toward diverse audiences. While most of the articles in this volume center on the novel, a greater appreciation of the multifarious aspects of "Three Kingdoms culture" in both traditional and contemporary China will enhance comprehension of the essays that follow.

THE HISTORICAL ORIGINS OF THE NOVEL

In Chinese history "Three Kingdoms" refers to the period during and immediately following the fall of the Han dynasty (206 BCE–AD 220). As the dynasty collapsed, three leaders gradually emerged as the most important, among the many warlords vying for power: Cao Cao (AD 155–220), the titular founder of the kingdom of Wei, occupying the northern part of the former Han empire; Sun Quan (AD 182–252), who founded the Kingdom of Wu in the south; and Liu Bei (AD 161–223) of the southwestern kingdom of Shu. The standoff between these three powers lasted for some sixty years (AD 220–280) and the empire was only fully— albeit temporarily—reunified after the Sima family deposed the Wei and founded the Jin dynasty (AD 265–320).[3]

Following a precedent established during the Han, the Jin Dynasty commissioned Chen Shou (AD 233–297) to write an official history of the Three Kingdoms period. The result was *Chronicle of the Three Kingdoms (Sango zhi)*. Over a century later, Pei Songzhi (372–451) supplemented Chen's history with annotations drawing from a variety of sources including unofficial histories, semihistorical accounts, and popular tales. Pei's annotations were three times as long as the actual history itself, and since most of the works Pei utilized are no longer extant his annotations provide valuable supplementary information about the people, places, and incidents described in the *Chronicle*.

The structure of *Chronicle of the Three Kingdoms* assumes that the kingdom of Wei was the legitimate successor to the Han dynasty. Only the chronicle of Wei contains a section of "annals" (*ji* = records of emperors and their families.) The life stories of Liu Bei and Sun Quan are titled biographies (*zhuan*), and the two men are referred to as "rulers" (*zhu*) rather than as "emperors" (*di*). Sima Guang (1019–86) concurred with this judgment—that the Wei was the legitimate successor to the Han—in his continuous history of China, *Comprehensive Mirror for Aid in Government (Zizhi tongjian)*. However, in *Outline and Digest of the Comprehensive Mirror for Aid in Government (Zizhi tongjian gangmu)* the Southern Song neo-Confucian Zhu Xi (1130–1200) argued that Liu Bei and his kingdom of Shu had the greater claim to moral legitimacy. Zhu Xi's stance is intimately related to the political situation of the Southern Song regime, a government that claimed legitimacy as the successor to the Northern Song but was continually threatened by a northern power occupying the traditional center of China.[4] The shift in sympathy seen in *Outline and Digest* anticipates the novel, which, as we have seen, focuses on and directs sympathy toward figures connected to the Shu camp. However, all the histories discussed above influenced the novel to some degree, while the novel in turn shaped, and continues to mold to this day, the common person's understanding of the history of the Three Kingdoms period.

In this collection, two essays explore the links between the novel and historiography in more depth. George Hayden's "The Beginning of the End" compares the descriptions of the last years of the Han dynasty in histories and in *Three Kingdoms*. Hoyt Tillman's "Selected Historical Sources for *Three Kingdoms*" focuses on two Song historians' appraisals of Zhuge Liang, and the impact of these appraisals on the fictional portrayal of Kongming. These essays illustrate how a rich array of historical sources was incorporated creatively within the novel.

A MILLENNIUM OF THREE KINGDOMS CULTURE

During the thousand-year span between the Three Kingdoms period and the advent of the novel, tales and traditions continuously accreted around the figures, places and events of the Three Kingdoms period. Prefiguring later historiography and the novel, sympathy was often directed toward the Shu cause. Literati poetry, popular religion, and popular entertainment all reflect aspects of folklore related to the Three Kingdoms period, and their influence is, in turn, evident within the novel.

The Three Kingdoms period served as the inspiration for a number of Tang poets; a number of their poems were incorporated into some editions of the novel. The great poet Du Fu (712–70) was particularly fascinated with Liu Bei's adviser, Zhuge Liang (Kongming), and wrote over twenty poems on that subject alone.[5] Speaking of Du Fu's poems on the Three Kingdoms, Moss Roberts says: "Long before the novel in any form, these poems had contributed much to the development of Liu Xuande [Liu Bei], Kongming, and others as defenders of an imperiled royal house; in later dynasties they were to become nationalistic symbols in the collective imagination of the Chinese."[6]

The poems of Du Fu and others were often inspired by a visit to a temple honoring one or another of the Three Kingdoms figures, and many figures were worshiped locally. Langzhong, the city where Zhang Fei once presided as magistrate, boasts a temple in his honor. A temple dedicated to Zhuge Liang erected adjacent to the site of Liu Bei's tomb in the city of Chengdu dates back to the seventeenth century and remains a popular tourist destination to this day. However, the Three Kingdoms figure that rose the highest within the official national pantheon was the Shu general, Guan Yu. State-sponsored worship of Guan Yu began in the Song-Yuan periods, reached maturity in the Ming dynasty, and continued throughout the Qing, thus paralleling the development of the novel.[7] The novel, which refers to Guan Yu as "Lord Guan" (Guan Gong), includes a scene describing Guan's apotheosis after his death.

Anecdotal evidence from the Song and Yuan dynasties indicates that Three Kingdoms was a subject regularly mined by popular entertainers. The earliest texts extant that developed out of popular entertainment date from the Yuan dynasty. The vernacular narrative *New Fully Illustrated Plain Speech on "Chronicles of Three Kingdoms"* (*Xin Quanxiang Sanguo zhi pinghua* hereafter referred to as the *Pinghua*) was published during the Zhizhi reign period (1321–23).[8] The text is written in alternating passages of prose and poetry, and as the title advertises, is accompanied by illustrations that occupy the upper third of every page. Another illustrated vernacular narrative drawing on the Three Kingdoms legend *The Story of Hua Guansuo* (*Hua Guansuo zhuan*) was published during the Ming Chenghua period (1465–1488).[9] There are three plays on Three Kingdoms themes among the thirty extant *zaju* play texts that date from the Yuan dynasty, and another nineteen *zaju* plays from Ming collections.

The very fact that these are all print texts suggests that they were not primarily aimed at a popular audience, and this is confirmed by what we know of the provenance of some of them. *The Story of Hua Guansuo* was discovered in the grave of the wife of a minor official. Many of the *zaju* play texts from Ming collections were originally copied from the Ming imperial archives. However, these texts do simulate popular performance, and the events described in these texts seem to spring from a tradition separate from historiography, as incidents not in any history appear multiple times.

Many incidents in these Yuan and early Ming vernacular texts became essential episodes within the novel. In her essay in chapter 6, Kimberly Besio examines the *zaju Bowang shao tun*, which features scenes from Zhuge Liang's early career, including Liu Bei's third visit to Zhuge's thatched hut. As discussed above, this is a pivotal episode within the novel. The famous "Peach Garden Pledge" (*taoyuan jieyi*) that begins the novel is described in the *Pinghua*, *The Story of Hua Guansuo*, and an early Ming *zaju* titled *The Peach Garden Pledge*.[10] The details of the incident are slightly different in each of these works, but also share many common features that suggest a similar origin.

In the novel this pledge exemplifies the competing values that play out within its pages, as will be discussed in the essays of Roberts, Tung, Cheung, and Yu. While the novel owes its basic story line to history, the multilayered portrayals of people and events within its pages are due to its assimilation of literary and folk materials from this millennium of Three Kingdoms culture.

THE NOVEL *THREE KINGDOMS*: EDITIONS AND INFLUENCE

There is a great deal we still do not know about the origins of the novel *Three Kingdoms*, as Bojun Shen discusses in the final chapter of this collection. The oldest extant edition of *Three Kingdoms* was published in 1522. The full title of this edition is *Sanguo zhi tongsu yanyi*; it is often referred to as the "tongsu edition" (TS), or the "Jiajing edition" by the period of the reign in which it was published. In this and all subsequent editions of *Three Kingdoms*, authorship is attributed to Luo Guanzhong, who was active in the latter half of the fourteenth century. Thus, there is a gap of over one hundred years between when Luo supposedly wrote the novel and the earliest extant edition. Further, a large gap exists between the depiction of Three Kingdoms incidents in the TS and the Yuan and early Ming vernacular texts discussed above. Shen points out that within contemporary scholarship a widely accepted theory of the origins of the novel posits an originary text authored by Luo from which descended a filiation of editions separate from the line of editions descending from the TS. These editions, published during the Ming and Qing periods, are referred to collectively as *zhizhuan* editions.

While the connections between these early editions of *Three Kingdoms* remain an important subject for academics to further clarify, the average modern reader knows the novel through Mao Zonggang's edition, published in the mid-1660s. Mao Zonggang put his stamp on the text through a number of editorial changes, as well as through prefatory instructions to the reader and interlinear notes.[11] Moss Roberts observes in the afterword to his translation, "The Mao edition seems to shift the history-fiction balance toward the 'purely literary' end of the scale . . ." (965). It is not coincidental that in the present volume the two authors most concerned with the literary qualities of the novel, Constantine Tung and Dominic Cheung, focus exclusively on the Mao edition. Moss Roberts based his translation on the Mao edition, but in his notes remarked on points where the Mao edition differed from the TS.

The Mao edition of *Three Kingdoms* quickly eclipsed the earlier editions of the novel as well as all previous vernacular works, decisively influencing drama and popular entertainment drawing from the story complex from the seventeenth century to the present. *Three Kingdoms* has played an important role in modern and contemporary Chinese culture, politics, and society. In his foreword to Moss Roberts's translation, John S. Service describes how the behavior of Sichuan warlords in the 1920s and the Communists and Nationalists during the 1930s and 1940s all seemed to take the novel as a template for political and military action (xiii–xiv.) References to *Three Kingdoms* are used to this day as a means to discuss politics, or as a metaphor for the universal human condition.

Three Kingdoms enters contemporary language through such expressions as "Speak of Cao Cao" (a phrase similar to the English "speak of the devil") or referring to a child as an "A Dou" when he or she is a disappointment to the parent.

As both Jinhee Kim and Junhao Hong discuss in their essays, the influence of *Three Kingdoms* now spreads well beyond the boundaries of China. *Three Kingdoms* is known to the world through print, television, and (especially) through a number of computer games based on the novel. Kim notes the popularity of these computer games in South Korea, and a Google search of English-language sites on the Internet reveals several elaborate Web sites devoted to these games. Due to modern technology *Three Kingdoms* is rapidly becoming a part of global culture; given the proven appeal of the novel and its characters, it might well continue entertaining audiences into the next millennium.

OVERVIEW OF THIS BOOK

The contributors to this collection of essays represent an array of disciplines including history, literature, philosophy, art history, theater, cultural studies, and communications, thus demonstrating the diversity of backgrounds from which study of *Three Kingdoms* can be approached. The essays are arranged into four groups: part 1, *Three Kingdoms* and Chinese Values; part 2, *Three Kingdoms* and Chinese History; part 3, *Three Kingdoms* in Chinese Drama and Art; and part 4, *Three Kingdoms* in Contemporary East Asia. Individually and collectively, these essays demonstrate the incredible hold that the novel and related Three Kingdoms material has had on the Chinese imagination over time and across various levels of society.

Moss Roberts has graced our collection with a foreword that is at once an elegant appreciation of the novel and an incisive summary of the contradictory values that animate *Three Kingdoms*. The implications of these contradictions are further explored throughout this volume but are the particular concern of the essays in part 1.

The three essays in part 1 all focus on the novel. The first two essays, by Constantine Tung and Dominic Cheung, respectively, explore the tragic elements of the novel as a means of illuminating the novel's universal appeal. In discussing the novel's tragic contradictions, Roberts, Tung, and Cheung all single out the dilemma of how to apply the value of *yi*, which Jiyuan Yu translates as "appropriateness." In the third essay in part 1 Yu concentrates on the philosophical significance of this concept in both the novel and early Confucian texts.

Constantine Tung sees the novel as an ethical and moral tragedy of epic grandeur in which cosmic will foreordains each hero's moral commitment to an impossible political condition. Since for Tung, the novel pits a man's will against the will of heaven, the *Three Kingdoms* heroes are doomed not "because they have tragic flaws, but because they refuse to compromise with cosmic preordination."

Dominic Cheung also focuses on cosmic foreordination, that is, the novel's assumption of an inevitable historical oscillation between decline and prosperity. This momentum is revealed in the opening lines of the Mao edition of the novel: "[T]he empire long divided, must unite; long united, must divide." The decline of Han despotism gave the warlords from various regions a golden opportunity to emerge as heroes. According to Cheung, the tension of the novel is created by the struggle between the intentions of the heroes' efforts and the realization of their failures.

In his essay, Jiyuan Yu begins with the assertion that *Three Kingdoms* "has been effective in popularizing Confucian moral ideals and instilling them in individual moral life and in the social structure." He reads the novel's treatment of "appropriateness" (*yi*) as a means of understanding how a concept from early Confucian philosophy was applied in a later period. The essay concludes that the novel's embodiment of Confucian virtue reveals a problem: the lack of hard-and-fast rules within this philosophy makes it difficult to sort out how to behave. There is no one right way to act that is applicable in all instances. However, Yu claims, this only demonstrates that Confucianism truly grasps "the complexities of human ethical life." As Roberts, Tung, and Cheung, and Yu all contend, the claim of *Three Kingdoms* to greatness springs precisely from its profound exposition of these complexities.

Part 2 consists of two essays that elucidate connections between history and the novel. This section begins with the beginning—both of the novel and of the story cycle itself. George Hayden's paper discusses the opening of the novel by comparing portents, responses, and choices of the emperors in historical records with the novelist's discretion in using them. Hayden concludes that the novel expresses "both admonition and testament to the human will" in the complexity of choice between freedom and fate. His conclusion thus harks back to the discussions in part 1.

In the second essay of part 2, Hoyt Cleveland Tillman studies the contributions of several historical sources to the transformation of the portrayal of Zhuge Liang (Kongming) in the novel *Three Kingdoms*. While the Jin historian Chen Shou's generally positive assessment of Zhuge Liang includes a criticism of his military abilities, in the novel Kongming is portrayed as a brilliant strategist and military commander, and even a "clever sage with tricks." Tillman considers the contributions of the Song historians Sima Guang and Chen Liang (1143–1194) to this transformation. Tillman's essay considers the complex role of shifting values in the transformation of Kongming, and thus proves the acuity of Moss Roberts's observation in the foreword: "*Three Kingdoms* can be read as a study of values in conflict."

The visual and performing arts have been powerful vehicles for spreading knowledge of characters and events from *Three Kingdoms* among the illiterate. While the novel was only accessible to the literate, the stories within it resonated with a broad range of the population. As the papers in part 3 demonstrate, a focus on *Three Kingdoms* can also lead to important insights concerning the history of drama and visual art in China.

By looking at two different editions—one Yuan and one Ming—of the *zaju* play *Bowang shao tun*, Kimberly Besio's essay explores dissimilar ideals of masculinity represented by characters from the Three Kingdoms story cycle. These diverging standards appear as differences of emphasis in the characterizations of Zhuge Liang and Zhang Fei in the two editions. She concludes that these differences, partially attributable to changes in the form and functions of *zaju* drama, at the same time reflect a shift (seen in the novel as well), toward a more orthodox Confucian definition of masculine virtue.

Catherine Pagani's investigation of the theme of *Three Kingdoms* in China's popular woodblock prints provides a new perspective on the study of the novel's influence in art forms. Pagani points out the close connections between the novel, popular drama, and popular visual art. She shows that characters and incidents from *Three Kingdoms* were "an ideal theme" for "New Year prints" (*nianhua*), a major popular visual art. For many of these prints, the most immediate inspiration was not the novel itself, but stage renditions of incidents from the novel; the prints themselves "employed theatrical conventions, of stage settings, costumes and makeup in their designs." Thus Pagani's study of these prints also provides insights into regional theater in late imperial China.

Elizabeth Wichman-Walczak also writes about *Three Kingdoms* on the stage, studying the contemporary Peking opera (*jingju*) *Cao Cao and Yang Xiu* (originally mounted in 1988), which was based on an intriguing episode in the novel. Her essay explores major factors underlying the critical and commercial success of *Cao Cao and Yang Xiu* and illuminates current possibilities for both *Three Kingdoms* material and the *jingju* theatrical form. As Wichmann-Walczak's paper attests, *Three Kingdoms* continues to play a vital role in contemporary Chinese culture.

The three papers of part 4 further examine the contemporary significance of *Three Kingdoms* and illustrate the expanding influence of *Three Kingdoms* beyond the borders of China. The first essay in part 4 discusses the tremendously successful television miniseries based on the novel. According to the author, Junhao Hong, over 1.2 billion people across the world have viewed this eighty-four-episode series. The numerical figures on both the production and the reception of the television series supplied by Hong confirm the important role television now has in disseminating traditional culture. But above and beyond the "gains and losses" Hong enumerates, we can also see the enduring hold, and yet constantly changing meanings, of the stories and characters of *Three Kingdoms* within the Chinese, and increasingly the world, imagination.

Jinhee Kim also emphasizes the enormous popularity and malleability of the novel as she draws on reception and reader-response theory to examine modern and contemporary Korean renditions of *Three Kingdoms*. She argues that in these works the reader is not a passive vessel; on the contrary, the Korean readers are as active as the author. These readers maintain their identity and differences in their reading, while also effectively crossing national, linguistic, and cultural boundaries.

In the final chapter, Bojun Shen, a highly accomplished authority on *Three Kingdoms*, assesses the state of contemporary scholarship on *Three Kingdoms*. Originally written in Chinese, this essay presents Shen's broad knowledge and keen perception of the accomplishments of scholars worldwide. Shen's discussion provides a fitting conclusion to this volume, as he not only describes the enormous vitality of *Three Kingdoms* studies in contemporary China, Japan, and the West but also suggests avenues for future development of the field. Shen proposes, among other things, that more attention be paid to the intimate relationship between the novel and Chinese culture as a whole. As the essays in this collection reveal, *Three Kingdoms* can serve as a resource for explorations of Chinese culture from a wide variety of approaches.

NOTES

1. The translation of this term is from Andrew Plaks, *The Four Masterworks of the Ming Novel* (Princeton, NJ: Princeton University Press, 1987). See chapter 5 for a comprehensive discussion of *Three Kingdoms* as vehicle for Ming literati values.

2. Luo Guanzhong, *Three Kingdoms: A Historical Novel,* trans. Moss Roberts (Berkeley: University of California Press/Beijing: Foreign Language Press, 1991). All citations from the novel in this introduction refer to Roberts's translation and will be incorporated into the text.

3. As Moss Roberts points out in the prologue, after the Jin collapsed China remained divided until the Sui dynasty (589–618), a period of almost four hundred years.

4. For more on the connections between historiography and politics see Moss Roberts, afterword to Luo Guanzhong *Three Kingdoms* (trans. Roberts), 948–953; see also Andrew Hingbun Lo *"San-kuo-chih yen-i* and *Shui-hu chuan* in the Context of Historiography" (PhD diss., Princeton University, 1981), 52–101.

5. Zhensheng Qiu, *Sanguo yanyi zongheng tan* (Beijing: Beijing Daxue, 1995), 19–25; Weisi Ye and Xin Mao, *Sanguo yanyi chuangzuo lun* (Jiangsu: Jiangsu renmin chubanshe, 1984), 11–15.

6. Roberts, afterword, 949.

7. Zhensheng Qiu, *Sanguo yanyi zongheng tan,* 43–45; see also Huajie Huang, *Guan Yu de renge yu shenge* (Taipei: Taibei shangwu yinshuguan, 1967); Gunter Diesinger, *Vom General zum Gott: Kuan Yu (gest. 200 n. Chr.) und seine "posthume Karriere"* (Frankfurt: Haag un Herschen, 1984); and Prasenjit Duara, "Superscribing Symbols: The Myth of Guandi, Chinese God of War," *Journal of Asian Studies* 47 (1988): 778–95.

8. For an introduction to the *pinghua* genre, see Wilt Idema, *Chinese Vernacular Fiction: The Formative Period* (Leiden: E. J. Brill, 1974).

9. Gail Oman King has translated this text as *The Story of Hua Guan Suo* (Tempe: Arizona State University Center for Chinese Studies, 1989); for more on the relationship between this text and the novel, see Anne E. McLaren, "Chantefables and the Textual Evolution of the *San-kuo-chih yen-i,*" *T'oung Pao* 71 (1985): 159–227; on the chantefable genre, see Anne E. McLaren, *Chinese Popular Culture and Ming Chantefables* (Leiden: E. J. Brill, 1998).

10. For the play and its relationship to the earlier narratives, see Kimberly Besio, "Enacting Loyalty: History and Theatricality in 'The Peach Orchard Pledge,'" *CHINO-PERL Papers* 18 (1995): 61–81.

11. For a translation of Mao Zonggang's prefatory comments, see David T. Roy "How to Read the Romance of the Three Kingdoms," in *How to Read the Chinese Novel,* ed. David L. Rolston (Princeton, NJ: Princeton University Press, 1990), 152–95.

I

Three Kingdoms and Chinese Values

1

Cosmic Foreordination and Human Commitment

The Tragic Volition in *Three Kingdoms*

CONSTANTINE TUNG

Three Kingdoms is a great tragedy that depicts the hero's fabulous defiance of cosmic foreordination. Linkages between the human world, cosmic design and the cyclical movement of the Five Agents (*wuxing*)—wood, fire, earth, metal, and water—play a decisive role in the hero's life in *Three Kingdoms*. The cyclical movement of the Five Agents manifests itself in history and in dynastic successions. A man's destiny is affected, though not necessarily determined, by the movement of the constellations, by the position and brightness of his star in the heavens, and by the order of succession of the Five Agents. The Chinese cosmic-human linkage begins with the Great Ultimate (*Taiji*), which consists of the Way (*Dao*) and gives rise to yin and yang. Interactions between yin and yang generate the Five Agents that in turn produce and sustain all matters, including the affairs of humankind. Unique signs from heaven manifest through unusual happenings on earth, therefore it is important for humans to understand the meaning of cosmic revelations and to chart a course of action accordingly. In *Three Kingdoms*, the Han dynasty belongs to fire, and fire is to be displaced by the agent earth, to which Cao Cao belongs. The leitmotif of the *Three Kingdoms* tragedy is the hero making the choice between following cosmic foreordination and executing his moral obligation.

Cosmic foreordination reveals the inevitable course of the future, but it differs from fate as it is presented in a Greek tragedy. Cosmic ordainment allows the hero to make choices so as to steer away from disaster. Cyclical successions of the Five Agents and the movement of the constellations are beyond the control of the human will, but are comprehensible to human intelligence. The hero makes

3

his choice and charters an appropriate course for the future. Cosmic foreordination is neutral, but the hero's choice gives meaning to his existence. *Three Kingdoms*, therefore, is a grand epic on the heroes' efforts to map their own courses in a world that is already charted by cosmic will (*tianyi*).

The opening statement of *Three Kingdoms*, "The Empire, long divided, must unite; long united, must divide," characterizes the novel's tragic theme.[1] The heroes and villains act and contend at a time when disintegration of the Empire is preordained. The hero's success or failure depends on his response to cosmic will. *Three Kingdoms* is not a neutral work of art; it takes stands, politically and morally, that define heroes and villains. The novel creates the most admired and beloved heroes in Chinese literature, (namely, Liu Bei, Guan Yu, Zhang Fei, and Zhuge Liang),[2] and the most infamous antagonist or villain (Cao Cao). The heroes commit themselves to a noble cause that unfortunately runs against the cycle of the Five Agents and the movements of the stars. The *Three Kingdoms* tragedy is the failure of the hero's noble commitment and of his defiance of the cosmic foreordination, but the meaning of this tragedy is ascribed to the hero's ethical principles and moral courage.

The motif of the *Three Kingdoms* tragedy, in the Hegelian ideal, is the hero's choice between equal values, not merely between good and evil. A Hegelian tragedy focuses on the hero's specific action and response. The significance in tragedy, as Hegel sees it, is not suffering as such but its causes. Aristotelian pity and fear are not necessarily tragic pity and fear to Hegel, whose definition of tragedy is focused on a conflict of ethical substance. This is the substance of the *Three Kingdoms* heroes' tragedy. Although aware of the cosmic preordination and historical cycle that decrees the empire is at its end, the *Three Kingdoms* heroes, nevertheless, make their political choices based on their moral convictions. They fail and are destroyed because their actions run against cosmic preordination. Their character flaws, indeed, make the tragedy a more intimate human experience, but often these flaws of the heroes are manifestations of cosmic will.

In chapter 14, "Cao Cao Moves the Emperor to Xudu" (Cao Mengde yijia xing Xudu), the cosmic sign shows its decisive and favorable influence upon the antagonist's decision-making. This cosmic sign is perceived to be heaven's sanction of Cao Cao's political aspirations. Thus, Cao Cao's act to place the emperor under his control is a cosmically sanctioned move. Cao Cao's action is an ironic revelation that the antagonist's ambition coincides with the cosmic will, while the novel's morals stand against the usurper. The heroes regard moving the emperor to Xudu as an act of betrayal, but the villain's accession to the supreme power in the empire is cosmically blessed. The conflict between the hero and the villain, therefore, is the hero's conscious defiance of cosmic will.

The future course of the contention is thereupon determined. The heroes—Liu Bei, Guan Yu, Zhang Fei, Zhuge Liang, and Jiang Wei—defy cosmic foreordination, which is personified in Cao Cao, the antagonist. This is a conflict between the villain, chosen by cosmic design as founder of a new political order, and the heroes, who are committed to a moral and political cause, the restoration of the Han. The *Three Kingdoms* heroes' commitment to the restoration of the Han is affirmed with their unswerving loyalty (*zhong*) to the empire, and this loyalty is solidified through the very personal brotherhood (*yi*). Brotherhood is the most highly regarded human relationship in the novel. Loyalty and brotherhood are the ethical principles adhered to by the *Three Kingdoms* heroes.

The *Three Kingdoms* heroes are doomed to fail in their struggles. Robert W. Corrigan says in his discussion of Sophoclean drama that the tragic view of life begins by insisting that heroes accept the inevitable doom of their fate, and that this fact is the mainspring of all tragic drama. While the hero may have to face and accept the reality of necessity, he also has an overpowering need to give a meaning to his fate. If man's fate, no matter how frightening, has no meaning, then why struggle?[3] The *Three Kingdoms* heroes understand the meaning of their action. The Sophoclean hero cannot escape from the tragic fate in *Oedipus the King*, but the *Three Kingdoms* hero makes his choice in spite of cosmic foreordination. The *Three Kingdoms* hero makes the choice, according to his free will, between adherence to the Daoist passive acceptance of inevitability (as Zhuge Liang does before Liu Bei's three visits), and taking the Confucian route of active involvement, (as Zhuge Liang does after Liu Bei's third visit).

Zhuge Liang and his Daoist friends know the consequence of defying cosmic foreordination. This tragic recognition is evident in Liu Bei's efforts to entreat Zhuge Liang. Sima Hui, a wise Daoist, responds to Liu Bei's inquiry about Crouching Dragon (Zhuge Liang) by comparing Zhuge Liang to the greatest statesmen of antiquity, Jiang Ziya and Zhang Liang. Comparing Zhuge Liang to the great statesmen in history instead of Daoist immortals is convincing evidence of Zhuge Liang's and his Daoist friend's secular concerns and aspirations. When Sima Hui learns that Xu Shu recommends Zhuge Liang to Liu Bei, he exclaims: "Why did Yuanzhi [the alias of Xu Shu] drag him out into this troubling business?"(37.308). This comment foretells a tragic event. As Sima Hui leaves, he reiterates his tragic premonition: "Alas, Crouching Dragon has found his lord but not the right time!" Sima Hui recognizes the futility of human struggles against the cosmic design at a particular historic moment (*tianshi*).

On one of his visits to Crouching Dragon, Liu Bei meets Zhuge Liang's friend Cui Zhouping. Cui Zhouping's response is illuminating:

> My lord, you are set to bring the chaos to an end. This is your benevolent intention, but since ancient times, chaos and order have come and gone unpredictably. When the High Ancestor (Emperor Gao Zu) killed the white serpent and led the righteous uprising to destroy the tyrannous Qin, it began the transition from chaos to order. It was followed by two hundred years of peace and prosperity. Then, Wang Mang usurped the throne and the empire again moved from order to chaos. Emperor Guang Wu restored the empire and led us out of chaos and back to order and to peace for the people lasting two hundred years. Now wars and

uprisings are again all around us. This is a time that we are moving from order into chaos, which will not end quickly. General, you wish to have Kongming to change the cosmic courses, and to mend the sky and earth. I am afraid it is not easy but only a waste of your mind and efforts. Don't you know that "one enjoys ease by following heaven, and one labors in vain by opposing it" and that "One can neither ignore one's fate nor can one fight against it"? (37.310)

Cui Zhouping illustrates the tragic notion of the futility of men's attempts to reverse cosmic foreordination and historical cycles. Cui Zhouping is no ordinary Daoist hermit; he is also an expert on warfare. In one of the final battles between the novel's last hero, Jiang Wei, and the Wei general Deng Ai, Deng Ai is stymied by Jiang Wei's battle formation based on Kongming's "Eight-Fold Position" (*bazhen*). Jiang Wei moves his *bazhen* swiftly into the "Long Snake Rolls Up the Earth" (*chang she juandi zhen*) battle position and succeeds in encircling Deng Ai who does not understand Jiang Wei's battle order. Another Wei force, led by Sima Wang, saves Deng Ai from annihilation. Asked how he knows Jiang Wei's battle order, Sima Wang tells Deng Ai: "When I was young, I studied at Jingnan, and became a friend with Cui Zhouping and Shi Guangyuan [another friend of Kongming], and we had studied this battle formation" (113.934). Zhuge Liang's Daoist friends all have worldly expertise, but they, except Zhuge Liang, are wise enough to remain aloft from intervening in the preordained course of the cosmic. This is Zhuge Liang's tragedy.

Cui Zhouping advises Liu Bei that a "wise" person should understand and accept heaven's course for his survival and peace. Liu Bei responds: "What you have said is certainly wise, but I am a scion of the Han and I am committed to restore the House of Han. How can I submit myself to fate?" (37.310). This noble choice eventually leads the hero to his disastrous defeat. The *Three Kingdoms* heroes' defiance of cosmic foreordination leads them into those areas of experience where man is at the limits of his sovereignty. Yet, they are determined to map out their own universe and to restore the Empire, and it leads to their utmost defeat.

For Zhuge Liang, Daoist escapism never entirely replaces Confucian commitment, and he often compares himself to Guan Zhong and Yue Yi, two famous historical statesmen. His Confucian sense of commitment eventually overcomes his Daoist escapism when he meets Liu Bei. In other words, Zhuge Liang's Confucian ethics and secular aspirations overcome his Daoist wisdom. Zhuge Liang's nickname, Crouching Dragon, denotes the hero's ambivalence between Daoist retreat and Confucian sense of duty, and this Confucian commitment eventually moves the Crouching Dragon out from his reclusive hiding place.

However, there is an equally powerful and more personal factor that obliges Zhuge Liang to come out of his hermitage. It is the very personal *yi*. In *Three Kingdoms*, *yi* denotes one's loyalty to the person who understands and appreciates one's value, and it constitutes the solid base of the brotherhood exemplified in the union of Liu Bei, Guan Yu, and Zhang Fei. *Yi* is a value that *Three Kingdoms* puts higher than *zhong*."[4] Liu Bei's persistent visits are a manifestation of his utmost appreciation, sincerity, and trust, and these qualities ultimately move Kongming.

Zhuge Liang's famous "Response at Longzhong" (Longzhong dui) demonstrates not only Crouching Dragon's comprehensive knowledge and understanding of the political situation of the world; it also shows that this crouching dragon already has strategic plans for rebuilding the disintegrating empire. Kongming is moved by Liu Bei's sincerity, and he also finds that Liu Bei's commitment meets his long-harbored wish and dream; in the words of Xu Shu, he [Kongming] often "compares himself to Guan Zhong and Yue Yi" (36.304).

In the "Response at Longzhong" Kongming maps out his geopolitical strategy for the restoration of the house of Liu, but he is aware of the unfavorable cycle of history and the cosmic ordainment. Of cosmic ordainment (*tianshi*) and human efforts (*renmou*), the two elements that Kongming attributes to Cao Cao's success, Kongming advises Liu Bei to concentrate on the latter. Kongming, nevertheless, accepts the task, despite his keen awareness of the inauspicious times and cosmic preordination. His Confucian secularism, his loyalty to the Han, and his gratitude for Liu Bei's appreciation supersede his preoccupation with self-preservation in the chaotic world.

Unlike them, Cao Cao, the archantagonist of *Three Kingdoms*, is blessed by the cosmic foreordination that manifests its decisive mystical favor at Huarongdao. Kongming's assignment of Guan Yu to try to ambush Cao Cao at Huarongdao is his attempt to wait out the cosmic ordainment. One may wonder why Kongming does not assign Zhang Fei or Zhao Yun to wait for and finish the desperate villain at Huarongdao. Liu Bei knows well that Guan Yu, with his strong sense of *yi*, will not be able to carry out this important mission to finish the villain. Kongming tells Liu Bei: "Last night I studied the constellations, and the traitor Cao's death was not shown there. So let Yunchang [Guan Yu] discharge the personal favor (*renqing*) [he owes to Cao Cao]" (49.409).

Clearly, Kongming knows that Cao Cao will not perish, no matter who is assigned to deal with him at Huarongdao. To assign Guan Yu to do this is Kongming's wise plan for the future. He feels that, after Huarongdao, Guan Yu's loyalty will not be compromised by his commitment to *yi* and indebtedness to favors (*en*) he owes to the archrival of Liu Bei. Kongming can only act according to the cosmic design by modifying his plan, and hoping for the cosmic signs to change.

The victory over Cao Cao at Red Cliff ironically marks the beginning of the greatest tragic episode in the novel. Kongming, the engineer of the Red Cliff victory, unwittingly leads his state toward catastrophe. Kongming, the wisest hero of all in *Three Kingdoms*, undermines his own grand strategy with each of his many clever moves and victories against his Wu opponents. The accumulation of the successful moves made by Kongming ends with the defeat of the mighty forces led by Liu Bei at the hands of young Lu Xun. It is a tragic drama of volcanic passion for revenge, and it is also a great tragic irony of men's struggle against the cosmic. Does Kongming have a choice?

After the battle of Red Cliff, Kongming takes Nanjun and other cities from the Cao forces without a fight, while Zhou Yu fights and defeats Cao's troops after a bitter struggle. Kongming then spoils Zhou Yu's plots repeatedly, and finally so angers Zhou Yu that he dies at the young age of 36. Although the novel portrays Zhou Yu as a less sympathetic contender, all these victories contradict the strategy of Kongming outlined in his "Response at Longzhong," that is, the principle of forming an alliance with Sun Quan against the North. Kongming, as wise as he might be, violates his own grand strategy and offends Zhou Yu and Sun Quan by taking the strategic Jingzhou region, which Zhou Yu and Sun Quan consider theirs.

Before leaving for Xichuan, Kongming reminds Guan Yu of the importance of maintaining good relations with Sun Quan. However, after piling repeated humiliations upon Sun Quan, Kongming's policy is now on very shaky ground. Kongming certainly does not have alternatives. Liu Bei, the only major contender without a home, needs a home base. Jingzhou, unfortunately, is the only available place, and its strategic location attracts all contenders' desires to possess it. Cao Cao's defeat at Red Cliff takes him out of contention for the time being, but at the same time Kongming turns his strategic ally into his adversary. The chain of cause and effect puts Kongming into an inextricable situation, and he is compelled to subordinate his strategic design to immediate tactical necessity. Kongming's wisdom cannot alter the historical and cosmic courses, and he is moving toward catastrophe.

The hero's flaws and errors manifest cosmic preordination, and they also heighten the emotional intensity of the tragic volition. The heroes are personally responsible for their failures and/or deaths. When Kongming must leave Jingzhou for Xichuan to assist Liu Bei, he entrusts the defense of Jingzhou to Guan Yu; in order to avoid warfare on two fronts he instructs Guan Yu to follow the strategic principle of "North, resist Cao Cao; East, peace with Sun Quan" (63.523). However, Guan Yu fails to abide by this strategic principle.

Arrogance is perceived in *Three Kingdoms* as a fatal character flaw that always leads a hero or a villain to his defeat or death. Zhao Zilong, the nearly perfect hero in the novel, suffers his only defeat at the hand of an inexperienced and impetuous Wei general, Xiahou Mao, simply because of his momentary arrogance (chapter 92). Arrogance is Guan Yu's mortal flaw. His request to have a duel with Ma Chao (chapter 65) and his resentment at Huang Zhong's promotion to be his equal as one of the five "Tiger Generals" (chapter 73) evidence Guan Yu's only, but nevertheless fatal, defect, as Chen Shou comments in *Chronicle of the Three Kingdoms* (*Sanguo zhi*).[5]

This catastrophic defect emerges when Guan Yu antagonizes Sun Quan with his insulting refusal of Sun Quan's proposal to have his son marry Guan's daughter. Guan Yu knows Sun Quan's long-cherished intention to take Jingzhou, but his arrogant temperament keeps him from seeing the necessity of diplomatic flexibility. The young and unknown Wu commander Lu Xun takes the advantage of Guan Yu's defect by flattering the great general with extreme humility, and he succeeds in lowering Guan Yu's alertness. This leads the great hero to his defeat and death.

Though his military situation is deteriorating hopelessly, Guan Yu's faith in *yi* remains. When he confronts Cao Cao's general Xu Huang in battle, the beleaguered hero asks Xu Huang: "Our friendship is indeed deeper than any other, but why have you driven my son time and again to the limit?" Guan Yu is utterly surprised when Xu Huang turns to his troops and cried out: "A thousand pieces of gold to the man who takes Yunchang's head!" Guan Yu asks: "Gongming, why do you say this?" Xu Huang answers: "Today this concerns the state, I cannot neglect my public duty because of our personal relations" (76.623). While saying this, Xu Huang charges toward Guan Yu.

Guan Yu's adherence to *yi* fails him again when he pleads to the Wu commander Lü Meng in the name of this value. Lü Meng replies via Guan's messenger: "My friendship with General Guan is personal, but today I am under the command of my superior, I am unable to do as I wish"(76.625). *Yi*, as Guan Yu understands it, transcends the line between enemy and friend. Guan Yu's display of *yi* over *zhong* at Huarongdao earns him great admiration of the readers, but ultimately *yi* fails to save the hero.

Liu Bei's death is most remarkable, and it makes him an Aristotelian tragic hero who at the moment of his death recognizes and repents the fatal mistake that leads him to disaster. Liu Bei's rejection of the advice by Kongming, ZhaoYun, and the others not to avenge Guan Yu's death begins the novel's most dramatic and tragic episode. Liu Bei's passion for revenge eclipses his rational judgment, undermines his grand design for unifying the empire, and costs him his own life. The bond of brotherhood takes precedence over the fortune of his new empire. Deeply humiliated by his defeat, Liu Bei, instead of returning to Chengdu, the capital of his empire, remains at Baidi ill.

Liu Bei's repentance of his mistake is at first revealed in dealing with his general Huang Quan's surrender to the Wei when advancing Wu forces blocked Huang's retreat. Huang Quan is convinced that Liu Bei will not persecute him and his family because of their mutual trust, *zhong* and *yi*. Liu Bei's not persecuting Huang Quan, however, is not entirely due to his adherence to *yi*, as Huang Quan believes. It is Liu Bei's first show of repentance for his mistake: "It is I who have done wrong to Huang Quan, not Huang Quan to me" (85. 693).

Touching Kongming's back, Liu Bei speaks his last words: "Since I had you as prime minister, I was fortunate to have accomplished the quest for the empire. How could I know that I was so foolish for not listening to your words, and ended in this defeat all by myself? I am sick because of my remorse, and I am now dying . . ." (85.695). These words reveal the hero's deep sense of humility and tortured repentance for his mistake. He holds himself responsible for the worst military defeat of his empire and the worst in the novel. His turbulent emotion and reflective moral understanding elevate Liu Bei to the status of an Aristotelian tragic hero.

The deaths of Guan Yu, Zhang Fei, and finally, Liu Bei conclude the tragic prediction stated in the very beginning of the novel's first chapter, "Feasting in the Peach Garden, the Three Heroes Pledged in a Sworn Brotherhood" (Yan taoyuan haojie san jieyi). This Sworn Brotherhood (*jieyi*) episode establishes the major moral principle and is a powerful theme of the novel. The pledge connects Liu Bei, Guan Yu, and Zhang Fei in a relationship that has commanded admiration and attracted imitations for centuries in China. However, their passion for this sworn brotherhood leads to the tragic conclusion of the novel's three most admired and beloved heroes.

The tragedy of the three sworn brothers corresponds to the Hegelian interpretation of tragedy. It is a conflict between the powers that rule the world of man's will and man's ethical substance, action. Hegel speaks of "equally justified" powers, and it is, therefore, tragic that observance of one would violate the other. To Liu Bei, Zhang Fei, and Guan Yu, loyalty to their sworn brothers and loyalty to the Empire are equally justified values. Guan Yu's letting the desperate Cao Cao go and Liu Bei's avenging his sworn brother's death exemplify the Hegelian view of conflict.[6]

Passion for brotherhood destroys Liu Bei, Guan Yu, and Zhang Fei, but defiance of cosmic preordination characterizes Zhuge Liang's tragedy. Wiser than the three fallen heroes, Zhuge Liang, like his friends who choose to remain in reclusion, understands that the cosmic movement is running against the cause for the restoration of the house of Liu, the Han dynasty. Yet, he accepts the call for his service to the impossible but noble cause.

When Kongming presents his "Petition for the First Expedition (xian chushi biao)," Grand Historian Qiao Zhou advises against the campaign, because he observes that "the constellation signs to the north indicate the height of vigor and the stars over the North are doubly bright." This is not the right time for war against the Wei, Qiao Zhou argues. Then he turns to Kongming: "Prime Minister, you have profound knowledge of the constellations, why do you insist to do so [against the cosmic will]?" "Heaven's way changes unpredictably, how can we hold ourselves to it?" Kongming responds (91.753). Qiao Zhou is a unique character in *Three Kingdoms*. He understands cosmic foreordination and signs in the constellations, yet he does not withdraw from the secular world as many wise Daoist recluses do. He serves in the Shu-Han imperial court, but avoids committing himself to the causes that violate cosmic foreordinations. He advises the Latter Emperor (Houzhu), Liu Shan, to surrender not because of his lack of loyalty, but because he reads and follows the cosmic signs.

Kongming's answer to Qiao Zhou reveals the dilemma between following cosmic dictates and fulfilling his commitment. Kongming only wants the unpredictable changes of the way of heaven (*tiandao*) to turn to his favor, and he is "*for the time being* [italics are mine] going to position the forces in Hanzhong and to watch the enemy's movements before taking action" (91.753). The tone suggests Kongming's uncertainty in his response to Qiao Zhou's remonstrance. His answer implies a compromise between his knowing the unfavorable sign of heaven's will and his commitment to the empire's reunification. Above all, his sense of *yi* obliges him to fulfill the late Emperor's trust in him.

When Kongming is ready for another expedition against Wei in AD 234, Qiao Zhou speaks again opposing Kongming's move, because of the unfavorable sign in the constellations. Sima Yi, Kongming's most formidable adversary, also reports to Cao Rui, the Wei emperor, about the same heavenly sign that is unfavorable to Kongming's offensive. He concludes: "Kongming indulges too much in his own talent and ability and acts against cosmic foreordination. He is defeating and destroying himself" (102.843–4). Sima Yi's prediction of Kongming's defeat is soon proved to be correct.

Zhuge Liang's tragedy—his failure to conquer Wei and his untimely death—results from the combined factors of unfavorable cosmic foreordination, his personal misjudgment, and the deterioration of human harmony (renhe) in the imperial court. Human harmony is a factor that Kongming in his "Response at Longzhong" considers vital for Liu Bei to compensate for Cao Cao's having "Heaven's time (tianshi)" and for Sun Quan's "geographic advantages (dili)."

Changes in Kongming's temperament from his early confidence, optimism, humor, and sometimes playful and cruel mischief to impatience and easily aroused anger after the failure of his first expedition against the Wei are reflections of the hero's frustration. Kongming's frustration comes not only from unsuccessful battles against Sima Yi, but also from his realization that he is running out of time. His confidence in dealing with Zhou Yu is shown with such expressions as "smile" (xiao) and "laugh aloud" (da xiao), expressions that demonstrate the hero's playfulness against his jealous and suspicious opponent. Confidence and optimism also inspire Kongming's theatrical talent. Kongming is a skillful actor (so is Liu Bei, by following Kongming's choreography), a talent exemplified in his dealing with Lu Su, who comes time and again demanding the returning of Jingzhou to Wu. At Zhou Yu's funeral, Kongming's eulogy and theatrical crying move all the hostile Wu officials and generals. Only Pang Tong, the Young Phoenix, sees through Kongming's drama and histrionics. Kongming "gives a big laugh (da xiao)" when Pang Tong points out to the deceptive performer this cruel theatricality. If fact, Kongming has plotted Zhou Yu's death. In the last round of the duel, Kongming laughed heartily and told Liu Bei that, "Zhou Yu is near his death. . . . When Zhou Yu comes, if he doesn't die, he will be mostly dead" (56.462).

Kongming's mood and self-assurance begin to change after the loss of Jieting. The presentation of emotions in *Three Kingdoms*, as in many novels of action, is simple. The most frequently used descriptions of moods are "smiling or laughing" (xiao), "laughing aloud or laughing heartily" (da xiao), "angry" (nu), and "furious" (da nu). In chapter 97, during the attack on Chencang, Kongming is "furious" four times even though he is about to win the battle. Later, he is also "greatly surprised" (da jing) by the loss of two of his generals and the defeat of his forces. After the loss of Jieting, Kongming confronts an increasingly difficult situation from without and within, and yet his loyalty and commitment remain unswerving.

During his last campaign against Wei, Grand Historian Qiao Zhou again tells Kongming of unfavorable constellation signs and natural omens for his new war. Again, Kongming rejects Qiao Zhou's advice: "Under the vital trust of the late Emperor, I should only do my best to fight the traitors. How can I give up the important cause of the Empire because of baseless evil omens?" (102.843). This is the hero's defiance of the limitations of being a man.

Previously, when fighting Cao Cao at Huarongdao, Kongming has modified his scheme in accord with cosmic will. Now Kongming attempts to prolong his life by defying the inevitability of cosmic will and he fails. Kongming's death concludes his struggle against the supreme will of the cosmos, the heavens. The hero has attempted to manipulate and to intervene in cosmic will in order to accomplish his unfulfilled commitment. Thus, Kongming is the only hero in *Three Kingdoms* who knowingly violates the will of heaven. Kongming's heroism and tragedy are his defiance of the state of being human.

Jiang Wei, the last hero of the *Three Kingdoms*, concludes the tragic drama with his unyielding virtues, *zhong* and *yi*. Fighting first on the side of Wei, Jiang Wei surrenders to Kongming when he has nowhere to turn. Jiang Wei is portrayed as an extremely filial son. A man of such a virtue does not belong in the camp of the traitors. Jiang Wei's loyalty to Kongming is solidified through his deep gratitude to Kongming's appreciation and Kongming's understanding of his talent and usefulness. Kongming claims that he finally has someone who can succeed him, and Jiang Wei abides by Kongming's wish. Jiang Wei says before launching another invasion of Wei: "When the late prime minister was still in his hut, he mapped out the tripartite division of the world. He led six offensives from Qishan in order to take the Central Plain, but unfortunately he passed away before accomplishing the task. I am now bearing his trust, and I must dedicate myself to continue his will and to serve the empire" (110.913). *Yi* is the paramount foundation on which *zhong* manifests. Jiang Wei's commitment leads the hero to the most violent death of all.

The *Three Kingdoms* tragedy is the heroes' "failure to map their universe," in Corrigan's words. The Sanguo heroes find themselves in a world, the Han empire, that they believe their forefathers have governed, civilized, and charted well. However, in their time the empire is disintegrating and falling apart.

The heroes' action is ethical in substance, yet it counters foreordination, and is the root of tragedy in Hegel's terms. They do so with their noble devotion to two ethical principles: loyalty (*zhong*) and brotherhood (*yi*). The struggle between Cao Cao (who is favored by cosmic foreordination) and Liu Bei, Guan Yu, Zhang Fei, Zhuge Liang, and Jiang Wei (who act in human rebellion against cosmic foreordination) has multiple meanings. As Robert W. Corrigan sees in Greek drama, these heroes are doomed by fate, which, in *Three Kingdoms*, is cosmic foreordination. In the heroes' defiance of this inevitability, there is "the affirmation of tragedy" that "celebrates a kind of victory of man's spirit over his Fate."[7] The Three Kingdoms heroes, "try nobly to impose a meaning on their own lives and on the world around them."[8] Liu Bei, Guan Yu, Zhang Fei, Zhuge Liang, and Jiang Wei are doomed not simply because they have tragic flaws, but because they refuse to compromise with cosmic preordination. Joseph Wood Krutch's ideal of tragedy affirms the meaning of the *Three Kingdoms* tragedy: "[I]t is that every real tragedy, however tremendous it may be, is an affirmation of faith in life, a declaration that even if God is not in his heaven, then at least Man is in his world. We accept gladly the outward defeats which it describes for the sake of the inward victories which it reveals."[9] *Three Kingdoms* is a monumental tragic novel. Its heroes' commitments and actions are based on high ethical principles, and their tragic failures are testaments to their moral courage. These elements make the novel powerful and moving with lasting impact on its readers.

NOTES

My discussion is based on the 1953 edition of *Sanguo yanyi*, edited by Zuojia chubanshe bianjibu (the Editorial Department of the Writers Publishing House), (Beijing: Zhujia chubanshe, 1953). Translations of the text quotations are mine.

1. In its chapter 120, the novel concludes, "The empire, long united, must divide, long divided, must unite." This signifies that the tragedy ends with the unification of the empire (*tianxia*), ruled by another house, the house of Sima.

2. I use both Zhuge Liang and his courtesy name Kongming alternatively in my discussion.

3. See Robert W. Corrigan, "Introduction: The Tragic Turbulence of Sophoclean Drama" in *Sophocles: Oedipus the King, Philoctetes, Electra, Antigone in Modern Translations*, ed. Robert Corrigan, 2nd ed. (New York: 1968), 11–27.

4. Professor Mu Qian, a noted historian, sees that Zhuge Liang's willingness to serve under Liu Bei, though due to political conviction, is more inspired by the "sincere friendship" that Liu Bei demonstrates during his "Three Visits" to Zhuge Liang. See Mu Qian, *Zhongguo zhishifenzi* (Hong Kong: Zhongguo wenti chubanshe, 1951), 11.

5. See Chen Shou, "Guan, Zhang, Ma, Huang, Zhao zhuan, diliu: ping 關張馬黃趙傳第六：評," in *Sanguo Zhi: Shu Shu*. Edition of reference is 8th ed. (Changsha: 1998), 757. In *Three Kingdoms*, Cao Cao's advisor Cheng Yu says the same about Guan Yu's strong sense of *yi* when they confront Guan Yu at Huarongdao. Cheng Yu asks Cao Cao to exploit Guan Yu's *yi* so that they can get away (50.414). At this critical moment, the novel's most esteemed virtue demonstrates its weakness.

6. Hegel's writings on tragedy are scattered throughout his works. I draw here from *Hegel on Tragedy*, ed. Anne Paolucci and Henry Paolucci, (New York: Anchor Books, 1962).

7. Corrigan, "Introduction," 15.

8. Ibid., 27.

9. Joseph Wood Krutch, "The Tragic Fallacy," in *European Theories of the Drama*, ed. Barrett Clark (New York: Crown, 1965), 520–21.

2

Essential Regrets

The Structure of Tragic Consciousness in *Three Kingdoms*

DOMINIC CHEUNG

On and on the Great River rolls, racing east.
Of proud and gallant heroes its white-tops leave no trace,
As right and wrong, pride and fall turn all at once unreal.
Yet ever the green hills stay
To blaze in the west-waning day.

Fishers and woodsmen comb the river isles.
White-crowned, they've seen enough of spring and autumn tide
To make good company over the wine jar,
Where many a famed event
Provides their merriment.
                                        —"West River Moon"

THE ROMANCE OF INCOMPLETION

Before mentioning the historical truth of "[T]he empire long divided, must unite, long united, must divide" that predicts the momentum of Chinese history, *Three Kingdoms* commences with sighs of regret. The opening poem, "West River Moon," imbues the tone of the novel with a consistent motif of vainglory, transient life, and fleeting time. Using the metaphor of the flowing Yangtze River, the author sets the stage for heroes to vie in the ebb and flow of unceasing time. Despite their ups and downs, all will perish, surge over surge, in relentless time.[1] The inconstancy of life further triggers the meaning as well as the meaninglessness of triumph and defeat, right and wrong, leading to a final comprehension of the Buddhist understanding of the unreality of life, in which the human world is nothing but a blush of sunset, charming and ephemeral, quick as a fleeting glance.

As to the white-headed fishermen and woodcutters, they are not only those who survived the trauma of history, but also those outside spectators recollecting events with a historical perspective. Thus, fishermen and woodcutters who live at the periphery of the mundane world—they cut wood in mountain forests and catch fish in mountain streams and rivers, selling them to the human world—pose as distant watchers of worldly affairs. Like the audience in Greek tragedies who came out of the play purged through pity and fear, they bring with them a didacticism that is inherent in the tradition of Chinese ethical values of loyalty, filial piety, chastity, and righteousness.

There is also a reason for the fishermen and woodcutters to be white-headed. To go through a long period of time and to witness the historical alternation of "spring air and autumn moon"—only then can these witnesses (fishermen and woodcutters, readers and historians alike) remain as "outsiders" and "see enough" from a distance. They are akin to the audience in Bertolt Brecht's "epic theater" in which the "alienation effect" is arrived at through the audience's dissociation with the dramatic events on stage, so that they can more closely watch the "performance" of actors and/or actresses.[2] This alienated audience is more sober than the characters on the world stage caught in the eternal cyclic changes of separation and reunion. The same logic of "long divided must unite; long united, must divide" continues with heroes and their separated kingdoms in the novel; incompletion begets regret, and regret begets tragedy.[3]

This paper posits as truth the historical oscillation that is revealed through a narrative structure of tragic consciousness in the disillusionment of heroes of the three nation-states of Shu-Han, Wei, and Wu. These essential regrets form the warp and woof of the novel in which the completion of tragedy is formed through the incompletion of regretful events.

ACHILLES' WRATH: THE ANGER OF A HERO

In Greek tragedies, fate controls heroes, whose final destruction is often caused by their tragic flaw or hamartia. Among the many shortcomings of the tragic hero, wrath or anger stands out as the most explosive and devastating. Homer's *Illiad* begins with the wrath of the hero in Book 1: "The Wrath of Achilles is my theme, that the fatal wrath, which, in fulfillment of the will of Zeus, brought the Achaeans so much suffering and sent the gallant souls of many noblemen to Hades, leaving their bodies as carrion for the dogs and passing birds."[4] The quarrel of the heroes continues and finally leads to Achilles' killing of Hector, the Trojan warrior, to avenge the death of his friend Patroclus. Before Hector died, he implored Achilles not to let his body fall prey to the dogs and birds, but to be taken back to Troy for a ransom of bronze and gold from Hector's parents. But the wrathful Achilles scowled and said,

> "You cur," he said, "don't talk to me of knees or name my parents in your prayers. I only wish that I could summon up the appetite to carve and eat you raw myself, for what you have done to me. But this at least is certain, that nobody is going to keep the dogs from you, not even if the Trojans bring here and weigh out a ransom ten or twenty times your worth, and promise more besides; not if Dardanian Priam tells them to pay your weight in gold—not even so shall your lady mother lay you on a bier to mourn the son she bore, but the dogs and birds of prey shall eat you up."[5]

Such is the feeling of wrath and vengeance with the heroes in *Three Kingdoms;* the word "in wrath" appears repeatedly, over a hundred times in the novel. Take Dong Zhuo's death, for example. After Dong fell for the ruse of the "double snare" (*lianhuan*) and was killed by his own stepson, Lü Bu, vengeance on Dong's corpse was no less wrathful than Achilles's action toward Hector—"Dong Zhuo's corpse was displayed on the main thoroughfare. There was so much fat in his body that the guards lit a fire in his navel; as it burned, grease from the corpse ran over the ground. Passing commoners knocked Dong Zhuo's severed head with their fists and trampled his body."[6]

Cao Cao was a suspicious man who would betray the world rather than let the world betray him. The classic illustration of this quality is the incident in chapter 4 when he killed Lü Boshe's whole family due to the suspicion that Lü intended to murder him.[7] However, when Cao Cao learned of the massacre of his father and family by the remnants of the Yellow Scarves who had surrendered to Tao Qian, prefect of Xuzhou, he fell to the earth with a great cry.

> As his attendants helped him up, Cao Cao gnashed his teeth and swore: "Tao Qian allowed his men to kill my father! The two of us cannot share the same sky. First I will put his city to the sword to quench my wrath.". . . When Chen Gong learned that Cao Cao intended to exterminate the populace of Xuzhou in his thirst for vengeance, he sought an audience. At first Cao Cao refused to see any man coming to plead for Tao Qian, but sentiment prompted him to hear out his former benefactor. Chen Gong appealed to Cao Cao: "They are saying that you are about to invade Xuzhou and avenge your father's murder by wholesale bloodshed. Let me attempt to dissuade you. Tao Qian is a humane and honorable gentleman and would never seek improper gain. Your father's death was Zhang Kai's crime, not Tao Qian's. Moreover, what enmity is there between the people of Xuzhou and yourself? Taking their lives would augur ill for your larger ambitions. I pray you, reflect on this. "Didn't you once abandon me?" Cao asked angrily. "How can you face me again? Tao Qian slew my whole family, and I mean to pluck out his entrails to satisfy my hatred. What you say in his behalf will not sway me." (10.81–82)

What happened to Ma Chao, a warrior belonging to an ethnic minority, was even more devastating. After Cao Cao killed his father, he bitterly but unwillingly retreated to his home territory of the Qiang tribes of Tangut for two years. After that he regrouped his men and recaptured cities and towns in the province of Shaanxi. Later, his generals betrayed him by attacking him from the rear. He found himself trapped between two armies and had a double battle to fight Worse still, At the height of the battle a new force had come into play. Xiahou Yuan, having received Cao Cao's command, had come to destroy Ma Chao. "Ma Chao's army was demolished by the combined strength of the three forces, and the remnant fled. Chao rode through the night, arriving at daybreak at the gates of Jicheng; demanding entrance, he was met with a storm of arrows and curses from Liang Kuan and Zhao Qu standing on the wall. They brought out his wife, Lady Yang, cut her down, and flung her corpse from the wall. Next, three of Ma Chao's infant sons and a dozen close kin were butchered one by one and pieces of their bodies were thrown to the ground. His bosom bursting, Ma Chao nearly toppled from his mount." (64.493).

But Ma's resilience and valor were almost superhuman. With only some three score of his followers left, he escaped and returned after midnight to the city. In the darkness, the city gate guards thought only of the return of their own men, opened the gates, and unwittingly let in the enemy. Once he entered the city, "Ma Chao began a chain of attacks inside the walls, beginning from the south end and sweeping through the commoners' quarters until he had reached the home of Jiang Xu. Xu's mother was dragged before him, but she showed no sign of fear. Pointing at Ma Chao, she reviled him, and Chao dispatched her personally. The households of Yin Feng and Zhao Ang were also put to the sword" (64.494).

What happened to Ma Chao in a matter of two nights and one day is almost a compression of the cycle of samsara. He was not only betrayed by his own generals and defeated in combat; but his wife and children were slaughtered right before his own eyes. "Rage and despair" do not suffice to describe his state of mind. Consequently, he ordered a massacre of the city he recaptured.

Thus, the essence of Achilles' wrath is the same as that of Cao Cao, Ma Chao, Zhang Fei, or Guan Yu. According to Freudian psychoanalysis, there is an aggression innate in human nature that is suppressed by civilization. In order to conform to society as social beings, men have to maintain a certain degree of "aim inhibition" in order to arrive at a "strong identification" with the masses.[8] But, the more they inhibit their aim or desire, the stronger the resistance arises in their subconsciousness. Freud has quoted an interesting passage from Heine, in which the poet confesses:

> Mine is a most peaceable disposition. My wishes are: a humble cottage with a thatched roof, but a good bed, good food, the freshest milk and butter, flowers before my window, and a few fine trees before my door; and if God wants to make

my happiness complete, he will grant me the joy of seeing some six or seven of my enemies hanging from those trees. Before their death I shall, moved in my heart, forgive them all the wrong they did me in their lifetime. One must, it is true, forgive one's enemies—but not before they have been hanged.[9]

Ever since the Hundred Schools contended in the Warring States, China had mutated into a highly inhibited society with strong ethical codes governing the behavior of men. This was especially the case in the Han dynasty when Confucianism had become the dominant trend of thought, transforming these with brutal instincts into a community of those with humanitarian ideals. Primitive libidos were transformed and sublimated, according to Freud, into "friendship" and this led, in *Three Kingdoms*, to the pledge of a blood-tie relationship called " sworn brotherhood" among men.

Yet all the above did not lead to the elimination of the human instinct for aggressiveness. The heroic character of Guan Yu demonstrates that, on the contrary, the more repression, the stronger the urge for aggression to release itself in the form of wrath or anger, leading to further destruction.

After the three friends—Liu Bei, Guan Yu, and Zhang Fei—pledged their oath to become sworn brothers in the Peach Garden, Guan's staunch loyalty and righteousness mediated between the benevolence of Liu and the rashness of Zhang. His loyal devotion to Liu is revealed in the incident where Guan forced his way into the rear garden when Cao Cao tried to corner Liu Bei to determine who were the heroes of the world. Later, when Cao Cao defeated the three brothers in Xuzhou, Guan failed to make his escape, and had to surrender to Cao under the condition that his loyalty remained with the emperor of Han instead of with Cao. As he tried to escort his two sisters-in-law to the capital of Xuchang, the treacherous Cao aimed to disrupt propriety between Guan and his sisters-in-law by deliberately arranging for them to stay in a single bedchamber. Guan stood outside all night, with a candle in his hand until dawn without any sign of fatigue.

In order to win Guan's heart, Cao showed unusual generosity toward him and his sisters-in-law during their sojourn in Xuzhou, giving Guan a small banquet every three days, and larger ones every five. There was one day that he noticed Guan's worn-out battle garb and presented him with a new one made from rare brocade. Although Guan accepted it, he still wore the old garb beneath the new one. When Cao teased him on his stinginess, Guan replied, "It is not frugality. The old dress was a gift from the Imperial Uncle Liu. I feel him near when I wear it. I could never forget my elder brother's gift on account of Your Excellency's new one. That is why I wear it underneath" (25.195).

Another gift from Cao evokes a similar reaction. Once Cao noticed Guan's horse was too lean to bear Guan's heavy body, he brought him the famed Red Hare steed to ride. Guan immediately showed his gratitude repeatedly to Cao, who was surprised and asked: "'I sent you beautiful women, gold, rolls of silk, one after the other, and never did you condescend to nod. Now I have given you a horse and you keep bowing and bowing. Do you value a beast above humans?' 'I admire this horse.' Lord Guan said, 'It can cover a thousand *li* in a single day. It is a gift that will enable me to reach my brother in a single day should his whereabouts become known'" (25.196). Such is Guan's unyielding devotion to his sworn brothers that even Cao Cao is touched by his determined loyalty.

As to Guan's courageous and undaunted martial skills of unsurpassed rivalry, his Red Hare steed was so swift that he rushed into the enemy forces and chopped off the head of Yan Liang, the leading general of Yuan Shao. In his first major test, Guan brought back the head of Dong Zhuo's general Hua Xiong before a goblet of warmed wine became cold. When Guan took leave of Cao Cao, he escorted his sisters-in-law on a solitary journey, slaying six generals at five passes. He has become the epitome of loyalty and righteousness. On the rational side, he was coolheaded enough to stop calm Zhang Fei when Zhang was about to explode over Liu Bei's three visits to Zhuge Liang's (Kongming's) thatched hut. On the sentimental side, his release of Cao Cao at Huarong Pass reflected his adherence to the virtue of righteousness rather than it did any leniency on his enemy.

But soon we find out that Guan Yu's character possesses the same tragic elements as western heroes. His tragic flaws are the flipside of his merits. His many victories due to his valor and martial skills have driven him to develop a subconscious narcissisism , which alienates him further from reality.[10] Once he drifts away from reality, his judgment begins to fail and a foolish stubbornness creeps in. When Liu Bei moved into Chengdu and promoted Ma Chao and Huang Zhong, Guan was indignant upon hearing the news and even wanted to return to Sichuan to fight a duel with Ma. When Liu Bei became the king of Hanzhong, he conferred upon Guan and the rest the title of Tiger general. Upon learning that the old veteran Huang Zhong was among the five, Guan discontentedly argued, "Zhang Fei is my younger brother; Ma Chao comes from a family of long-standing eminence. [Zhao] Zilong has followed my elder brother for many years and is as good as my younger brother, too. For them to have a position equivalent to my own is perfectly understandable. But who is Huang Zhong to rank alongside me? No self-respecting warrior would ever league himself with an old common soldier" (73.559). He then refused both title and seal.

It was fortunate that the messenger finally convinced Guan that "In this case, although the king of Hanzhong has named you as one of the 'Five Tiger Generals,' there is also the bond of brotherhood between you and him. To him, you and he are one. General, you are as good as king of Hanzhong; and the king of Hanzhong, you. How could you be classed with those others?" (73.559–560). Guan then understood and thanked the messenger for having prevented him from making an error, and received the seal with great humility. Nonetheless, his "elitist mentality" was totally exposed. By the time he was defeated by the Cao army and retreated to Maicheng, the whole sequence was in fact caused by his arrogance and subjective judgment in which he acted and behaved like a wounded beast in a cage. When his right arm was wounded by a poison arrow and was treated by the renowned physician Hua Tuo, the physician advised him that he must avoid all emotional excitement for a hundred days. It was a warning about his uncontrolled wrath—a wrath that led not only to his defeat but also his eventual death.

Whatever wrath the heroes in *Three Kingdoms* may have, it is not necessarily a total spirit of vengeance. Instead, it is more appropriate to look at their wrath as a resistance to inhibition of human aggressiveness. Moreover, their wrath comes quite spontaneously as a part of the heroic temperament. We can even assume that wrath is an artificial way for heroes to boost their courage, and repress sexual desire— particularly for the *Three Kingdoms* heroes who deliberately shunned women. The abstention from women may not be as extreme as the misogynist practices in *The Water Margin* (*Shuihu Zhuan*), but the emphasis on brotherhood over women is all the more obvious in *Three Kingdoms*. The characters of Guan Yu and Zhao Yun (Zilong) are true exemplars of this ethos.[11]

While Guan and Zhao are truly heroes who would not risk their careers for the sake of women, negative characters such as Cao Cao and his son Cao Pi are vicious womanizers, or at least their casual relationship with women in the novel is contradictory to Han practice. The straightforward heroes are those who observe virtues and show no interest in women as a general practice, while treacherous heroes are those who seduce women whenever they wish to. In the early career of Cao Cao, he made a mistake in having an illicit relationship with a woman, and it caused the death of his beloved bodyguard Dian Wei (16.130–131). After a victory with his father in a besieged city, Cao Pi found an extremely beautiful lady among the captives. She was the daughter-in-law of the defeated lord. Pi kept her privately and presented her to his father later. Cao Cao looked at her intently and said, "The perfect wife for my son" and told Cao Pi to take her as his wife (33.253).

For the positive heroes in *Three Kingdoms*, wrath becomes the catalyst that creates the tragic flaws that drive them toward failure or destruction. Zhao Yun's wrath upon hearing a proposal to marry his sworn brother's sister-in-law is an exception that implies social ethics. Besides, Zhao Yun as a hero in the novel has far fewer flaws than the others, and therefore is presented as too perfect to qualify as tragic.

FROM DIVINE TO HUMAN: HERO FATIGUE

In AD 227, Kongming submitted his "First Memorial" (Xian chushi biao) to the young Shu-Han emperor urging a military expedition to the north. He implored the young emperor to practice good Confucian virtues of heeding worthy advisors and repelling evil courtiers. The tone of the memorial is sad, desperate, weary and full of nostalgia of the past. He said of his early career:

> I began as a common man, toiling in my fields in Nanyang, doing what I could
> to keep body and soul together in an age of disorder and taking no interest in

making a name for myself among the lords of the realm. Though it was beneath the dignity of the late Emperor to do so, he honored my thatched cottage to solicit my counsel on the events of the day. Grateful for his regard, I responded to his appeal and threw myself heart and soul into his service.

Hard times followed for the cause of the late Emperor. I assumed my duties at a critical moment for our defeated army, accepting assignment in a period of direst danger. Now twenty-one years have passed. (91.701)

Though a short passage, it summarizes Kongming's career and his frustration with the Shu-Han kingdom. When Kongming wrote this memorial, he was forty-six, an age when he should have been at the height of his career, although life expectancy in ancient China was different from present-day life expectancy. Instead, his fatigued voice lingers like an old person in the conclusion of the memorial—"I now depart on a distant campaign. Blinded by my tears falling on this petition, I write I know not what" (91.701).

Lu Xun, a prolific modern writer and also known for his critical study of classical Chinese fiction, is only partially correct in his judgment of Kongming's character. In his study of classical Chinese fiction, Lu Xun commented on *Three Kingdoms* characters by saying, "Luo Guanzhong wished to make Liu Bei a kind man, but draws a character that seems a hypocrite. Wanting to depict Zhuge Liang's wisdom, he makes him appear a sorcerer."[12]

To describe Liu Bei's kindness as hypocritical is an overstatement. If we took him as nothing more than a run down distant relative of the Han emperor, we would be surprised by his resilience and perseverance. His far-reaching insight, abundant benevolence, and royal lineage are all that he has to compete with other powerful warlords. Perhaps, witty may be a better word than hypocritical to describe Liu.[13]

Kongming's great analytical ability and boundless knowledge, as well as his dexterity in manipulating the geography of the three political centers of China, help give Liu Bei the opportunity to establish himself as one of the strong contenders. As soon as he stepped out of his hermitage and became Liu's chief advisor, Kongming took Qingzhou, and later besieged Sichuan, or the Riverlands, in order to establish a home base for the Shu-Han kingdom. His military strategy is beyond comparison. Famous ruses such as inciting Zhou Yu to form an alliance against the Cao army, borrowing arrows from the enemy's navy, and supplicating the east wind to set fire to the enemy's linked ships lead to astonishing military successes and are due to his meticulous calculations. The philosophy of yin-yang with its application to the Five Elements, geomancy of ghosts and spirits, and the use of talismans to seek protection were prevalent in the Han period, many of Kongming's strategies are carried out under the guise of these practices. Kongming always competes with his archrival Sima Yi by watching the stars to learn the destiny of man. Kongming could even keep Sima Yi in awe after he had died, as Sima Yi believed that Kongming was still alive with his master star high in heaven. In order to achieve the high confidentiality of military actions, Kongming often appeared to be mysterious and unpredictable like a sorcerer.[14]

The heroes in Greek mythology were said to be of divine birth and the semidivine nature of Kongming is in fact a reflection of his natural intelligence. While Liu Bei's royal Han lineage reconfirms the mandate of heaven, Kongming's deification is a result of his superhuman ability to carry out his military operations in such a precise and cunning manner that all his generals think of him as semidivine.

But then the question arises as to why such a divine figure expresses such enormous fatigue in his two famous memorials. In Greek tragedies, there are the three unities of time, place, and action; Hero frustration or depression comes and goes in an instant of time, and empathy is achieved right after the fall of the hero. With Kongming, time is much longer and more tedious. He has gone through struggles for twenty-one years since he left his cottage. During this long stretch of time serving as chief advisor and administrator, Kongming has eaten little and slept less. After he entered the Riverlands, he made a southern expedition to capture the barbarian leader Menghuo. He made no rest stops but continued to head northward to attack Wei. Six times, Kongming made northern expeditions and six times he failed. We can almost assume that the northern expedition had become his everlasting obsession.

Kongming's fatigue is not accompanied by inertia; rather, it shows a constant striving and struggling. But soon we discover that human limitations dominate the fate of the individual. Kongming is, after all, more human than divine. His essential regrets are attributed to his own destiny and his limited life span. Providence refers to a human destiny that is predetermined. The destiny of a tragic hero is often a result of his resistance to fate. Consequently his success or failure is less important than his human attempts to reverse fate, an effort that becomes the ultimate emblem of human existence.

The limited span of life, however, determines the rule of the game. There is only one life to live, whether for hero or commoner. The ultimate challenge is to achieve goals within that limited time, be it a long or a short life. Kongming wants to defy the rule by altering his fate. He makes arrangements to address his prayer to the Big Dipper. If his master lamp stays lit for seven days, he might live for another year. Superficially, the plan fails because of the carelessness of Wei Yan, who dashes into the tent and reports the invasion of the northern enemy. He accidentally kicks over the master lamp, and it goes out. In reality, it is a reaffirmation of the game rule that no human can defy the rule of heaven. In preparing his final testament to the young emperor, Kongming admits, "Mortality is man's common lot; his years are numbered" (104.806).

Thus, we are back to the ontological quest of the ancient Greeks and Romans, which is similar to Zhuang Zi's Taoist paradox of seeking limitless knowledge in a limited life. The greatest disillusionment of the *Three Kingdoms* heroes involves the cruelty of time, both in the senses of bad timing and of running out of time. When Kongming said that mortality is man's common lot, he was mourning the limited time in which man can achieve his goal. In discussing the vision of Western tragedy, Richard Sewall brought forth the concept of "human boundary" and pointed out that the tragic vision impels the man of action to fight against his destiny, kick against the pricks, and state his case before God or his fellows. The "human boundary" is encountered when human possibility reaches its limit, when human existence is confronted by an ultimate threat.[15] Kongming has reached his human boundary when he comes to the end of his life and feels the ultimate challenge of his human existence. The ultimate question he is addressing is no longer a cognitive quest of "who am I?" but more of an existential outcry of "what else can I do?" The completion of his essential regrets indeed is the tragedy of all heroes in the *Three Kingdoms*.

NOTES

1. For "West River Moon," see Moss Roberts, trans., *Three Kingdoms: A Historical Novel* (Berkeley and Los Angeles: University of California Press; Beijing: Foreign Language Press, 1991), 3. Translations in the text are from this edition. See also the Chinese original in Luo Guanzhong, *Sanguo Yanyi* (Hong Kong: Xianggang Youlian chuban youxian gongsi, 1969).

2. What Brecht refers to as "A-effect," or "V-effect" (*Verfremdung*) is the sense of alienation from the audience's point of view. It arises when one watches the action on stage and one eliminates empathy. Such a procedure, of course, counteracts the intended cathartic effect of Greek tragedies. It was said that Brecht arrived such understanding of alienation from watching an offstage performance by the famous Chinese opera singer Mei Lan-fang, who performed before an audience in Moscow in 1935. For more information, see John Willet, *The Theatre of Bertolt Brecht: A Study in Eight Aspects* (New York: New Directions, 1959).

3. Regrets that are essential are not only the *hamartia* or tragic flaw of the heroes; they are closely associated with the mythical cycles of seasons. The woodcutters and fishermen who have seen "enough / Spring air and autumn moon" reminiscent of Northrop Frye's "mythos of seasons" and the attribution of the four seasons to comedy, romance, tragedy, and irony, and satire, repectively. See Northrop Frye, *Anatomy of Criticism* (New York: Atheneum, 1969), 206–23.

4. Homer, *Illiad*, trans. E.V. Rieu (Harmondsworth, England: Penguin, 1950), 23.

5. Ibid., 406.

6. Roberts, *Three Kingdoms*, 9.73. Hereafter all citations will be incorporated into the text.

7. For a more detailed description of this incident and a discussion of its depiction in New Year's prints, see Catherine Pagani's essay in this volume.

8. "The element of truth behind all this, which people are so ready to disavow, is that men are not gentle creatures who want to be loved, and who at the most can defend

themselves if they are attacked; they are, on the contrary, creatures among whose instinctual endowments is to be reckoned a powerful share of aggressiveness . . . As a rule this cruel aggressiveness waits for some provocation or puts itself at the service of some other purpose, whose goal might also have been reached by milder measures. In circumstances that are favorable to it, when the mental counter-forces, which ordinarily inhibit it, are out of action, it also manifests itself spontaneously and reveals man as a savage beast to whom consideration towards his own kind is something alien. Anyone who calls to mind the atrocities committed during the racial migrations or the invasions of the Huns, or by the people known as Mongols under Jenghiz Khan and Tamerlane, or the capture of Jerusalem by the pious Crusaders, or even, indeed, the horrors of the recent World War—anyone who calls these things to mind will have to bow humbly before the truth of this view." Sigmund Freud, *Civilization and Its Discontents* (New York, W. W. Norton and Company, 1961), 68–69.

9. Ibid., 67–68n.3.

10. According to Freud, libido further develops into narcissism. See ibid., 76n.10. Guan Yu's majestic appearance, which suggests the magnitude and glory of a hero, is given the beginning chapter of the novel; "Xuande [i.e., Liu Bei] observed him: a man of enormous height, nine spans tall, with a two-foot-long beard flowing from his rich, ruddy cheeks. He had glistening lips, eyes sweeping sharply back like those of the crimson-faced phoenix, and brows like nestling silkworms." Roberts, *Three Kingdoms*, 1.9.

11. Zhao Yun's refusal to marry his sworn brother's sister-in-law is an example of the heroic ethics in *Three Kingdoms*. When Liu Bei and Kongming tried to persuade Zhao to change his mind, Zhao resisted:"'In the first place,' [Zhao] Zilong answered, 'marrying my brother's sister-in-law would provoke contempt. Secondly, it is her second marriage; I would be causing her to forsake the life of chastity proper to a widow. And thirdly, it's not easy to read the intentions of someone who has just surrendered. Lord Liu has just taken control of the area around the Jiang and Han rivers, and he is preoccupied with a difficult situation. How could I put aside my lord's great cause for the sake of a woman?'" (52.398). Chinese scholars have tended to agree that Zhao is a less tragic character than Guan Yu, because he possesses fewer flaws and is too perfect as a human character. See Zhenjun Zhang, *Chuantong xiaoshuo yu Zhongguo wenhua* (Guangxi: Guangxi shifan daxue chubanshe, 1996), 177.

12. Xun Lu, *Zhongguo xiaoshuo shi lüe* (Hong Kong: Sanlian Shuju, 1958), 100. I have adopted Hsien-yi Yang and Gladys Yang's translation of Lu's *A Brief History of Chinese Fiction* [1964] (reprint Westport, CT: Hyperion, 1973), 168.

13. On his deathbed, he confided in Kongming and said, "'If my heir proves worthy of support, support him. If he proves unfit, take the kingship of the Riverlands yourself.' Kongming broke into a sweat; in extreme agitation, he prostrated himself again. 'Could I do otherwise,' he said tearfully, 'than serve him as aide and vassal, persevering in loyalty unto death?'" (85.647).

14. In fact, the Russian folklore scholar Boris Riftin has pointed out that as far as the Western epical motifs in *Three Kingdoms* are concerned, Kongming played the roles of an advisor, administrator, magician, and sorcerer. See Boris Riftin (Li Fuqing), *Sanguo yanyi yu minjian wenxue chuantong* (Shanghai: Shanghai guji chubanshe, 1997), 79.

15. Richard Sewall, *The Vision of Tragedy* (New Haven, CT: Yale University Press, 1959), 5 and 151n.10.

3

The Notion of Appropriateness (*Yi*) in *Three Kingdoms*

JIYUAN YU

Appropriateness (*yi*, also translated as "righteousness," "duty," or "morality") means "what is suitable," or "what is appropriate." It is one of the major values that *Three Kingdoms* seeks to embody. "Forming appropriateness in the Peach Garden" (*Taoyuan jieyi*, also known as the "Peach Garden Pledge") is one of the best-known stories in Chinese literature. Appropriateness is also a central virtue in Confucian ethics. In Confucius's *Analects* we read: "For the gentleman it is appropriateness that is supreme" (17:23); and "In dealing with the world the gentleman is not invariably for or against anything. He is on the side of what is appropriate" (4:10).[1] Being appropriate is an essential quality of a gentleman. Confucianism is the main moral system in China. *Three Kingdoms*, as one of the most important representative works in Chinese literature, has been effective in popularizing Confucian moral ideas and instilling them in individual moral life and in the social structure.

This paper attempts to show how the conception of appropriateness in *Three Kingdoms* is related to the philosophical conception of appropriateness in classical Confucianism, with a focus on the relationship of the Peach Garden brothers (Liu Bei, Guan Yu, and Zhang Fei). I will show that the author of *Three Kingdoms* makes a clear effort to embody this Confucian virtue in creating and describing his characters and their relations. By studying how the value of appropriateness operates behind a number of tragic conflicts in *Three Kingdoms*, we can also better understand the vagueness and tensions inherent within the Confucian theory of appropriateness.

APPROPRIATENESS AND KINGSHIP

Appropriateness, etymologically related to "to fit" (*yi*), can be interpreted either as "what is appropriate to do," or as "the quality of doing things appropriately." In the former sense, appropriateness is an attribute of ethical action; and in the latter sense, it is a quality of the agent (a virtue of judging and choosing what is appropriate). These two aspects are, of course, connected. Possessing a sense of what is appropriate enables a virtuous agent to decide how to act appropriately.

"What is appropriate to do," however, is first of all determined by the rites (*li*), the mores or customs of the society, and in particular, the rites of the Zhou Dynasty which is Confucius' ideal social structure. The core of the Zhou rites is a human social hierarchy modeled on family relationships. "Let the ruler be the ruler, the subject the subject, the father the father, the son the son" (*Analects* 12.11). Confucius even claims: "Do not look unless it is in accordance with the rites; do not listen unless it is in accordance with the rites; do not speak unless it is in accordance with the rites; do not move unless it is in accordance with the rites" (*Analects* 12.1). To be a virtuous person, one must internalize traditional values, and this is accomplished through adherence to the rites.

Usually, appropriate behavior is also behavior that is in accordance with social rites.[2] Mencius groups rites and appropriateness together (*liyi*) as the norms governing all kinds of relations.[3] Yet they are not completely identical. Confucius is not a rigid conservative and does not demand that one cling to the rituals rigidly and mechanically. Ritualization is not a matter of blind observance, but involves intellectual reflection. He himself approves certain changes.[4] A moral agent is allowed to deviate from the conventional social rites under certain circumstances. In applying the regulations to certain particular circumstances, the agent should take into account what is called for in that circumstance. In situations where an explicit rule might not be available, individual judgment and evaluation should be exercised. When Confucius says that the gentleman is not invariably against anything but is always on the side of appropriateness, and when he says that appropriateness is supreme, it is clear that appropriateness is the only thing that can never be overridden. Implicitly, social rites lack such an imperative. In short, while we generally follow social rites, there are also occasions on which what is right does not seem to be what the ritual norm requires. When this occurs, right comes before the rites. The departure from social rites, however, cannot be as dramatic as abandoning faith in the fundamental efficacy of social rites.

The faculty for determining what is truly appropriate even when one departs from social rites is also called appropriateness. The *Doctrine of the Mean* (chapter 20) explicitly defines appropriateness as "what sets things right and proper." In the *Analects*, "The Master said: 'Appropriateness the gentleman regards as the essential stuff (*zhi*) and the rites are his means of putting it into effect'" (15.17). *Zhi* literally means "basic stuff." Here it is related to the gentleman and hence cannot be taken as something inborn. I read it as a reference to the cultivated second nature, and read this remark to be saying appropriateness is the cultivated nature, which determines how to apply the ritual norm.

Hence, appropriateness involves more than simply obeying what the social rites prescribe, and it has a dimension of sensitivity and flexibility. In Mencius, this sense of flexibility is also called *quan* ("discretion" or "weighing"). For instance, social rites prescribe that man and woman should not touch each other. Yet Mencius claims that one can even touch one's sister-in-law if he is saving the latter from drowning, for that is a matter of discretion.[5]

Appropriateness is not to violate social rites, but to make them more appropriate. Nevertheless, classical Confucianism does not clearly specify the conditions under which one should exercise appropriateness or discretion to justify the departure from rites. Conceivably, this opens the door for moral conflicts and dilemmas.

Three Kingdoms relies heavily on the discrepancy between rites and appropriateness. The Liu Bei–Cao Cao conflict is the central theme of the novel. The basic evaluation of *Three Kingdoms* is that Liu Bei is the legitimate successor of Han, whereas Cao Cao is a usurper. At first glance, this position is highly biased. Although Cao Cao has held the Han emperor in thrall, he stops short of establishing himself as emperor. In contrast, although Liu Bei claims to restore the collapsing house of Han, it is not a secret that what this really means is to elect Liu Bei himself as the emperor of Han rather than to restore the dignity of the existing Han emperor. The novel makes Liu's ambition clear in the opening chapter, where we are told that when Liu was a child playing with other children, he climbed up into the huge mulberry tree near his house and proclaimed himself to be emperor mounting his chariot. Given his ambition and real goal, one might wonder how Liu's pursuit could square with the demands of rites. It is a rebellious act for Liu Bei, as a subject, to seek to be a ruler.

Three Kingdoms designs two strategies to justify Liu's pursuit. First, it takes pains to paint the image of Liu Bei as a righteous ruler who rules by compassion rather than by force and who wins men's hearts. This serves to build up the moral basis for Liu's kingship. In chapter 41 when Liu is defeated by Cao Cao, he insists on withdrawing together with his people rather than abandoning them. It is a decision that puts him in great danger. In the face of a strong objection from his generals, Liu replies: "The human factor is the key to any undertaking. How can we abandon those who have committed themselves to us?" (41.315). This image of Liu Bei's benevolence is effectively reinforced in *Three Kingdoms* by its frequent and sharp contrast with the behavior of Cao Cao who is described as holding the motto "Better to wrong the world than have it wrong me!" (4.38). The novel uses Liu Bei's own words to summarize how he is different from Cao Cao: "The man who is my antithesis, who struggles against me as fire against water, is Cao Cao. Where his means are hasty, mine are temperate; where his are violent, mine are humane; where his are cunning, mine are truehearted. By maintaining my opposition to Cao Cao, my cause may succeed" (60.460).

The second strategy is to put particular emphasis on the point that Liu Bei is a scion of the imperial family. When Liu first introduces himself to Zhang Fei in the opening chapter, he begins by claiming: "I am related to the imperial family" (1.9). This membership is mentioned repeatedly throughout the novel. *Three Kingdoms* includes the story that Liu is recognized by the emperor as an uncle by descent, and thus becomes the "imperial uncle" (20.156–157).

As a man of surpassing benevolence, Liu Bei is credited with moral legitimacy. As a scion of the house of Han, he is granted some degree of political legitimacy.

While it is not clear to what extent the second strategy is present in the spirit of Confucianism, the first, and also the most effective strategy, is certainly guided by Confucian value. When the Zhou house overthrew its predecessor, the Shang dynasty, its justification was that the Shang dynasty had forfeited the Mandate of Heaven (*Tian Ming*) through its misrule. From that time on, the loss of the Mandate of Heaven became the major justification for the change of dynasty. How, then, can one determine where the Mandate of Heaven lies? According to Confucianism, the most decisive clue is to see whether the ruler wins over the hearts of the people. Mencius says: "It is through losing the people that Jie and Zhou lost the empire, and through losing the people's hearts that they lost the people. There is a way to win the Empire; win the people you win the Empire. There is a way to win the people; win their hearts and you win the people. There is a way to win their hearts; amass what they want for themselves; do not impose what they dislike on them."[6] Clearly, *Three Kingdoms* follows this theory to establish Liu Bei's moral strength.

One problem, however, still remains. At the time of our story, the emperor is still on the throne, albeit in name only. If Liu assumes the throne, he would still violate what the rites demand—that a ruler should be a ruler and that the subject should be the subject. Liu Bei himself is fully aware of this, so when his officers propose for him the title of emperor after he conquers Sichuan, he responds: "You are quite mistaken. I may be of the royal house, but I am a subject nonetheless. If I do this, it will be an act of opposition to the dynasty [of Han]" (73.555). Even the chief advisor, Zhuge Liang, who pushed hard to make Liu accept the title of emperor, agrees that by refusing this, Liu "avoids suspicion and maintains appropriateness." Liu is then praised for taking "appropriateness as the fundamental principle of his whole life" (my translation). Thus, it seems to be a common understanding that to take the title of emperor is not an action in keeping with appropriateness. In these passages, appropriateness is meant in the sense of what is in accordance with the rites.

Liu Bei, then, is asked to assume the title of "king of Hanzhong" temporarily. To this suggestion, Liu Bei's initial response is: "Though you would all honor me as king, without the Emperor's public edict, it would be usurpation" (73.556). To call oneself king without the edict of the existing emperor would still not be an appropriate thing to do. This time, however, Zhuge Liang no longer backs off; rather he argues: "It would be more appropriate to depart from the norm in this case. Do not cling to convention" (73.556). Here discretion determines what is appropriate even though the agent departs from the rites. With this Confucian idea of discretion, Liu is persuaded to accept the title of king. There is no explanation, however, about why the idea of discretion can be used to justify the taking of the title of "king of Hanzhong," yet cannot be used to justify the taking of the title of emperor.

This is by no means an isolated case in which *Three Kingdoms* applies the notion of discretion arbitrarily. Liu Bei needs to take land, yet all the lords are members of the house of Han. The rites require that one cannot take land from a lord with the same surname. If this rule were strictly followed, Liu Bei would accomplish little. What should he do, then? *Three Kingdoms* presents conflicting stories at this point. In chapter 40, Zhuge Liang advises Liu Bei to seize the district of Liu Biao as a base, but Liu Bei firmly refuses: "I would rather die than do this thing which is not appropriate" (my translation). In chapter 60, when the strategy for seizure of Sichuan, which was the district of Liu Zhang, is proposed and contemplated, Liu Bei initially is still not willing to take the move: "I cannot risk the loss of the trust and appropriateness to the world for a trifling personal gain" (my translation). Yet this time *Three Kingdoms* appeals to the theory of discretion through Pang Tong, the second advisor to Liu Pei. Pang Tong counsels: "My lord, that accords well enough with sacred universal principles. But in a time of division and subversion, when men strive for power by waging war, there is no high road to follow. If you cling to accustomed principles, you will not be able to proceed at all. It is suitable to follow discretion and be flexible" (60.460). Liu Bei is persuaded and says to Pang Tong: "Your memorable advice shall be inscribed on my heart."

It remains unclear, however, why the theory of discretion could not be used in taking Liu Biao's district. The relationship between what is appropriate in the sense of following the rites and what is appropriate as a result of discretion is vague in Confucianism; it is equally vague in *Three Kingdoms*.

APPROPRIATENESS: BETWEEN KINGSHIP AND KINSHIP

Confucius writes: "Make it your guiding principle to be loyal to others (*zhong*) and to be trustworthy in what you say (*xin*)."[7] To be loyal and trustworthy are two major Confucian virtues. In *Analects* 1.4 Zengzi claims that they are two of the three things on which he examines himself every day (the third is whether he teaches others something that he has not tried out himself). In *Analects* 1.7 Zixia asserts that they are two of the four things for him to judge whether a person is educated (the other two are the appreciation of men of excellence rather than of beautiful women and the service of one's parents with utmost effort). Put in a general way, to be loyal is a virtue in dealing with one's lord or superior, and to be trustworthy is a virtue in dealing with one's friends. Both are within the requirements of appropriateness. (In *Analects* 12.9, after saying that one should take to be loyal and trustworthy as guiding principle, Confucius adds: "move yourself to where appropriateness is"). In Chinese, these virtues are called loyalty-appropriateness (*zhongyi*) and trustworthiness-appropriateness (*xinyi*), respectively. In *Analects* 1.13 Youzi directly connects trustworthiness and appropriateness: "[T]o be trustworthy in word is close to appropriateness in that it enables one's words to be repeated."

However, trustworthiness and loyalty could be in tension under certain circumstances: to be loyal, one sometimes has to violate trustworthiness, and vice versa. What is the guiding principle in order to do the appropriate thing under such a circumstance? Confucianism does not say.

A careful reading suggests that the above Confucian ideas of loyalty-appropriateness and trustworthiness-appropriateness and the tension between them underlie the characterization in *Three Kingdoms* of the relationship among the Peach Garden brothers (Liu Bei, Guan Yu, and Zhang Fei). When Liu, Guan, and Zhang take the oath of brotherhood, they swear: "We three, though of separate ancestry, join in brotherhood here, combining strength and purpose, to relieve the present crisis. We will perform our duty to the Emperor and protect the common people of the land. Although we dare not hope to be together always but hereby vow to die the selfsame day. Let shining Heaven above and the fruitful land below bear witness to our resolve. May Heaven and man scourge whosoever betrays appropriateness or forgets kindliness!" (1.9).

This oath amounts to a contract of appropriateness. A careful look reveals that it contains a potential moral dilemma. On the one hand, "to perform our duty to the Emperor and protect the common folks of the land"—which means in this context to restore the house of Han—is the moral basis of appropriateness.[8] On the other hand, the oath of brotherhood has its special requirement: they should die together. Yet to die together is not a necessary condition for the serving the state. Rather, it makes this bond imply a serious dilemma—if one of the three brothers is dead before the house of Han is reestablished, what should the other two do? For the sake of restoring the house of Han, they should continue to fight; yet if they do not die together, they will have violated the oath itself.

This contradiction becomes sharper once we understand the real nature of this oath. It was mentioned earlier that the real goal of Liu Bei is not simply to restore the house of Han, but to become emperor of the Han himself. Hence, the relation of brotherhood is also a relation between the prince and the ministers. All three brothers are fully aware of this aspect of their relationship. In chapter 26, when Zhang Liao asks Guan Yu to compare their relationship with Guan's relationship with Liu Bei, Guan replies: "You and I are just friends. Xuande [Liu Bei] and I are friends to begin with, brothers in the second place, and, finally, lord and vassal. The relationships are not comparable" (26.203). Indeed, it is questionable whether three brothers are really friends when they join in brotherhood. When these three swear to die together, they had just met for a few hours and barely know each other. Yet Guan is right that his (and Zhang Fei's) relation to Liu Bei is in the meantime a relation between minister(s) and prince. In chapter 2, when the uprising of the "Yellow-Scarves" is suppressed and Liu Bei is appointed to the post of magistrate of the Anxi district, Guan and Zhang follow Liu Bei there to take the job. The novel describes their relationship in this way: "While in office Xuande shared bed and board with his brothers, and they stood beside him throughout long public sessions" (2.17). The fact that when Liu Bei conducts public affairs the two younger brothers stand in attendance indicates the two aspects of their relationship: whereas privately they are brothers, in public the relation is that of master and subordinates.

If this is the case, the tension mentioned earlier in the contract of appropriateness turns out, more specifically, to be the tension between Liu Bei's kingship and the sworn oath-kinship of the three. If one of them is dead, what should the other two do? In my reading, one of the most important themes of *Three Kingdoms* is the unfolding and materialization of this potential tension.

To have this dilemma materialize, the one who dies first cannot be Liu Bei, since his death would remove the tension itself. Guan Yu is killed by Wu, and Liu Bei and Zhang Fei react.

When Liu Bei learns about the death of Guan Yu, he "utter[s] a dreadful cry and [falls] unconscious to the ground" (77.589). When he revives, his first words are: "I took an oath of brotherhood with Lord Guan and Zhang Fei. We vowed to die as one. With Lord Guan gone, what meaning do wealth and honor have for me?" (78.590). The bond of appropriateness in the sworn brotherhood calls. To follow the contract of appropriateness, Liu Bei should attack Wu to seek revenge. Liu Bei, however, is persuaded by Zhuge Liang not to move in that direction. Zhuge is concerned about Liu Bei's political interest. The alliance between Liu Bei and Sun Quan of Wu is Zhuge's master strategy to help Liu to achieve his eventual dream. In chapter 80 Cao Pi, the son of Cao Cao, openly deposes the emperor and establishes the state of Wei. Upon hearing this, the officers of Liu Bei, headed by Zhuge Liang, immediately urge Liu to succeed the dynasty of Han as emperor. Liu Bei, after some modest gestures, formally declares the founding of the state of Shu-Han and proclaims himself emperor. After all this is done, he starts planning to attack Wu, realizing fully that his failure to do so would put him at risk of violating the oath to die together (chapter 81). Yet many of his officers argue against this action. Zhuge proposes that Liu Bei, instead of going himself, can dispatch one top commander to conduct the war. Then, we read: "In view of Kongming's [Zhuge's] strenuous objections, the Emperor was experiencing some uncertainty about the invasion" (81.613).

Clearly, Liu Bei is caught in the dilemma between kingship and kinship. His repeated expression of the intention to attack Wu indicates that he knows well the bond of trustworthiness-appropriateness, but the fact that he is repeatedly persuaded suggests that he takes his own kingship as top priority. Before Zhang Fei challenges him, Liu's determination to seek revenge does not appear to be firm.

Zhang Fei's attitude, however, is rather different; he grants absolute priority to kinship. When he is still at his post to receive the messenger that Liu Bei sends to summon him, Zhang Fei asks: "My will to avenge my brother's murder is deep as the sea. Why have the members of court made no appeals to the throne for a general mobilization?" (81.613). When he is told that most of them urge Liu Bei to destroy Wei before attacking Wu, Zhang cries out furiously: "We three brothers took an oath to live and die as one. Now the second brother has passed from us before his time. What do wealth and station mean to me without him? I shall see the Son of Heaven [i.e. Liu Bei] myself and offer to serve in the vanguard. Under the banner of mourning I shall wage war upon the south, bring the traitor home to sacrifice to my second brother, and thus fulfill the covenant" (81.613). When he returns to the court, he immediately complains to Liu Bei in a sharp and tough tone: "Today Your Majesty reigns, and already the Peach Garden Oath is forgotten! Can you leave our brother unavenged?" To this Liu Bei answered: "Many officers oppose taking revenge. I cannot act rashly." Upon hearing this, Zhang Fei replies in a firm tone: "What do others know of our covenant? If you will not go, I will seek revenge whatever the cost to myself. Should I fail, I shall be content to die and see you no more" (81.613).

Chinese popular culture venerates Zhang Fei as the model of courage. Zhang Fei is brave not only in battlefields, but also in defending the value of the oath of brotherhood. He openly expresses his dissatisfaction with Liu Bei for putting the interest of his kingdom before the value of appropriateness. This is remarkable if we keep in mind that at that time Liu Bei has become the emperor of Shu.

Zhang Fei's defiance forces Liu Bei into a corner. His own ultimate goal of becoming the emperor of the whole empire is important. Yet it is also important to be faithful to one's oath and not to violate trustworthiness-appropriateness. This is especially significant for Liu Bei, since the image of being a moral person is Liu Bei's major strength, as was discussed in the first section of this paper. Liu Bei cannot afford to lose the image of being a person of appropriateness. Confucius had said, "I do not see how a man can be acceptable who is untrustworthy in word."[9] Zhang Fei's challenge makes Liu's excuses appear to be weak and insincere. As a result, Liu has to attack Wu for the sake of trustworthiness-appropriateness.

The tension implied in the contract of appropriateness is illustrated in the contrast between "great appropriateness" and "small appropriateness." For many, to restore the house of Han is a matter of great appropriateness, whereas to seek revenge for the death of a brother is a matter of small appropriateness. One reason that the general Zhao Yun has to oppose Liu's attack on Wu is precisely that "War against the traitors to Han is a public responsibility. War for the sake of a brother is a personal matter. I urge Your Majesty to give priority to the empire" (81.612). Another officer, Qin Mi, even says explicitly that to seek revenge for the death of Guan Yu is to follow small appropriateness. Liu surely realizes this, and indeed he must be thinking in the same way before Zhang Fei's urging. When he decides to attack Wu, his judgment of great appropriateness and small appropriateness seems also to change. Hence, he scolds his officer Qin Mi, who argues that it is a matter of small appropriateness to avenge the death of Guan: "Yunchang is I—in sacred union—and I am Yunchang. Who could forget the great obligation this entails?" (81.613).

This decision to attack Wu sets both Zhang Fei and Liu Bei on a tragic course. It makes Liu and Zhang fulfill their oath of dying as one and thus their obligation to the contract of appropriateness. By sacrificing his ultimate goal of reestablishing the house of Han and bringing about a reunification of the empire, Liu Bei preserves his image of being a person of appropriateness.

This is how the tension implicit in the Peach Garden Oath develops. This development is one of the most successful and influential points in *Three Kingdoms*. Initially, kinship is a means to kingship, but in the end kingship is sacrificed for the sake of maintaining the appropriateness of kinship. We are left, however, with a puzzle about what is really "great appropriateness" and what is "small appropriateness."

APPROPRIATENESS BETWEEN THE SWORN-BROTHERHOOD AND OTHER RELATIONSHIPS

The tension discussed in the previous section is one that is internal to the relationship of appropriateness among the Peach Garden brothers. Yet each of these brothers is inevitably related to other people. It is likely that one of them will enter into a relationship involving trustworthiness-appropriateness with someone who happens to be an enemy to one of his brothers. If one of the brothers followed trustworthiness-appropriateness in his relationship with such a person, he would violate trustworthiness-appropriateness in his relationship with his brothers. What should this person do in such a circumstance? The Confucian theory of appropriateness does not provide clear guidance.

Three Kingdoms artistically embodies this dilemma in another high point of the story. The brother who is caught in this dilemma is Guan Yu, who enters into a relationship of appropriateness with Cao Cao, the archenemy of Liu Bei. To this conflict we now turn.

In chapter 24 Liu Bei is defeated by Cao Cao at Xu Zhou, but he escapes and seeks protection from another warlord, named Yuan Shao. Guan Yu, who is assigned to protect the wives of Liu, is surrounded by the army of Cao Cao, with the certainty of death if he does not yield. Cao Cao, who admires Guan very much and hopes to recruit him, sends Guan's friend Zhang Liao to persuade Guan to surrender. At first Guan Yu is not moved: "I will die, devoted to loyalty-appropriateness" (25, my translation.). Cao is Liu's enemy, and since Guan is Liu's minister, Guan's initial attitude is in line with the Confucian demand that one should value appropriateness more than one's own life. As Mencius said: "Fish is what I want; bear's palm is also what I want. If I cannot have both, I would rather take bear's palm than fish. Life is what I want; appropriateness is also what I want. If I cannot have both, I would rather take appropriateness than life."[10]

Zhang Liao disputes Guan's belief that his death is in the spirit of loyalty-appropriateness. Zhang argues that if Guan dies at that moment, he will be guilty of three faults: "In the beginning, when you, brother, and Protector Liu bound yourselves in fraternal allegiance, you swore to share life or death. Now your brother has been defeated, and you are about to die in combat. If Xuande [i.e. Liu Bei] survives and seeks your aid in vain, won't you have betrayed your oath?" (25.193). This is the first offense. The other two are that Guan's death will leave Liu's wives unprotected and will waste his military skill. If that happens, Zhang asks, "[H]ow have you fulfilled your appropriateness?" (25.193). Clearly, in Zhang's understanding, the oath that Guan is bound to assist Liu is the basis for determining what loyalty-appropriateness is.

In the end, Guan is willing to submit if three conditions are met. He says to Zhang,

> First, the imperial uncle, Liu Xuande, and I have sworn to uphold the house of Han. I shall surrender to the Emperor, not to Cao Cao. Second, I request for my two sisters-in-law the consideration befitting an imperial uncle's wives. Nobody, however high his station is, is allowed to get close to the gate of their residence. And third, the moment we learn of Imperial Uncle Liu's whereabouts, no matter how far he may be, I shall depart forthwith. Denied any of these conditions, I shall not surrender. Please return to Cao Cao with my terms. (25.193)

Of these, the first and the third are particularly relevant insofar as the value of appropriateness is concerned. At first glance, Guan Yu appears a bit disingenuous in raising the first condition, since it has been an open secret that Cao controls the throne. Even Cao Cao himself responds to this condition by saying: "I am the prime minister of Han. The Han and I are one. This then may be granted" (25.193). However, the first condition is subtler than this. What Cao Cao fails to realize is that between the house of Han and himself there is a significant moral boundary. Loyalty-appropriateness requires that one cannot surrender to two masters or dynasties. As Zhang Fei claims: "A loyal vassal prefers death to disgrace. What self-respecting man serves two masters?" (28.216). Apparently, to surrender to Cao entails a serious betrayal of Liu Bei, and even Liu Bei himself takes it this way. When Liu learns that Guan is in the camp of Cao, he writes him a letter, saying, "In the Peach Garden you and I once swore to share a single fate. Why have you swerved from that course, severing the bond of grace and appropriateness?" (26.204). By insisting that he submits to Han, rather than to Cao, Guan is not open to the charge that he serves two masters. Thus, his surrender cannot be judged to violate the appropriateness of the oath. It is precisely this moral boundary between Cao Cao and the house of Han that enables Guan to maintain the image of being appropriate. Cao Cao demurs at the third condition, but is eventually persuaded by Zhang Liao for the following reason: "Liu Xuande treats Guan with generosity and consideration—no more. If Your Excellency extends a greater largess to bind his love, need we fear his leaving us?" (25.194).

Guan surrenders when all three conditions are granted. Cao indeed treats Guan with extreme kindness. He arranges for Guan to get the rank of general from the emperor, entertains him with banquets and feasts that follow each other in quick succession, offers him presents of silks and gold and silver vessels, provides him with ten lovely serving girls, and even sends Guan a specially made fine bag to protect Guan's beard. When Cao notices that Guan's green embroidered robe is badly worn, he has a new one made of fine brocade and presents it to Guan. When he sees that Guan's horse is old and skinny, Cao gives him as present his best horse named "Red Hare." Cao does everything that he can possibly think of, yet the only gift for which Guan bows to show gratitude is the horse. And Guan's gratitude makes Cao feel deeply regretful about his gift, because Guan's reason for being grateful is that." It can cover a thousand li in a single day. It is a gift that will enable me to reach my brother in a single day should his whereabouts become known" (25.196). When Guan Yu finally learns where Lu Bei is, he immediately abandons his rank in the camp of Cao, sends back all gifts except the horse, and leaves Cao without any hesitation.

The kindness of Cao Cao toward Guan is a test of Guan's virtue of appropriateness. *Three Kingdoms* creates here a story that represents the Confucian position on the relation between appropriateness and personal advantage or profit. For Confucianism, one of the basic features of appropriateness is that it is in opposition to personal advantage or profit: "The gentleman understands appropriateness; the small man understands what is profitable."[11] One chooses to do a thing of appropriateness simply because it is the right thing to do, not because it might bring about good and beneficial consequences. The demand of appropriateness is imperative. Guan survives the test because he holds on to this principle of appropriateness without being shaken. In his farewell letter to Cao Cao, Guan says, "Now I have discovered that my first liege is in the army of Yuan Shao. Our covenant is ever in my thoughts; to betray it is unthinkable. Despite the great favor you have bestowed on me of late, I cannot forget the appropriateness of the past" (26.205). Although Guan fails to die for loyalty-appropriateness, he becomes a paradigm of loyalty-appropriateness in Chinese popular culture because of his virtue in upholding the original oath and resisting the temptations offered by Cao.

Nevertheless, to be treated with kindness establishes a kind of relation of appropriateness. Guan Yu apparently owes Cao Cao for the latter's kindness. His debt becomes greater when, on his way to rejoin Liu, he forgets to obtain the necessary travel document because he is in a hurry. Guan then has to kill six generals of Cao at five military passes. Confucius said that one should "repay a good turn with a good turn."[12] Appropriateness demands that Guan return the favor to Cao. Otherwise, he would be perceived as a person who is "not (bu) appropriate." Guan fully understands this obligation, as he concludes his farewell letter to Cao Cao as follows: "For whatever benefaction I may yet remain in your debt, kindly defer the accounting until some future day" (26.205).

This moral obligation comes due at a moment when Guan has an opportunity to capture Cao Cao. When Cao is defeated by the allied forces of Wu and Liu Bei, Guan Yu is assigned by Zhuge Liang to ambush Cao Cao at Huarongdao. When, true to Zhuge's prediction, Cao Cao and his handful of surviving soldiers indeed show up and are blocked by Guan Yu, Cao and his exhausted soldiers no longer have the energy and will to fight, and there is no chance to run away, either. It is clear that the last and only means that Cao Cao has to save his life is through a personal appeal to Guan. Cao Cao is not shy about reminding Guan of the past kindness he bestowed on him: "My army is defeated and my situation is critical. At this point I have no way out. But I trust, General, you will give due weight to our old friendship" (50.383). Guan Yu struggles to argue against this reasoning, and replies, "In the present situation I cannot set aside public duty for personal considerations." Cao Cao continues: "A man worthy of the name gives the greatest weight to trustworthiness and appropriateness." At that, says the novel, "'Lord Guan, whose sense of appropriateness was as solid as a mountain (*Yi zhong ru shan*), could not put Cao Cao's many obliging kindnesses he had received or the thought of the slain commanders from his mind. Moved, despite himself, at the sight of Cao's men distracted and on the verge of tears, Lord Guan softened. He swung away his mount and said to his soldiers, "Spread out on all sides," clearly signaling his intent to make way" (50.384).

Guan Yu, mindful of Cao's past generosity, purposefully spares Cao Cao. By doing this, he is judged to be performing an action of appropriateness, as is indicated clearly by part of the title of chapter 50: "Guan Yunchang Releases Cao Cao Out of Appropriateness." However, by doing this, Guan in the meantime commits a serious violation of the oath of brotherhood with Liu Bei. The oath's moral basis is to restore the house of Han, and Cao Cao is the main enemy in this great cause. If Guan had captured Cao Cao at that time, Liu Bei could have gained the whole empire and realized his dream. Clearly, Guan's appropriateness in releasing Cao Cao has a disastrous impact upon the great cause of the oath of brotherhood.

Furthermore, by releasing Cao, Guan violates military rules. When taking the job of staging the ambush at Huarongdao, he signs a military decree that if he fails to capture Cao Cao he will be executed. By releasing Cao, Guan allows his personal appropriateness to take precedence over the demands of the law. When he returns to headquarters empty-handed, he faces the death penalty from Zhuge Liang. But Liu Bei saves his life. Liu gives the following reason: "When my brothers and I pledged mutual faith, we swore to live—and to die—as one. Now Yunchang has broken the law, but I haven't the heart to go against our former convenant. I hope you [i.e., Zhuge Liang] will suspend the rule this time and simply record his fault, allowing him to redeem his offense by future merit" (51.386). It is an irony that Guan Yu betrays his oath to Liu, yet Liu saves him by means of the oath. It is quite a tradition in China to put appropriateness above the law, and Guan's release of Cao sets up an influential model.

We see here two conflicts in the notion of appropriateness: (1) the conflict between appropriateness with respect to Liu and appropriateness with respect to Cao; and (2) the conflict between appropriateness and the law. It is through this complicated picture that Guan Yu's image of being a person of appropriateness is established. It is appropriate for Guan to refuse to stay in the camp of Cao and return to Liu; and it is also appropriate for him to spare Cao Cao by repaying his previous kindness. If he had chosen not to do either of these two conflicting things, Guan's image would have been seriously damaged. Yet although Guan has been venerated in Chinese popular culture as the incarnation of the value of appropriateness, we are left with a conundrum: how can it be the case that performing these contradictory actions constitutes a demonstration of appropriateness?

CONCLUDING REMARKS

The above discussion of appropriateness in *Three Kingdoms* and its relation to Confucianism should indicate that the author of *Three Kingdoms* was well versed in Confucianism and had a plan to embody the Confucian theory of appropriateness in his novel. In his creation of these characters and his description of their goals, beliefs, and reasons for acting, he embodies the various different and even incompatible aspects of the Confucian notion of appropriateness. No doubt, the unfolding of these tensions and conflicts contributes significantly to the greatness of *Three Kingdoms*.

What, then, does this situation tell us about Confucianism? At first glance, it reveals a problem in Confucianism: namely, that it cannot provide practical guidance when moral conflicts occur. From the standpoint of modern Western rule-based moral theories, Confucianism clearly fails to establish some universal moral principles that all agents should follow under all circumstances. Nevertheless, the popularity and profound influence of *Three Kingdoms*, to a great extent, demonstrates that the Confucian view of morality cannot be dismissed easily. If characters such as Liu Bei and Guan Yu held only one universal moral principle and applied it mechanically in every situation, if they were indifferent toward friendship, love, affection, and so forth—if, for instance, Liu simply refused to avenge the death of Guan in order to preserve the interest of the kingdom, or if Guan simply captured Cao Cao out of his sense of duty—it is inconceivable that these characters would be so appealing, and the literary value of *Three Kingdoms* would be significantly reduced. Hence, we have reason to believe that human life itself is more complicated than what a single principle can govern. There is no single principle to guide one to do what is appropriate throughout one's life. Given the demonstrated relationship between Confucianism and *Three Kingdoms*, success of *Three Kingdoms* may indicate that Confucianism, in its refusal to establish universal moral principles that can be used to guide all actions and in its focus on the character and virtues of a moral agent, grasped the true complexity of human ethical life.

NOTES

1. Unless otherwise noted, in this paper, translation of the *Analects of Confucius* is based on D. C. Lau's *Confucius's Analects* (Hong Kong: Chinese University Press, 1983); translation of the *Mencius* is based on D. C. Lau's *Mencius* (Hong Kong: Chinese University Press, 1984); and translation of *Three Kingdoms* is based on Moss Roberts' *Three Kingdoms: A Historical Novel* (Berkeley and Los Angeles: University of California Press; Beijing: Foreign Language Press, 1991). One modification I make is to translate *yi* consistently as "appropriateness" whenever it appears. (Both Lau and Roberts translate *yi* in various ways. Lau uses "morality," "what is moral," "duty," and so on, and Roberts alternates among "honor," or "duty," "obligation," or "allegiance," etc.).

2. *Analects* 1.13, 2.24, 5.16, 7.3, 12.10, 12.20, 13.4, 15.16, 16.11. *Mencius*, 1a/3; 1a/7, 3a/4, 4a/27, 6a/5, 7/15, 7b/24.

3. *Mencius* 1a/7, 4a/10, 6a/10, 7b/12.

4. *Analects* 3.4, 9.3.

5. *Mencius* 4a/17; 7a/26.

6. *Mencius* 4a/9; cf. 5a/5.

7. *Analects* 1.8.

8. As Guan Yu remarks clearly: "My brother and I swore in the Peach Garden to make common cause in upholding the house of Han" (66.504).

9. *Analects* 2.22.

10. *Mencius* 6a/10.

11. *Analects* 4.16, cf. also, 19.7; 7.15; 14.13.

12. *Analects* 14.34.

II

Three Kingdoms and Chinese History

4

The Beginning of the End

The Fall of the Han and the
Opening of *Three Kingdoms*

GEORGE A. HAYDEN

Well before the formal beginning of the Three Kingdoms era upon the close of the Latter or Eastern Han in 220, the three kingdoms were already taking shape in the persons of Cao Cao, Sun Quan, and Liu Bei. The tripartite fragmentation of the Han itself was the formation of an uneasy balance of power, a settling of a more chaotic condition resulting from the loss of imperial authority and prestige at an earlier time. The search for an answer to the question of when and how the Han began to fall leads to two kinds of source material and two different approaches to historical fact and interpretation. One type of source is traditional Chinese historiography: *Chronicle of the Three Kingdoms* (*Sanguo zhi*) by Chen Shou, *Hou Han ji* by Yuan Hong, *Hou Han shu* by Fan Ye and Sima Biao, and *Comprehensive Mirror for Aid in Government* (*Zizhi tongjian*) by Sima Guang. The other type of source is historical fiction in the form of Luo Guanzhong's *Three Kingdoms*.

Traditional Chinese historians have tried to present as much important factual data as possible for a designated historical period and have tended to forego simple explanations; the guiding principle is complexity. Through a mass of events and individuals in annals and memoirs and with the aid of only sporadic commentary by the compiler/author, we are to form our own opinions on historical causes. Even such summarization as can be found tends toward some complexity.

An example is Sima Guang's summary of the decline of the Eastern Han. Six symptoms of moral decline have their start with Emperor He, who reigned from 89 to 105:

1. excessive power in the hands of imperial in-laws

2. indulgence of imperial favorites

3. a lack of standards in reward and punishment

4. open bribery

5. confusion in judging the worthy and the inept

6. a confounding of right and wrong

The responsibility for these symptoms, in accordance with Confucian tradition, rests with the emperor; even bribery, if not actually committed by him, was tolerated by him and was in any case the reflection of widespread degeneration beginning at the top. The itemization is not specific, because it covers the reigns of several emperors. Sima Guang's point is that the first three emperors of the Eastern Han—the emperors Guang Wu (r. 25–57), Ming (r. 58–75), and Zhang (r. 76–88), had such a beneficial effect on public morality that certain conscientious officials of later, more benighted regimes managed to shore up the dynasty in spite of the rot at the highest levels and, but for the absence of a good man on the throne, could have worked miracles. Only with the reigns of the emperors Huan (r. 147–67) and Ling (r. 168–89) does he use labels of disgust—"stupidity and cruelty," (*hun nüe*)—in reference to two rulers who in his opinion went out of their way to favor the wicked and destroy the good. Public anger during this time resulted in the misguided call by He Jin for outside armed help against the eunuchs, which in turn brought the disasters caused by Dong Zhuo, Yuan Shao, and other warlords and the irrecoverable loss of the "great mandate" of the Han.[1] Although specific on He Jin's mistake as the proximate cause of the downfall of the Han, Sima Guang is less specific on the ultimate causes, but he presents more than ample documentation in the body of his history.

The concerns of the novelist lie elsewhere: in threading action and speech together into a single line of narrative on the fall of the Han and the rise and fall of the three kingdoms. The line must have a starting point and a conclusion, and this starting point should explain as succinctly as possible how it all began to go wrong. The version of the novel with the title *Sanguo zhi tongsu yanyi*, hereafter to be called the TS, opens the narrative with the accession of Emperor Ling in 168, the manipulation of power by the eunuchs Cao Jie and Wang Fu, the failed plot against them led by Dou Wu and Chen Fan, and the subsequent domination of the court by the eunuchs, all in a short paragraph of four sentences as punctuated in a modern edition.[2] This introduction leaves out Emperor Huan entirely. An account of portents and their interpretations follows and leads to mention by name of the eunuch leaders as the "Ten Regular Attendants" (*Shi changshi*). The narrative then shifts to Zhang Jue and the Yellow Scarves (*Huang jin*). In this narrative development transition words between topics do not appear; the technique might be called causation by contiguity. Excessive power in the hands of eunuchs leads to portents and calamities; when the emperor ignores these, he only helps to consolidate eunuch privilege, which leads in turn to the Yellow Scarves. The connection between the Yellow Scarves and the eunuchs is made concrete by mention of the two eunuchs acting as a fifth column for Zhang Jue in the palace. The edition published by Mao Zonggang, called *Sanguo zhi yanyi* or *Sanguo yanyi*, draws a smoother connection between the eunuchs and the Yellow Scarves by first pointing to the moral decay and banditry resulting from eunuch pollution and then proceeding directly to Zhang Jue without the common sign of a shift of topic, the "*que shuo*" of the TS.[3]

With the Yellow Scarves rebellion of 184 comes detailed narrative instead of introductory summary, and the reader begins to participate as witness to the fall of the Han through the Yellow Scarves uprising and its suppression, the massacre of the eunuchs, and the seizure of power by various strongmen beginning with Dong Zhuo and ending with Cao Cao. All this is a necessary condition to the rise of Liu Bei and his brotherhood with Guan Yu and Zhang Fei, pledged to support the beleaguered emperor as well as the long-suffering people. The three heroes arise as a consequence of and in response to the growing chaos, and their struggle offers resolution. And it all starts with the eunuchs. Now we know how the Han fell, but in a sense we still do not know why it did so.

The Mao version keeps the eunuchs as a cause but traces misplaced confidence in them back to Emperor Huan. It identifies him and Emperor Ling as the ultimate sources of trouble and refers more specifically to two mutually corresponding practices of Emperor Huan that Emperor Ling continued under eunuch instigation: proscription of good men from office and trust in eunuchs. The blame of these two emperors for the decline of the Han may derive immediately from Sima Guang's comments mentioned above, but such blame has been of long standing at least since Zhuge Liang's first memorial to the second emperor of Shu-Han at the outset of the northern expedition: "Welcoming worthy subjects and keeping petty men at a distance: this is how the Former Han flourished. Welcoming petty men and keeping worthy subjects at a distance: this is how the Latter Han declined. When the former emperor [Liu Bei] was alive and spoke with me of such matters, he never failed to sigh in pained regret over Huan and Ling."[4] At the very beginning of the Mao version, before its identification of the human sources of the downfall of the Han, comes a statement on the cyclical movement of history: "It is the way of the world that what is long divided must unite and what is long united must divide." Subsequent to this opening, the end of the Han appears in the broad sweep of history since the Warring States divided the realm of the Zhou. After unification by Qin came the struggle between Chu and Han, reunification under the first emperor of the Han, revival under Emperor Guang Wu, and final division into three kingdoms during the reign of Emperor Xian.[5] We now have a suprahuman reason as to why the Han fell: it had ruled long enough in unity, and now it was time for disunity to set in. This cyclical view of history is evident in Mencius: "Life in the world has endured a long time now, sometimes in order and sometimes in confusion."[6]

During the Former Han, Dong Zhongshu adopted into Confucianism the phraseology of Zou Yan of a century earlier and described the passage of time as the alternation of yang and yin, and as the orderly succession of the five agents of earth, metal, water, wood, and fire. This alternation is an endless series of evolutions and reversions, like the passage of season to season and year upon year, in which yang and yin, order and confusion, are interdependent and mutually generative phases of the same organism, the way of nature.

The difference between the cycle of the seasons and the cycle of the dynasties is a matter of regularity and predictability. In Mao Zonggang's scheme, in contrast to the two centuries of division during the Warring States era is the unity of the Qin, lasting only fifteen years and followed by a relatively brief period of civil war and then by two centuries of unity in the Former Han. This is hardly the orderly succession of the seasons. One question that arises is whether this irregular pattern is haphazard, self-determined, or caused by some such higher power as heaven. If it is purely random, then the word "long" (*jiu*) has no standard at all. If it is self-determined, then how long is "long"? Why is "long" a matter of two hundred years in one instance and fifteen in another? Did unity under the Qin have some such quality as inhumanity that curtailed its duration from perhaps a normal span of two hundred years? Was disorder after the Qin so short for any particular reason, such as the appearance of an extraordinary individual in the person of Emperor Gao of the Han? What then, if anything, determined Qin administrative policy or the arrival of Liu Bang? Why, for that matter, should the so-called normal span of a dynasty be two hundred years or any other stretch of time? An elaborate chain of material causation could be worked out for these questions, but Mao Zonggang's opening to the novel is more poetic than precise. No explanation is forthcoming. This does not mean, however, that it can be dismissed as having nothing to do with the rest of the novel.

We might wonder as well about the end of the Han. The cause may lie with the emperors Huan and Ling, but what made them favor the eunuchs and persecute the antieunuch faction in the first place? Were these actions the result of a gradual accumulation of power by influential eunuchs? If so, then the ultimate cause goes back to an earlier time, and these two emperors are less culpable than Mao suggests. If the origin of the problem is an individual quirk of Emperor Huan, which his successor, Emperor Ling, voluntarily perpetuated, then the topic of free choice turns up. On the subject of eunuchs Cao Cao is quoted in the novel. "The trouble with eunuchs has always existed; it is just that the ruler should never give them so much influence and favor that things might come to this."[7] This quotation is based on what is supposed to be an actual statement by Cao Cao to the effect that the office of eunuch has rightly existed for all time, and if extremes of privilege are avoided, no disaster need occur.[8] Cao Cao thereby dismisses any inevitability of the eunuch problem, which he ascribes simply to poor judgment.

The question of causality is still unresolved, however. The poor choices of the emperors Huan and Ling may not have been free at all but forced by an overwhelming decline into disorder, of which the eunuch problem is an inevitable symptom. This particular symptom appears at this particular time and with an impetus not to be averted or overcome by human agency. The emperors were just part of the process, in which all is fated and no human volition is free.

The issue of causality recurs in the novel immediately after introduction of the eunuch problem. During the reign of Emperor Ling, in the years 169, 171, and 178, eight natural anomalies or disasters occur.

For the year 169:

* a sudden appearance and disappearance of a huge blue-green serpent in the emperor's presence

* an accompanying storm of thunder, rain, and hail

For the year 171:

* an earthquake in the capital

* a tidal wave.

For the year 178:

* the transformation of a hen into a rooster

* a black miasma that enters the palace

* a rainbow, also in the palace

* an avalanche

The list is a condensation of many more such instances as recorded in *Hou Han ji*, *Hou Han shu*, and *Comprehensive Mirror*, and as such it illustrates the predilection of historical fiction for simplification and focus. The reader may receive the impression from the novel that only in the reign of Emperor Ling did such events begin to occur, whereas a reading of the historical sources reveals otherwise. A survey of the annals in *Hou Han shu* for the 160 years of the Latter Han up to the year 184 and the outbreak of the Yellow Scarves rebellion shows a pattern of disasters or at least a pattern of their recording. These disasters include more categories than the novel mentions: solar eclipses; droughts; asteroids; floods; plagues; insect infestations; fires in imperial palaces, stables, and tombs; windstorms; and famines, as well as the earthquakes, hailstorms, tidal waves, and avalanches mentioned in the novel. They begin as early as the reign of Emperor Guang Wu but increase, sometimes alarmingly so, during the latter half of the 160-year period, as if the record keepers were becoming increasingly anxious over the fate of the Han and increasingly eager to cite divine intervention the longer the dynasty lasted.

The frequency of such entries in the historical sources is testament to the seriousness with which people at the time took these anomalies. To many they were signs from heaven. Dong Zhongshu explains a belief of great antiquity: "When the first indications of error begin to appear in the state, Heaven sends forth ominous portents and calamities to warn men and announce the fact. If, in spite of these warnings and pronouncements, men still do not realize how they have gone wrong, then Heaven sends prodigies and wonders to terrify them. If, after these terrors, men still know no awe or fear, then calamity and misfortune will visit them. From this we may see that the will of Heaven is benevolent, for it has no desire to trap or betray mankind."[9]

A statement attributed to Dong Zhongshu in a biography on him by Ban Gu claims the origin of calamities and anomalies to be an imbalance in yin and yang reflecting disharmony between the will of Heaven above and evil on earth below, a disharmony caused by unjust punishment.[10] It is clear that to Dong Zhongshu human error and injustice are the motive force behind disturbances to a delicate cosmological balance and that in human hands lies the possibility for correction. In response to such warnings the Han emperors often called on officials to point out defects in the government or proclaimed such remedial measures as amnesty, relief, and exemption from taxes.

The historical sources record all eight events as having taken place, as well as opinions on their significance from officials consulted by Emperor Ling. From the four advisors to the court whose memorials to the throne are recorded in the sources, the TS quotes two in part: Yang Ci and Cai Yong. The gist of the memorials is that the rainbow and the transformation of the hen to a rooster are warnings from Heaven that undesirable elements control the court. Palace ladies, eunuchs, and a coterie of petty litterateurs favored by the emperor are mentioned by Yang Ci, while Cai Yong concentrates on women, as in the following excerpt from the TS: "Your servant humbly regards all of the anomalies as prodigies of a dying state. Heaven has never ceased to care for the Han and for that reason produces many supernatural changes to serve as reproaches, in the hope that the ruler will come to realization and transform danger into security. The rainbow and the transformation of the chicken were both caused by involvement of women in government. . . ."[11]

In a further effort at simplification and focus the Mao version deletes Yang Ci and his memorial entirely and uses only the last sentence in the excerpt of Cai Yong's memorial translated above, changing *'furen"* (women) to *"fu si"* (women and eunuchs). This version thus ascribes to Cai Yong Yang Ci's condemnation of eunuchs and gives a better rationale for attempts by the eunuchs to punish Cai Yong in both versions of the novel.

In the orthodox historical sources the interpretations of the strange phenomena are more varied than the novel suggests, but they do share a common theme in the yin principle. From some of the memorials and especially from Sima Biao's treatise on the five agents in *Hou Han shu*, we can appreciate the common assumptions regarding all of these portents. During the Han serpents were seen as feminine symbols. The advisor Xie Bi makes this identification in a memorial on this particular serpent, although his point has nothing to do with eunuchs but explains its appearance

as a result of the resentful spirit of Dowager Empress Dou.[12] He quotes two lines
from *Shi jing* in which images of snakes have reference to women.[13] On the appearance of a second serpent in 172 (not included in the novel) Yang Ci cites the same
lines and uses an example from history to show a connection between serpents and
female interference in government.[14] Sima Biao then ties this serpent specifically to
eunuchs.[15] Sima Biao uses a statement by Liu Xiang that hailstorms are signs that
yin is overwhelming yang and blames three severe hailstorms—the one in question
in 169 and two others in 171 and 181, respectively—on the eunuchs.[16] With reference to floods and tidal waves he says that when water, a symbol of *yin*, loses its
original nature, it creates disasters, and participation in government by petty men is
the cause.[17] He also associates heavy rainfall with eunuchs.[18] Earthquakes and avalanches in a similar fashion are signs that earth has lost its original nature, and the
earthquake of 171 he ascribes to the malign influence of the eunuchs led by Cao Jie
and Wang Fu.[19] He leaves it unsaid that earth, as against the yang of Heaven, symbolizes yin. On the transformation of the hen, Sima Biao quotes Cai Yong as saying
that a wonder of the same kind in the Former Han portended Wang Mang's usurpation. This time the cock's comb has not formed, indicating that another attempt
to usurp the Han will be unsuccessful. If the emperor does not reform his government, however, the cock's comb may form and result in disaster. To Sima Biao this
is a prediction of the Yellow Scarves rebellion, which, although unsuccessful, was
followed by severe taxation, administrative malfeasance, and ultimate collapse.[20]
Sima Biao conflates the black miasma and the rainbow and quotes Cai Yong, who
on the basis of prophecies shows that secondary rainbows indicate control over the
ruler by the yin principle of empresses and consorts; the five colors of rainbows in
the palace foretell warfare. No comment apparently is necessary on black as symbolic of yin. Sima Biao in this way uses both the miasma and the rainbow to predict
not only the Yellow Scarves but also the pernicious influence of Empress He, con-
sort of Emperor Ling, and her two brothers, Jin and Miao. It is He Jin who sets the
Han on an irremediable course to perdition by bringing Dong Zhuo and his troops
into the capital to help wipe out the eunuchs.[21]

Taken as a whole, the portents mentioned, among hundreds of others, are
interpreted as having a double function: to reflect current defects in government
and to predict further disaster if those defects go uncorrected. In the interpretations we can see how advisors bolstered their arguments on policy with omens
indicating the way of nature or the will of heaven. The novel provides no such
precise interpretations as Yang Ci, Cai Yong, and Sima Biao offer, although Mao
Zonggang's commentary fills in some gaps.[22] Rather, the author seems to assume
comprehension of the symbolism on the part of the reader. The monitory function
of the portents is clear nevertheless. With understanding of the predictive function
of the eight portents, the lead-in to the Yellow Scarves and to Dong Zhuo is all the
more clear-cut.

In the novel the portents play another role besides the reflective and predictive functions taken over from history: to show the emperor's reaction. The initial

reaction of Emperor Ling to the accumulation of these signs is alarm; hence his proclamation for interpretations. Upon reading memorials by Yang Ci and Cai Yong (by Cai Yong only in the Mao version) suggesting that he distance himself from his favorite palace women and eunuchs, he sighs, rises, and leaves to "change his clothes" (*geng yi*), a euphemism for relieving himself. After this comes retaliation by the eunuch faction on Cai Yong. The implication is obvious: the emperor will do nothing about the problems indicated by the portents, and the worsening moral decay brought on by the eunuchs leads immediately to the Yellow Scarves.

Another implication is clear in the portents themselves and the emperor's response or, rather, lack of response. The emperor has a chance to break free of the weight of custom and strike out on a path of reform, but he must make a choice between action and inaction. Unless we assume absolute fatalism, a temporal determinism that sets the course of the Han inexorably toward collapse and in the process decrees that the emperor participate in that collapse by doing nothing, the emperor's choice is free—difficult, to be sure, but free all the same. In other words, mankind is either free or bound to fate. If it is free, then Emperor Ling could in that one moment have changed the course of history. In response to omens brought perhaps by Heaven but caused ultimately by his own misguided actions, he could have averted the train of events culminating in the end of the Han. Instead he adds to the momentum of disunion, destruction, and misery, against which Liu Bei and Zhuge Liang will struggle bravely but in vain. In this regard *Three Kingdoms* is both admonition and testament to the human will.

NOTES

1. Sima Guang, *Zizhi Tongjian, juan* 68, Han ji 漢紀 60, Xian di Jian'an 24 nian (219) (Beijing: Zhonghua shuju, 1956), 5:2173, 2174.

2. Luo Guanzhong, *Sanguo zhi tongsu yanyi* (hereafter "TS"), *juan* 1, Ji tiandi taoyuan jieyi 祭天地桃園結義 (Shanghai: Shanghai guji chubanshe, 1980), 1:1.

3. Luo Guanzhong, *Sanguo zhi yanyi* (hereafter "Mao edition"), chap. 1 (Hong Kong: Shangwu yinshuguan, 1962), 1:1.

4. Chen Shou, *Sanguo zhi, juan* 31, Shu shu 5, "Zhuge Liang zhuan" (Beijing: Zhonghua shuju, 1982 ed.), 4:920.

5. Luo Guanzhong, Mao edition, chap. 1, 1:1.

6. *Mengzi* 孟子, "Teng Wen gong 滕文公," *xia* 下: 9.

7. Luo Guanzhong, TS, *juan* 1, "Dong Zhuo yi li Chenliu wang 董卓議立陳留王," 1:21. Mao edition, chap. 3, 1:16.

8. A citation by Pei Songzhi from *Wei shu* 魏書 in Chen Shou, *Sanguo zhi juan* 1, 1:5; and Sima Guang, *Zizhi Tongjian juan,* 59, Han ji 51, Ling di Zhongping 6 nian (189), 5:1897.

9. Dong Zhongshu 董仲舒, *Chunqiu fanlu* 春秋繁露, 30, *juan* 8, as translated in *Sources of Chinese Tradition,* comp. W. Theodore de Bary, Wing-tsit Chan, and Burton Watson (New York: Columbia University Press, 1960), 187.

10. Youlan Feng, *Zhongguo zhexueshi* (Shanghai: Shangwu yinshuguan, 1935), 2:531.

11. Luo Guanzhong, TS, p. 2.

12. Yuan Hong, *Hou Han ji jiaozhu,* ed. Tianyou Zhou, *juan* 23 (Tianjin: Tianjin guji chubanshe, 1987), 641. Fan Ye, *Hou Han shu, juan* 57 (Changsha: Yuelu shushe, 1994), 1: 798, 799. Sima Guang, *Zizhi Tongjian juan* 56, Han ji 48, Ling di Jianning 2 nian (169), 4:1814, 1815.

13. *Shi jing* 詩經, Xiao ya 小雅, "Si gan" 斯干. Sima Guang, *Zizhi Tongjian.* In an interlinear note to Sima Guang, Sanxing Hu 胡三省 misidentifies the song as "Xiao yang" 小羊. The lines are "A serpent, a snake:/Favorable signs for women" 維虺維蛇，女子之祥.

14. Yuan Hong, *Hou Hanji jiaozhu, juan* 23, pp. 660, 661. Fan Ye, *Hou Han Shu, juan* 54, 759, 760. Fan Ye in his annals and Sima Guang do not record this occurrence; Sima Guang includes Yang Ci's memorial with Xie Bi's for the appearance of the serpent in 169.

15. Sima Biao, Zhi 17, Wuxing zhi 五行志 5, in Fan Ye, *Hou Han shu,* 2: 1467.

16. Ibid., Zhi 15, Wuxing zhi 3, in Fan Ye, *Hou Han shu,* 2:1455, 1456.

17. Ibid., pp. 1453–1455.

18. Ibid., Zhi 13, Wuxing zhi 1, in Fan Ye, *Hou Han shu,* 2:1437.

19. Ibid., Zhi 16, Wuxing zhi 4, in Fan Ye, *Hou Han shu,* 2:1462.

20. Ibid., Zhi 13, Wuxing zhi 1, in Fan Ye, *Hou Han shu,* 2:1440.

21. Ibid., Zhi 17, Wuxing zhi 5, in Fan Ye, *Hou Han shu,* 2:1469, 1470.

22. Luo Guanzhong, Mao edition, chap. 1, 1: 2. According to Mao, the omen is fitting because first males, or "roosters," were changed into females, or "hens," and later these "hens" tried to change into "roosters" by meddling in government, rightfully exclusive to the yang.

5

Selected Historical Sources
for *Three Kingdoms*

Reflections from Sima Guang's and Chen Liang's
Reconstructions of Kongming's Story

HOYT CLEVELAND TILLMAN

Attention is often drawn to performance literature (like dramas and plays and storytelling) as the principal sources for *Three Kingdoms* (*Sanguo yanyi*); without minimizing the relevance of those sources, I would like to highlight two historians' contributions to reconstructed images of heroes from the Three Kingdoms era in the third century. The particular hero chosen for this case study is Zhuge Liang (often called Kongming, 181–234), not only because of his historical importance but also because of his crucial role in *Three Kingdoms*. Since historians over the centuries have wrestled with major questions about Zhuge Liang, interpretations of Zhuge Liang have changed over time as historians retold his story from the vantage point of their own periods and issues. Sometimes even recorded and remembered "facts" changed, too, as historians reimagined the hero's life and deeds. Although numerous historians contributed significantly to Chinese understandings of Zhuge Liang, I am here focusing on the two historians who arguably had a particularly significant impact on the character of Kongming as portrayed in the historical "novel." The baseline for assessing the transformation of Zhuge Liang is, of course, the "historic" Zhuge Liang in Chen Shou's *Chronicle of the Three Kingdoms* (*Sanguo zhi*). Despite a generally positive portrayal of Zhuge Liang, Chen Shou rendered a negative evaluation of Zhuge's military abilities: Zhuge Liang "made campaigns every year without achieving results. It would seem that resourceful generalship in response to changing situations was not his forte."[1] Against the

backdrop of the Chen Shou's *Chronicle*, the Kongming of *Three Kingdoms* is more
talented as a strategist and military commander; moreover, he emerges as a Daoist
sage or even a clever trickster. The novel's hero is also a much more stern administrator of legal punishments and military discipline than the man in Chen Shou's
biography of Zhuge Liang. What and how did Sima Guang (1019–86) and Chen
Liang (1143–94) contribute to these transformations of Zhuge Liang? And what
role in this transmission did Zhu Xi's (1130–1200) *Outline and Digest of the Comprehensive Mirror for Aid in Government* (*Zizhi tongjian gangmu*) possibly play?

I.

In the *Comprehensive Mirror for Aid in Government* (*Zizhi tongjian*), Sima Guang's
reconstruction of Kongming's story projected Zhuge Liang as a stern upholder
of law and punishments.[2] Compared to the *Chronicle*, the *Comprehensive Mirror*
significantly enhanced Kongming's role in several executions. Yong Kai's death is
perhaps the simplest and clearest case of Sima Guang's changes; moreover, it is a
change that apparently enhances Zhuge Liang's credit in suppressing a rebellion.
Chen Shou's *Chronicle* had clearly stated that the rebel Yong Kai was killed by
another rebel, Gao Ding (d. 225).[3] The *Huayang guozhi*, a source included in Pei
Songzhi's commentary to the *Chronicle*, presented Gao Ding's troops as killing Yong
Kai and afterwards Zhuge Liang executing Gao Ding.[4] There is no evidence, either
in Yan Yan's *Zizhi tongjian bu* or in Lu Bi's *Sanguo zhi jijie*, for Zhuge Liang killing
Yong Kai.[5] Moreover, no known early source had assigned Zhuge Liang responsibility for executing Yong Kai. Nevertheless, Sima Guang credits Zhuge Liang with
killing not only Gao Ding but also Yong Kai.[6] One could explain this discrepancy
as a simple narrative device for moving the story along. Neither Yong Kai nor Gao
Ding were the main rebel leaders, and Sima Guang could be seen as using them
merely to set the stage for the larger story of Zhuge Liang's capture and release of
Meng Huo (fl. 220s). However, it seems to me that the stage could have been set
even better by preserving the distinction that Gao Ding killed Yong Kai, for these
conditions would have underscored Zhuge Liang's reasons for executing Gao Ding,
while repeatedly pardoning other leaders of this rebellion. What perspective on the
death of Yong Kai did *Three Kingdoms* take?

As if deliberately combining the contradictory accounts in the *Chronicle* and
the *Comprehensive Mirror*, *Three Kingdoms* elaborated upon Zhuge Liang's role
in Yong Kai's death, but with a surprising twist in the larger story. Chapter 87
of *Three Kingdoms* recounts Zhuge Liang's disposal of Yong Kai and Gao Ding's
rebellion. Yong Kai, the governor of Jianning, began the rebellion in league with
Meng Huo, the king of the Man people; moreover, the governor of Zangke district,
Zhu Bao, and the governor of Yuesui, Gao Ding, quickly surrendered their cities
to Yong Kai and joined forces with him. When Zhuge Liang's army captured Gao
Ding's vanguard and leader, E Huan, Zhuge Liang proclaimed that Gao Ding was
"a honorable man—whom Yong Kai has led astray and into rebellion." Kongming

further announced: "I shall release you now so you may get Governor Gao Ding to resubmit to our authority and spare himself the gravest consequences."[7] Gao Ding hesitated, but still joined with Yong Kai in the next assault on Kongming's camp. Quite a number of their troops were captured, but Zhuge Liang again released them when they professed to be Gao Ding's men. While releasing those who were actually Gao Ding's men, Kongming remarked that Yong Kai had sent a messenger with an offer to behead both Gao Ding and Zhu Bao; however, Kongming claimed that he did not have the heart to accept Yong Kai's surrender on these grounds. After hearing these accounts from his men, Gao Ding sent spies to Yong Kai's and Kongming's camps. Kongming's men apprehended the spy, and Kongming pretended to mistake him for Yong Kai's man. Besides complaining that Yong Kai had missed the promised date for delivering Gao Ding's and Zhu Bao's heads, Kongming gave the spy a letter urging Yong Kai to act promptly. Deceived by such evidence, Gao Ding attacked Yong Kai, and E Huan intercepted and beheaded the fleeing rebel leader. Presenting Yong Kai's head, Gao Ding surrendered, but Kongming ordered Gao Ding's execution on the grounds that the surrender was only a pretense. Kongming waved a letter allegedly from Zhu Bao offering to surrender and claiming that Gao and Yong were too close for them to forsake their joint rebellion. Thus, Kongming tricked Gao Ding into offering to catch Zhu Bao in order to prove his sincerity. With similar tactics to the attack on Yong Kai, Gao Ding berated Zhu Bao from the front while E Huan cut him down from behind. Thereupon, Kongming appointed Gao Ding as governor of Yizhou, and these three rebellions were quelled.

Beyond the entertaining details that *Three Kingdoms* creates and adds in its elaboration on the suppression of Yong Kai's rebellion, it is particularly noteworthy that the novel builds upon Sima Guang's suggestion that Zhuge Liang executed Yong Kai. The novel is faithful to Sima Guang's apparently inventive assertion that Zhuge Liang was responsible for Yong Kai's death; yet, the novel does not contradict the accounts in the *Chronicle* and the *Huayang guozhi* that credit Gao Ding's men with the deed. The key to the solution in *Three Kingdoms* is Kongming's manipulation of Gao Ding into acting as his agent against Yong Kai. Moreover, Kongming cleverly compels Gao Ding to attack the third rebel and return with Zhu Bao's head. Thus, Zhuge Liang still precipitates the death of two rebels. Reflecting historical sources, the novel also presents Kongming as ordering the execution of Gao Ding. Nevertheless, contrary to early historical accounts, Gao Ding not only lives but is also made the governor of Yizhou. His survival is central to Kongming's clever strategy for dispensing with the two more dangerous rebels. Overall, this solution reflects the novel's larger re-creation of Kongming as clever trickster and practical strategist. As such, the novel produced a far different hero than the one whose military talents and results Chen Shou criticized.

Omitting Chen Shou's criticism of Zhuge Liang's understanding of expediently flexible tactics in response to changing situations (*quan*), Sima Guang's narrative laid the groundwork for regarding Zhuge Liang as a notable military strategist and commander. Often Sima Guang's means for constructing a much more positive picture was to lift details from various sources preserved in Pei Songzhi's commentary and incorporate them into the grand narrative. For instance, writing almost as though the Southern Campaign had been a fairly simple matter, Chen Shou had merely noted: "In the spring of 225, Liang led his troops southward in a rebellion suppression campaign, and by the autumn all were pacified."[8] He did not include such stories as Zhuge Liang's capture and release of Meng Huo seven times, but Sima Guang use this story, which was preserved in Pei Songzhi's (372–451) commentary.[9] This brief story suggested that Zhuge Liang brilliantly and handily overwhelmed the non-Han peoples, but it did not provide details. By drawing from Pei Songzhi's commentary this brief story of Zhuge Liang's capturing and releasing Meng Huo seven times, Sima Guang elevated the visibility of this story and placed it in an authoritative position in the official grand narrative. From this position of elevated historical authenticity, the brief account of Meng Huo in the *Comprehensive Mirror* could more easily be elaborated upon in the novel.

Three Kingdoms vastly expanded the brief paragraph from the *Comprehensive Mirror* into four chapters (87 through 90) of detailed stories of Kongming's strategies and summaries of the battles. Sitting in his camp, Kongming orchestrated the battles and their outcomes. For instance, claiming that his vanguard generals Zhao Zilong and Wei Yan were too old, Kongming announced that junior commanders would attack Meng Huo's vanguard, but Kongming's aim actually was to provoke his two senior commanders to act swiftly and boldly. Foreseeing that Zhao Zilong and Wei Yan would be provoked into breaking into the enemy's camps and smashing Meng Huo's vanguard, Kongming secretly arranged for the junior commanders to play supporting roles and set ambushes to capture Meng Huo's fleeing chiefs. Unaware of Kongming's plans, Zhao Zilong and Wei Yan reported their own success and presented the head of one of Meng Huo's vanguard chiefs, but their troops gave excuses for failing to capture the other two chiefs. When Kongming explained his strategy and how the two chiefs had fallen into his trap, the commanders bowed to the ground and proclaimed, "Not even the gods could fathom Your Excellency's calculations!" (87.665). Meng Huo himself was repeatedly captured, but refusing to surrender, he blamed his failures on Kongming's "tricky schemes" or sought other excuses. Responding to Kongming's gracious pardons, some of Meng Huo's commanders and clansmen captured Meng Huo and delivered him to Kongming some of the seven times. When one of Meng Huo's allies attacked with wild beasts, Kongming waved his fan to cause the wind to change direction and unleashed hosts of weird mechanical beasts belching fire and breathing black smoke to overwhelm the genuine beasts of the Man region. Imagination about Kongming's ingenuity and sagely powers soared to the point of anachronistically crediting him with deploying gunpowder in his final victory over the Man people. After luring the rebel's vanguard into a narrow valley, Kongming's firepower wiped out the 30,000-man vanguard of seemingly invincible rattan-armored troops. The key was a large number of black wagons that "had been loaded earlier with fire launchers called 'earth thunder,' each containing nine missiles. The mines were buried thirty paces apart and connected by fuses—bamboo tubes packed with powder. On firing, the hills crumbled and the rocks split" (90.691). With such a demonstration of firepower, it is not surprising that his commanders again bowed before him and proclaimed, "Your Excellency's marvelous ingenuity is more than even the gods and spirits could fathom" (90.692). Unfortunately, the devastation was so extensive that Kongming wept and predicted that the slaughter arising from this "trick" would surely shorten his life span; thus, the novel prepared the reader for Kongming's untimely death, which ended his later campaign against the Wei in the North.

Tales in *Three Kingdoms* about Kongming's campaigns against Wei also apparently owed something to the *Comprehensive Mirror*. For instance, sources preserved in Pei Songzhi's commentary further augmented the drama of Zhuge Liang's final campaign against Wei in 234; moreover, Sima Guang's incorporation of such stories into the text of his officially commissioned history strengthened their credibility and increased their circulation in later texts, including the novel. Sima Guang incorporated stories about Kongming's sending a woman's bonnet to Sima Yi (often called Zhongda, 179–251) in an attempt to provoke the Wei commander into coming out of defensive positions to do battle in the open with the Shu army.[10] Another colorful story related how Sima Yi at first pursued the retreating Shu army, but pulled back when it appeared that Zhuge Liang might still be alive. If Zhuge Liang were alive, the feigned retreat might be a ruse to draw Sima Yi out of his defensive stronghold for a battle. When the common people observed what transpired, they composed the famous ditty: "A dead Zhuge has put a live Zhongda to flight!"[11] Because these two stories could be regarded as lauding Sima Yi's wisdom, they were in the early Tang dynasty already written into Sima Yi's biography in the official history of the Jin dynasty. Two additional stories make such a reading of these stories even more obvious. One recounts how Sima Yi had correctly predicted that if Zhuge Liang's invasion were to be directed against Wuzhangyuan, the Wei generals under Sima Yi would have nothing to worry about and could easily take a defensive position to block him. The other story recounts how Sima Yi, after hearing about Zhuge Liang's work habits, remarked: "Zhuge Kongming troubles himself with small matters, so will he be able to last long?"[12] The previous story could be said to be a critical comment about Zhuge Liang's mistake in military strategy, and the latter story could be said to express his obsession with managing details personally; therefore, one might certainly assert that these two entries present Sima Guang's ultimate agreement with Chen Shou's critical evaluation of Zhuge Liang's abilities as a military commander. Despite the obvious logic in that assertion, I surmise that these stories are adequate for letting the reader come to a quite different conclusion: all four of these stories taken together could also be regarded as commending Zhuge Liang's dedicated loyalty "to strive until death comes" and also as acknowledging Sima Yi's affirmation of Zhuge Liang's military genius. Indeed, Sima Yi's reluctance to confront Zhuge Liang on the field of battle suggests his awe for Zhuge Liang as a military commander.

It would appear that the author of *Three Kingdoms* came to a similar conclusion when incorporating these stories into the historical novel to augment Kongming's fame. The novel cites and elaborates on these four stories (chapters 103 and 104); however, the larger context trumpets Kongming's greater talents and tactics. For instance, just before recounting three of these stories, the novel portrays Kongming almost succeeding in destroying Sima Yi in Shangfang Gorge. Despite Sima Yi's caution about Kongming's traps and schemes, Kongming manages to lure him into the gorge where he is attacked by fire and exploding mines. Unexpectedly, a sudden storm extinguishes the fires; therefore, "The mines lay silent; the incendiary devices ceased functioning" (103.800). Thus, only the intervention of the heavens enabled Sima Yi to escape Kongming's ingenious scheme. Projecting Kongming's cleverness, the story even credited him—very anachronistically—with having gunpowder explosives. When he earlier fled to Shanggui to escape another of Kongming's traps, Sima Yi reverently sighed as he acknowledged, "Kongming's maneuvers are as subtle as those of gods and demons" (101.781). In this trap, Kongming managed to confuse Sima Yi so thoroughly that he concluded that Kongming's troops were "supernatural."

II.

The emphasis in *Three Kingdoms* on the supernatural character of Zhuge Liang's abilities and tactics might well have been inspired by Chen Liang's historical essays: *An Inquiry into History* (*Zhuogu lun*), and the *Chronicle Record of the Three Kingdoms* (*Sanguo jinian*). Both works contain significant biographies of Zhuge Liang. According to Chen Liang, Zhuge Liang developed invincible military orders of battle. For instance, he described Kongming's "Formation of Eight Hexagrams" or "Eightfold Array" (*bazhen tu*):

> With his eightfold military formation arrayed facing forward, it had four heads and eight tails, and any point of contact with the enemy would become a head. It would not advance too quickly or retreat too hurriedly. Shock brigades were unable to break through its front, and armies that seemed to come from nowhere would not be able to go round to strike its rear. An army in ambush could not isolate its wings, and pursuing troops could not attack its rear by surprise. Spies would have no way to reconnoiter, and cunning tricks would have no facility. Any troops blocking its way would be attacked and destroyed, and any attacking army would be defeated. Even though the two armies had not yet engaged, Zhongda's abilities were already frustrated.[13]

Thus, Kongming's battle arrays were far superior to Sima Yi's.

Chen Liang's description of Zhuge Kongming's Formation of Eight Hexagrams might well have inspired an episode in *Three Kingdoms* in which Sima Yi opted to test orders of battle against Kongming. At Kongming's invitation to attack the formation, Sima Yi selected three commanders and gave them instructions on how to lead their men into the formation: "Kongming has deployed his forces in a square with eight gates—Desist, Survive, Injure, Confound, Exhibit, Perish, Surprise, and Liberate. I want you three to attack through the eastern gate, Survive, and fight your way through the western gate, Desist, and then back to the northern gate, Liberate. His formation can be broken, but you must use all due caution" (100.775).

The results proved the superiority of Kongming's hexagram formation:

> When the three Wei commanders entered the Riverlands formation, they found it a continuous wall which they could not penetrate. The three commanders hurriedly led their men around the base of the formation in an attempt to break out from the southwest, but Riverlands archers checked their advance. The formation was like a maze, with multiple and intersecting lanes, each having its own entrance and exit. Who could tell the four directions any more? The three commanders lost contact and could only hurl themselves wildly along the lanes. But all they saw were brooding clouds that struck fear in their hearts and a dense mist closing in on them. As war cries rose around them, the northern troops were seized and bound one by one and then delivered to the main Riverlands camp. (100.775)

When Kongming released the captured horsemen with a message to Sima Yi to brush up on his military manuals and pay closer attention to tactics, the Wei high commander was so enraged that he led his mighty host in a direct assault on the Shu army. The battle went so poorly that Sima Yi panicked and retreated, but he still lost six or seven of every ten troops. Afterward, he did not emerge again from his defensive positions. In short, this account in the novel could well reflect what Chen Liang crystallized as Sima Yi being "dispirited" when confronted by Zhuge Liang's orders of battle.

Zhuge Liang's use of tricks is a major difference between Chen Liang's first Kongming essay in the *Inquiry into History*, on the one hand, and *Three Kingdoms*, on the other hand, but this difference opens the way to perceiving a possible trajectory of influence. Mainstream historical assessments rooted in Chen Shou's *Chronicle* had established the view that flexible strategies in meeting changeable situations was not Zhuge Liang's forte; therefore, Chen Liang's effort to promote Kongming as a military hero went against the main current of historical scholarship and the weight of recorded facts. Chen Liang accomplished a reevaluation of Kongming's strategic skills in a rather surprising way. According to Chen Liang, Sima Yi was the one who "was as unpredictable as a spirit and always won by surprise tactics." Therefore, Sima Yi possessed self-confidence in his abilities, and even Sun Quan (182–252) feared him. Having set Sima Yi up as an almost invincible strategist, Chen Liang then justified Kongming's stance against Sima Yi:

> Sima Yi excelled in cunning and tricks. If Kongming were to adopt these same methods, he would be relying on sheer intelligence to counter intelligence

and courage to counter courage, then there would be no way to predict which would be fated to victory or defeat. Wasn't it better to use rectitude (*zheng*) to attack intelligence and to use what was right (*yi*) to assault courage? This was Kongming's determined policy, so how could he have dared merely to seek quick results! Therefore, Zhongda used treachery, but Kongming used loyalty; Zhongda used self-interest, but Kongming used public spiritedness; Zhongda used cruelty, but Kongming used humaneness (*ren*); and Zhongda used cunning, but Kongming used trustworthiness (*xin*). Even before troops arrived, Zhongda was already dispirited.[14]

Chen Liang's statement might appear as hardly more than calling on standard Confucian virtues to provide cultured civility (*wen*) with a "moral victory" to compensate for actual weakness in confronting the martial military (*wu*). However, in his preface to his inquiry, Chen Liang had railed against the trend to contrast civil and military talents, as well as the tendency for civil and military officials to belittle one another. To him, managing affairs and dealing with enemies were interrelated aspects of the same skills.[15] That Chen Liang had in mind a transvaluation of these talents or virtues is suggested in his Zhuge essay through contextual explanation of "rectitude" or "correctness" (*zheng*) in terms of military training: "The defining abilities of a intelligent man are his unlimited tricks and inexhaustible strategies. A hero dispenses with tricks to manifest the great rightness and sets aside clever strategies to win by rectifying (*zheng*) the army; these [actions] are what is beyond the ability of the [merely] intelligent man." Rectification of the army produced practical military results: even before Kongming's troops arrived, Sima Yi was already dispirited. Moreover, as illustrated in Kongming's development of the Eight Hexagram Formation (discussed above), he frustrated Sima Yi's strategies. From other biographies in the *Inquiry into History*, it is clear that Chen Liang was not at all averse to clever strategies per se; for example, he set forth strategies and tricks that Liu Bei (162–223, reigned 220–223) and Cao Cao (155–220) should have used to avoid defeats and achieve greater success.[16] Indeed, Chen Liang's preface asserted his own focus on military strategy as the basis for his essays: "My fondness is simply for grand strategies of hegemons and kings, and it seems I have some insight in regard to the pluses and minuses of military options. Therefore I am able to follow and discuss places in early histories where heroes did not attain [success] or where they did achieve [success], but later commentators were not able to understand them. I make their successes and failure crystal clear, in order to be observed and to serve either as models or as warnings."[17] Thus, in the context of the whole *Inquiry into History*, it is clear that Chen Liang does not intend to denigrate military strategy when his Kongming essay asserts that: Instead of Kongming having to rely on cunning strategies, the key to his success was attacking Sima Yi's weaknesses in virtue and discipline.

In short, based on all this reasoning, Chen Liang could assert that Kongming was actually good at clever strategies (*qi mou*), but chose not to use them. Chen

Liang wrote: "Commentators have regarded Kongming to be best at control of the army but poor at using clever strategies, for even a clever person knows never to use his weakness. I am of the opinion that Kongming was actually good at clever strategies, but deliberately didn't use them; his purpose was to avoid Zhongda's strength and to attack his weakness."[19]

Since Chen Liang boldly ventured to claim that Zhuge Kongming was actually good at clever strategies, it is quite possible that he set a direction of interpretation that eventually culminated in the novel's stories and details of Kongming's schemes and tricks that eclipsed even Sima Yi's.

Suggested linkage regarding Kongming's supernatural abilities as a strategist might be found in Chen Liang's and the novel's shared assumption that Kongming was sagely, for sages were believed to have special wisdom and abilities. Whereas the novel's Kongming took on the manner of a Daoist sage with supernatural powers, Chen Liang struggled against mainstream interpretations to assert that Zhuge Liang patterned himself after ancient sages and followed their principles of kingly governance (wangdao). Historians, beginning with Chen Shou's Chronicle, often quoted Zhuge as claiming to be comparable to the likes of Guan Zhong (died 645 BC), who had enabled his lord to become the regional hegemon or strongman of North China. Although this was a somewhat positive model, it did not reach the level of such sagely ministers as the mythical Yi Yin (sixteenth century BC) and the legendary Duke of Zhou (died ca. 1033 BC), who helped establish the Three Dynasties in the golden age of antiquity. In his belated 261 eulogy to Zhuge Liang, Liu Shan (207–71, reigned 223–63) explicitly compared his deceased prime minister with these two legendary sages. Portraying Zhuge as uniquely combining both civil and martial leadership, Liu Shan exclaimed that: Zhuge "alone embodied and held responsibility for both civil administration and military command. . . . Falling ill and dying just as victory was near, how could such a calamity occur!"[19] Even though Sima Guang had projected Zhuge Liang as more able in military affairs than Chen Shou had done, Sima Guang was too sober a historian to embrace Liu Shan's inflated metaphors.[20] Chen Liang not only advanced Zhuge Liang's military genius to a level beyond what Sima Guang had ascribed to him, but he was also probably the first historian to adopt the notion that Zhuge was sagely like Yi Yin and the Duke of Zhou. Chen Liang argued:

> Kongming followed the model of Yi Yin and the Duke of Zhou. . . . Having accepted the task of being entrusted by Liu Bei with the heir to the throne, he neither ignored the heir's nurture nor deposed him, so people had no room for complaint. His authority approached that of the ruler, but his superior was not suspicious of him; his power surpassed the host of officials, but his subordinates harbored no jealousy. With enthusiasm and dedication, he administered Shu, and social customs and education became respected. . . . Kongming was always careful to do these things [exemplified by the ancient sages], so he truly modeled himself on Yi Yin and the Duke of Zhou.[21]

Since Chen Liang promoted Zhuge Kongming to the sagely level, he had to portray Kongming's military effectiveness as grounded upon virtue rather than upon deception (*jue*) or expediently (*quan*) adapting principles to changing situations. "Therefore, Kongming commanded his troops properly, did not employ expediency or deception, and did not depend upon petty advantage; but his opponent [Sima Yi] said, 'Liang has a great ambition but doesn't understand battle opportunities, has many strategies but lacks decisiveness, is good at battle but is not able to adept principles to changing situations.'"[22]

There are obvious differences between Chen Liang's Kongming as a "Confucian" sage and the rather "Daoistic" sage in *Three Kingdoms*. Nonetheless, by portraying Zhuge Kongming's sagely qualities as making him superior in military affairs to Sima Yi, Chen Liang's transformation of Kongming into a sage might well have been a turning point in the evolution that eventually yielded the sagely Kongming in the novel.

Sima Yi's disparaging remarks about Kongming suggest another difference between Chen Liang's historical essays and *Three Kingdoms*, but again there might be a possible connection. Chen Liang complained that the reason some historians and commentators regarded Kongming as an inferior adversary of Sima Yi was simply that they were deceived by Sima Yi's statements. "Some have even regarded him as not an equal opponent of Sima Zhongda; this is indeed a childish judgment. Don't they say this just because of what Zhongda himself said? They don't understand that such statements by Zhongda were deceitful. Zhongda could not use his deceit to entrap Kongming; therefore, he often spied on Kongming's comings and goings for an opening to make some boast in order to deceive his own subordinates."[23]

Thus, having failed to entrap Kongming, Sima Yi resorted to grasping any opening to boast in order to fool his own subordinates. For instance, he made the famous statement (which Sima Guang elevated from Pei Songzhi's commentary): If Kongming marched to Wuzhangyuan, the Wei army could easily rest in its defensive positions. According to Chen Liang, Sima Yi made such contrived statements to suggest that he could predict military events and that Kongming was incompetent. Despite Sima Yi's repeated efforts to fool his own troops with the allegation that Kongming did not understand military strategy, he unconsciously revealed his true feelings after Kongming's death. While inspecting the orderliness of Zhuge Liang's abandoned encampment, he saluted and sighed, "a world-class genius!" Commentators and historians over the centuries, however, had been fooled by the empty claims Sima Yi made to justify his own failure to confront Kongming in battle. In contrast, *Three Kingdoms* has Sima Yi make many statements expressing his awe of Kongming and give warnings to his commanders about Kongming's military genius. Moreover, as discussed above in the section on Sima Guang, the novel even puts Sima Yi's negative assertions and predictions about Kongming in contexts that redound to Kongming's reputation. Perhaps Chen Liang's debunking of the more conventional readings of Sima Yi's statements helped to liberate the novel's author from the early mainstream tradition of awe for Sima Yi's genius.

According to Chen Liang's historical essays, Sima Yi was driven to seek excuses and deceive his own subordinates because he realized that he dared not fight Zhuge Liang. As Sima Yi became aware of his inability to compete with Kongming, he retreated to defensive positions and refused to fight—even though he had a far larger army and much shorter supply lines. Sima Yi "was in charge of a mighty army, but only took the defensive under the pretext of 'waiting for Kongming to become exhausted.' . . . If Kongming had died one or two years later, what excuse could Zhongda have offered?" Sima Yi discerned that the only thing he could do was to stall for time and hope that Zhuge Liang would either die or would run out of provisions and retreat. By the time of the campaign in 234, Zhuge Liang's inventions of mechanical "wooden bulls" and "gliding horses" for aiding transport had solved the problem of supplies that had forced earlier campaigns to end; moreover, he had established soldier-farmer colonies inside Wei territory. According to Chen Liang, there was surely a limit to how long Sima Yi could dissemble and avoid fighting. "If a general doesn't fight battles, his ruler will suspect him, his colleagues at court will censure him, the people will belittle him, he himself will feel uneasy, his macho spirit will have no expression, so there would be no way to avoid fighting; but if he fought he would be defeated."[24] Thus, Sima Yi was caught in a dilemma.

Whereas Sima Guang only provided an account from which one could infer that Zhuge Liang might have been successful if he had lived longer, Chen Liang's thesis explicitly claimed that Zhuge would have defeated Sima Yi and unified China; thus, Chen Liang provided historical grounds for the novel's assumptions about these matters. Chen Liang proclaimed: "Therefore, I have said that if Kongming had not died, Zhongda would have been defeated, the land within the passes would have been pacified, Wei could have been subdued, Wu could have been incorporated, and sagely ritual institutions and cultural music could have been restored."[26]

Similarly, in *Three Kingdoms* Kongming's brilliant march toward victory is frustrated by his illness and untimely death. The novel goes further in presenting Kongming on the verge of victory a couple of times earlier, but treachery by Gou An and Li Yan (died 234) forced Kongming to disengage. In short, Chen Liang's historical essays prefigured the novel both in making Sima Yi into Zhuge Liang's chief adversary and in claiming that Kongming was on the verge of certain victory when death ended his campaign.

III.

Some might wonder if the author of *Three Kingdoms* ever actually read either Sima Guang's master narrative or Chen Liang's essays on Kongming, for they might assume that the novel simply drew from the *Zizhi tongjian gangmu* (*Outline and Digest of the Comprehensive Mirror for Aid in Government*). Among the reasons for this assumption, two stand out. First, Zhu Xi set the guidelines or organizing principles (*fanli*) for this historical work, which were then implemented by his students; moreover, since Zhu Xi was the center of state orthodoxy in China after 1241, writers of a historical novel would be expected to turn to the history associated with his authoritative cultural voice.[26] Second, besides the weight of orthodox authority, several matters of political ideology align the novel with Zhu Xi's *Digest*. Zhu Xi objected not only to Sima's inadequate attention to traditional, moralistic "praise and blame" historiography but also to some of Sima's historical judgments. Regarding the Three Kingdoms era, Zhu Xi strongly condemned Sima Guang for dismissing the issue of the legitimate succession of dynasties (*zhengtong*) and for taking the Wei dynasty as the convenient reference point for recording events. The *Digest* championed Liu Bei's Shu (Han) regime as the continuation of the Han dynasty because of Liu Bei's lineage connection to the Han royal house and because of its relatively virtuous leaders, particularly Liu Bei and Zhuge Liang. Besides the general point regarding which ruler or regime deserved official recognition, Zhu Xi paid close attention to the denotation and connotations of different terms employed. For instance, Zhu Xi vehemently criticized Sima Guang for using the term "invade" (*kou*) in connection with what Zhu Xi classified as Zhuge Liang's legitimate punitive expeditions against Wei rebels (*fa Wei*). Even though the *Comprehensive Mirror* sometimes wrote that Zhuge "came out" of a certain place or "attacked" (*gong*) Wei, the expression "invade" (*kou*) was used on three occasions in referring to Zhuge Liang's campaigns.[27] Although *kou* can be read as simply another term for "to attack militarily," the term also connotes bandits and pillaging. Zhu Xi complained that the *Comprehensive Mirror* was thereby denigrating Shu Han's ethical and political status: "The Han prime minister Liang's leading the troops to punish the unlawful rebels was described as *rukou*, and this was not just on one occasion; this is incomprehensible."[28] Zhu Zi made sure that in the *Digest* Zhuge Liang's five campaigns were termed legitimate punitive expeditions against Wei rebels.[29] Moreover, on one occasion, Wei's military action is labeled as an invasion (*kou*) explicitly as an expression of respect for the (Shu) Han as the legitimate government.[30] *Three Kingdoms* adopted the same view of the legitimacy of Zhuge Liang's rulers and his military campaigns against the Wei.

The specific information and views discussed about Zhuge Liang yield a more complex picture. First, ignoring the *Chronicle* fact that Yong Kai was killed by the fellow rebel Gao Ding, the *Digest* simply accepted at face value the assertion in the *Comprehensive Mirror* that Zhuge had killed Yong Kai, but the *Digest* replaced Sima's inclusion of "and Gao Ding" with the simple unspecified "etc." (*deng*). Moreover, the only significant comment made was the insistence that the "beheading" (*zhan*) be termed an "executing" (*zhu*) to highlight the proper legality or morality of the act.[31] As seen in the discussion earlier, the novel portrays Zhuge Liang as tricking Gao Ding into killing Yong Kai and ultimately as rewarding Gao Ding with an official position in exchange for delivering the head of a fellow rebel. Thus, the novel exercised creativity in negotiating these contested historical views and in enhancing the story beyond what any of the standard historical accounts could offer. Second, by lifting the story of Zhuge's capture and release of Meng Huo from Pei Songzhi's commentary, Sima Guang had elevated the brief story into the master narrative, and the *Digest* continued to preserve this brief story in its commentary. Again, the novel creates lively details recounting how Zhuge managed to capture and release Meng Huo seven times. Third, as mentioned, Sima Guang's narrative about Zhuge Liang's campaigns, as well as his and Sima Yi's comments, could encourage the reader of the *Comprehensive Mirror* to see Zhuge Liang as a more effective and more dedicated military leader than he was portrayed in Chen Shou's *Chronicle*. The *Digest* and the novel apparently had a similar reading, but it is again unclear whether the novel's author was reading the *Comprehensive Mirror* or the *Digest*. Fourth, the novel's presentation of Kongming as a stern administrator of justice and punishment points toward the *Comprehensive Mirror*, because the *Digest* was not overly concerned about this matter.

Fifth and most revealing, there is the matter of the more grandiose military claims on Zhuge Liang's behalf. Explicitly addressing Chen Shou's negative evaluation of Zhuge Liang's military strategies and results, the *Digest* specifically claims not only that Zhuge in the 231 campaign "defeated Sima Yi and cut down General Zhang He," but also says more sweepingly that Sima Yi deployed his troops very cleverly, "so he was not easy to contend with, but was defeated by Liang every time."[32] Moreover, in its culminating section on Zhuge Liang, the *Digest* again twice briefly proclaims Zhuge "defeated Sima Yi and killed Zhang He."[33] The only place where the *Digest* clearly acknowledges the defeat of Zhuge's campaign is in regard to the battle of Jieting, but responsibility is, following convention, assigned to Ma Su (died 227).[34] In short, the *Digest*'s claims for Zhuge Liang's military success do go beyond the implications of Sima Guang's *Comprehensive Mirror*. But the *Digest* does not go as far as Chen Liang's essays in making Zhuge Liang into a sagely military genius. Moreover, the *Digest* does not contain the level of detail that the novel needed to draw upon to create its intriguing accounts of Kongming's military strategies and battles. The novel's author needed thicker historical details, and the *Comprehensive Mirror* and Chen Liang's essays provided both more detail than the *Digest* and a better-digested synthesis than the scattered details searchable in Pei Songzhi's commentaries to Chen Shou's *Chronicle*. Chen Liang, in particular, transformed Zhuge Liang into a sagely strategist capable of clever and flexible schemes, and his portrayal of Kongming's sagely eight hexagram battle arrays appear to have inspired the novel's fuller exposition of those battle arrays and the sagely strategies and clever tricks Kongming employed. Chen Liang also apparently began the trend to frame the climatic story as Zhuge Liang's contest with Sima Yi. The novel took the same stance as Chen Liang on Sima Yi's heartfelt admiration and awe of Zhuge Liang. Chen Liang was likely the first historian[35] to set forth the thesis that only an untimely death prevented Zhuge Liang from certain victory against Sima Yi. The novel embraced these themes and elaborated on them with creative stories. It seems to me quite likely that besides the ideological commitment to the Shu Han as the legitimate government of the era, the *Digest*'s most important contribution to the novel might well have been the impression that Zhu Xi's authority endorsed revising Chen Shou's sober assessment of Zhuge Liang's military results on the grounds set forth by such Song historians as Sima Guang and Chen Liang. Even the *Digest's* brief assertion that Sima Yi "was defeated by Liang every time" might well have been read by the novel's author to validate the grandiose claims made by someone like Chen Liang that Kongming was winning against Sima Yi and the Wei.

IV.

In conclusion, if we look at *Three Kingdoms* from the perspective of a long evolution from the *Chronicle of the Three Kingdoms*, we could say that Sima Guang's *Comprehensive Mirror for Aid in Government* and Chen Liang's *An Inquiry into History* provided some of the key milestones along the road toward Kongming's brilliance and clever tricks in the novel. *Three Kingdoms* certainly benefited from Sima Guang's combination of Chen Shou's diverse biographies into a grand narrative that highlighted the exploits of major figures, especially one like Kongming. By elevating and lending credibility to stories preserved in Pei Songzhi's commentary, Sima Guang also took preliminary steps in laying a foundation for a more hopeful perspective on Kongming as a military commander. Nonetheless, Sima Guang did not present Kongming as a sage, like Yi Yin, but rather reinforced Chen Shou's quotation in which Kongming likened himself to Yue Yi and Guan Zhong. Thus, Sima Guang's Zhuge Liang was a model, specifically a model commander of troops and administrator of punishments. As if echoing Chen Liang's historical essays, *Three Kingdoms* goes far beyond the *Comprehensive Mirror* in portraying Kongming's military abilities—especially the supernatural quality of Kongming's military tactics and genius. Chen Liang made Kongming into a superb strategist with clever plans and military formations that were beyond Sima Yi's comprehension. Rejecting the tradition of placing Kongming on a level with Yue Yi and Guan Zhong, Chen Liang argued that Zhuge Liang was comparable to sagely ministers like Yi Yin and the Duke of Zhou. Chen Liang likened Kongming to sagely ministers and portrayed Kongming as deploying his army in accord with Confucian virtues; these claims could be read as implicitly building upon a tradition—first articulated in Liu Shan's 261 eulogy—that praised Kongming as sage and as an extraordinary leader combining cultural civil and martial military quality. But Chen Liang further contributed to fleshing out images of Kongming's strategic genius. Besides his account of the impact of Kongming's Eight Hexagram Formation upon Sima Yi, Chen Liang argued for Kongming's superiority to Sima Yi despite the latter's renowned abilities for clever strategy and spiritlike surprises. Moreover, Chen Liang's claim that Zhuge Liang was actually good at clever strategies surely facilitated later writers' imagination of Kongming's actual exploits. Chen Liang's reconstruction of Kongming's story shifted the focus of the Three Kingdoms story to the confrontation of Kongming versus Sima Yi, and the novel also focuses on this confrontation. Kongming's apotheosis as a Daoist sage and trickster in the text of *Three Kingdoms* probably owes something to Chen Liang's historical essays that transformed Kongming into a spiritlike genius and successful military commander. Chen Liang himself had argued that Confucius (Kongzi, 551–479 BCE) had washed the historical record clean (*xi ganjing*) in compiling the classics to make grand models (*zhengda benzi*) and to inspire later generations.[36] One of Chen Liang's aspirations was to do something of the same with selected Han and Tang heroes. We could say that *Three Kingdoms* fulfilled that aspiration. The fact that Sima Guang was one of China's greatest historians and Chen Liang was known for his historical studies made their reconstructions and transformations of Kongming more believable as history, and thus prefigured the creativity and trajectory of *Three Kingdoms*. Thus, despite the creativity of performance literature, literary work was at least facilitated, and perhaps even inspired, by the historical changes and myths about Kongming that these Song historians (among others) created in retelling his story.

NOTES

This essay was drafted at the University of Munich in 2001 while I was enjoying an Alexander von Humboldt Foundation Award, and Margaret Tillman edited that draft. Ms. Jean Han, librarian at the University of California's East Asian Library in Berkeley, generously facilitated timely use of the computerized Siku quanshu edition of the *Zizhi tongjian gangmu*. My research base on Zhuge Liang as a hero has been sponsored at various points since the early 1980s by the Fulbright-Hayes Program of the Department of Education, the Committee for Scholarly Communications with the PRC, the American Council of Learned Societies, the National Endowment for the Humanities, the Chiang Ching-Kuo Foundation, and the Center for Chinese Studies at the National Central Library.

1. *Sanguo zhi* (Beijing: Zhonghua shuju, 1982), 35.934; Achilles Fang, trans. *The Chronicle of the Three Kingdoms (220–265): Chapters 69–79 from the "Tzu Chih T'ung Chien" of Ssu-ma Kuang*, 2 vols. (Cambridge, MA: Harvard University Press, 1952 and 1965), 1:439.

2. For a detailed discussion of Zhuge Liang in the *Zizhi tongjian*, see Tian Hao (Hoyt Tillman), "Shixue yu wenhua sixiang: Sima Guang dui Zhuge Liang gushi de chongjian" [History and Culture: Sima Guang's Reconstruction of Zhuge Liang's Story], *Lishi Yuyan Yanjiusuo jikan* [Bulletin of the Institute of History and Philology, Academia Sinica] 73, no. 1 (March 2002): 165–98.

3. *Sanguo zhi*, 43.1048.

4. *Huayang guozhi* (Shanghai: Shangwu, 1929), 4.4b; see also *Sanguo zhi*, 43.1048.

5. Yan Yan, *Zizhi tongjian bu* (1876), 71.2b; Lu Bi, *Sanguo zhi jijie* (1957; Beijing: Zhonghua shuju, 1982), 43.7b.849.

6. *Zizhi tongjian* (Beijing: Zhonghua shuju, 1956), 70.2224.

7. *Three Kingdoms*, chap. 87; translated by Moss Roberts in *Three Kingdoms: A Historical Novel*, attributed to Luo Guanzhong and translated from the Chinese with notes and an afterword by Moss Roberts (Berkeley and Los Angeles: University of California Press; Beijing: Foreign Language Press, 1991), 661. Hereafter all citations will be incorporated into the text.

8. *Sanguo zhi*, 35.919.

9. Ibid., 35.920; *Zizhi tongjian*, 70.2224–25.

10. Story is from *Wei shi chunqiu* 魏氏春秋 as included in Pei Songzhi's commentary to the *Sanguo zhi*, 3.103; quoted in *Zizhi tongjian*, 72.2295.

11. Story is from the *Han Jin chunqiu* 漢晉春秋 as included in Pei Songzhi's commentary to the *Sanguo zhi*, 25.927; *Zizhi tongjian*, 72.2296.

12. Fang Xuanling, *Jin shu* (Beijing: Zhonghua shuju, 1974), 1.8, 9; *Zizhi tongjian*, 72.2292, and 2295–96.

13. *Chen Liang ji*, rev. ed. (Beijing: Zhonghua shuju, 1987), 6.61–62; this would be chapter (*juan*) 7 in conventional collections of Chen Liang's writings, so adjust *juan* numbers for the *Zhuo'gu lun* if the reader uses other editions.

14. Unless otherwise noted, all quotations in this paragraph are from "Zhuge Kongming, shang 諸葛孔明上 ," in *Chen Liang ji*, 6.61–63.

15. "Zhuo'gu lun, xu," in *Chen Liang ji*, 5.50.

16. *Chen Liang ji*, 5.53–55 on Cao Cao, and 5.58–60 on Liu Bei.

17. "Zhuo'gu lun, xu," in *Chen Liang ji*, 5.50.

18. "Zhuge Kongming, shang," in *Chen Liang ji*, 6.62.

19. *Sanguo zhi*, 35.927.

20. Sima Guang only noted the posthumous title bestowed in the eulogy; see *Zizhi tongjian*, 72.2298.

21. "Zhuge Kongming, xia" in *Chen Liang ji*, 6.63.

22. Ibid., 6.64.

23. Unless otherwise noted, references in this paragraph are to "Zhuge Kongming, xia," 6.63–64.

24. "Zhuge Kongming, shang" in *Chen Liang ji*, 6.62.

25. Ibid., 6.62.

26. For an account of the rise of Zhu Xi's views, see Hoyt Cleveland Tillman, *Confucian Discourse and Chu Hsi's Ascendancy* (Honolulu: University of Hawaii Press, 1992). For a study of Zhu Xi's views of Zhuge Liang in his collected writings and statements to his students, see Hoyt Cleveland Tillman, "One Significant Rise in Chu-ko Liang's Popularity: An Impact of the 1127 Jurchen Conquest," *Chinese Studies* [*Hanxue yanjiu*] 14, no. 2 (December 1996): esp. 13–24.

27. *Zizhi tongjian*, 71.2239, 72.2267, and 72.2291.

28. Zhu Xi, *Zhuzi wenji* (Taipei: Yunchen wenhua chubanshe, 2000), 22.812–813.

29. Zhu Xi, *Yupi Zizhi tongjian gangmu* (Taipei: Shangwu, 1983), 15.1a–4b, 6a–7a, 8ab, 17ab, 28ab, 29a–30a, and especially 15.35ab.

30. Ibid., 15.15a.

31. Ibid., 14.83a.

32. Ibid., 15.15a.

33. Ibid., 15.35a and 35b.

34. Ibid., 15.1a–4b.

35. For a study of a poet with a pioneering upward reevaluation of Zhuge Liang, see Hoyt Cleveland Tillman, "Reassessing Du Fu's Line on Zhuge Liang," *Monumenta Serica* 50 (2002): 295–313.

36. *Chen Liang ji*, 28.352; this would be chapter 20 in conventional collections of Chen Liang's writings.

III

Three Kingdoms in
Chinese Drama and Art

6

Zhuge Liang and Zhang Fei

Bowang shao tun and Competing Masculine Ideals within the Development of the Three Kingdoms Story Cycle

Kimberly Besio

As sweeping in scope as the classic novel *Three Kingdoms* is, it actually represents only a select portion of the Three Kingdoms story cycle—that is, the complex of literary and popular traditions that accreted around historical figures and incidents from the Three Kingdoms period (AD 220–265). By the time the novel made its appearance, the Three Kingdoms story cycle comprised materials from a wide range of literary genres including history, semifictional anecdotes, poetry, and, from the Song dynasty (960–1206) on, fictional narrative and drama. This complex provides a wealth of resources on a variety of topics in literary history and cultural studies. One topic on which the story cycle can offer particularly valuable insights is constructions of masculinity.

Chinese men from Mao Zonggang to Mao Zedong have traditionally looked to the characters within the Three Kingdoms story cycle as models of masculine behavior. Even today, these characters—whether revered as wisdom incarnate or the epitome of honor and righteousness (as Zhuge Liang and Guan Yu are), or reviled as an unscrupulous schemer (as Cao Cao is)—immediately evoke within the Chinese imagination patterns of male conduct. However, these patterns and the attitudes toward them have not remained fixed but have varied, as the qualities associated with the various figures and the importance ascribed to them have changed. The relative malleability of these patterns, as well as the long history of the story cycle and the rich array of materials connected to it, makes the story cycle a particularly fruitful arena for an exploration of differing ideals of masculinity over time and between different audiences.

In this essay I undertake such an exploration by comparing two editions of a single play, the Yuan *zaju Bowang shao tun*. The two texts, one a printed edition published in the Yuan and the other a manuscript transcribed in the late Ming, represent different phases in the development of the *zaju* genre.[1] Thus, this comparison is valuable for what it confirms about changes in the forms and functions of *zaju* drama from the Yuan to the Ming.[2] The Yuan edition of *Bowang shao tun*, one of only thirty commercially printed Yuan editions still extant, offers important insights concerning the early textual traditions of Yuan *zaju*. The Ming manuscript, transcribed in 1616 from the archives of the Imperial Palace by Zhao Qimei for his private collection, provides valuable evidence for how the Three Kingdoms story cycle was deployed on the Imperial stage. However, on another level, the play is also notable for the clash that it features between two different models of masculinity, and for the change in the nature of these models from the Yuan edition to the Ming edition.

In *Bowang shao tun* two male characters stand out—Zhang Fei, the straightforward man of action, and Zhuge Liang, the artful strategist.[3] In the Ming edition of the play we witness an increased focus on a subplot within the play that portrays a battle of wills between these two figures. Although the confrontations between Zhuge and Zhang are clearly shaped by dramatic convention, once we have identified those aspects of the play related to developments within drama, we can still see within these encounters a paradigm for a modification of masculine ideals that accompanied the formation of the novel. That is, characters tended to be reshaped to better accord with Confucian orthodox values.[4] The slightly different emphases in the two editions of *Bowang shao tun*, particularly their differing characterizations of Zhuge, reflect this shift, and thus provide valuable insights into the multivalent meanings these characters and the story cycle possessed over time and among different audiences.

ZHUGE LIANG AND ZHANG FEI IN HISTORY AND FICTION

Of all the outstanding figures that made their mark on the history of the Three Kingdoms period, Liu Bei's adviser, Zhuge Liang, has the most consistently excited the Chinese imagination. The story of Zhuge's life is recorded in the dynastic history, *Chronicle of the Three Kingdoms (Sanguo zhi)*. The author of this history, Chen Shou, considered Zhuge so important to Liu Bei's cause that he accorded Zhuge a separate biography. However, as recent scholarship has shown, Zhuge's perceived importance and the qualities associated with him have varied somewhat over time.[5] Hoyt Tillman has traced the trajectory of Zhuge's popularity among literati through references to Zhuge in poetry and in history. He suggests that while Zhuge's popularity fluctuated at different historical moments, it generally rose over time. Moreover, rises in Zhuge's status tended to take place in moments of national crisis when, as a symbol of loyalty and national reunification, Zhuge's image was especially compelling.[6] Zhuge was a favorite among the common people early on, as is evidenced by the erection of a temple in his honor only twenty-nine years after his death and various anecdotes cited by Pei Songzhi in his commentary on the *Chronicle*.[7] The vernacular narrative *Plain Speech on Chronicle of the Three Kingdoms* (*Sanguo zhi pinghua*, published 1321–23, hereafter referred to as the *Pinghua*), drew on folk tradition to portray Zhuge as a Daoist immortal capable of performing magical feats.[8] The novel retained only a small number of the more fantastic attributes ascribed to Zhuge in the earlier narrative, and shaped an image more in accord with that in the dynastic history and poetry, which has proved definitive. Zhuge's depiction in the novel, regularly cited as one of the book's great achievements, is that of a wise statesman and a brilliant military tactician who labors tirelessly for his cause even as he realizes it is doomed.[9]

Zhang Fei's role within the story cycle followed a very different trajectory. Zhang appears in the *Sanguo zhi* in a group biography devoted to Liu Bei's five most important generals. While Chen Shou recorded several incidents that became staples in a portrayal of Zhang as a martial hero, defiant himself and appreciative of defiance in others, Chen finally deemed Zhang "violent and merciless (*bao er wu en*)."[10] Zhang is clearly viewed with much more affection in the Yuan *Pinghua* and in drama from the Yuan and early Ming periods. In the *Pinghua* and in many *zaju*, Zhang is a central figure, and while he is still depicted as violent and defiant of authority, he is also a vibrant and lively character whose rude behavior was highly entertaining.[11] However, in the novel Zhang's rash behavior is depicted as problematic at best, disastrous at worst; and many of the incidents that feature Zhang as a hero in the *Pinghua* were either left out of the novel or were drastically rewritten.[12]

At all points in the historical development of these two figures, Zhuge and Zhang are contrasting types. Whether represented by magic feats or acts of moral superiority, Zhuge's strength resides in his superior understanding, while Zhang relies on his physical prowess. As representatives of contrasting characterizations of male behavior they share the stage in many dramatic renditions of incidents from the story cycle, among which is the play *Bowang shao tun*.

THE TWO EDITIONS OF *BOWANG SHAO TUN*— SAME PLOT, DIFFERENT FORMS AND FUNCTIONS

The plot of the two editions of *Bowang shao tun* consists of a series of events connected to Liu Bei's recruitment of Zhuge as a military advisor. The first act portrays Liu Bei's third and final visit to Zhuge's hut. During this visit Liu succeeds in meeting with Zhuge, and eventually persuades Zhuge to join his cause. Acts 2 and 3 concern Zhuge's first test as a military adviser when he deploys Liu's troops against Cao Cao. The title of the play is based on the ensuing battle, in which

Zhuge has Liu's men burn a Cao encampment at Bowang. The fourth act of the
play demonstrates Zhuge's skill in diplomacy—he outwits an emissary sent to
persuade him to transfer his loyalties to Cao Cao.

While the plots of the two editions remain essentially the same, their for-
mats differ markedly, representing specific examples of formal trends in drama
texts, and reflecting changes in the function of *zaju* texts between the Yuan and
the mid-Ming period. At the same time these differences in form and function
changed the characterization of the main figures in the play, an issue I will explore
in more detail below.

The Yuan edition conforms to a type that Stephen West has dubbed "production driven." Not only the song sets, but also the stage directions, the cue lines,
and the speeches of the *zheng mo* (lead singer), Zhuge, are provided; speeches
by other characters are identified by stage directions but are not written out.[13]
The significance of this textual form for *Bowang shao tun* is that it turned the
spotlight almost exclusively on the actor playing Zhuge. In this play the *zheng
mo's* part calls for fifty-eight specific actions (leaving out general stage directions
such as "says = *yun*" or "sings = *chang*"), compared to thirteen specific actions by
all the rest of the characters combined.[14] The Yuan edition of *Bowang shao tun* has
twenty-two more songs than the later manuscript edition. Again, this difference
represents a general trend.[15] The focus on the *zheng mo* part in the Yuan edition
reflects what other Yuan evidence implies about the constitution of acting troupes
during this period—that they consisted of a single star, who was supported by a
"family" of actors.[16]

While these formal features constitute this edition's "production-driven"
nature, they also support a characterization of Zhuge quite different from his characterization in analogous narratives. As we will see below, in the Yuan edition not
only is more information supplied about Zhuge's motivations than we see in other
accounts, particularly in the scenes devoted to Liu Bei's visit to the thatched hut and
Zhuge's first deployment of Liu's forces, but also these motivations are revealed as
more practical and less highminded than is congruent with later images of Zhuge
as a dedicated and selfless statesman.

The Ming version of *Bowang shao tun* contrasts with the Yuan edition; in this
version, the actor playing Zhuge performs within the context of an ensemble troupe,
and has few songs. In the Ming manuscript, the lines of all the characters are provided in full detail; supporting characters conduct lengthy dialogues and act out
scenes without Zhuge present on stage. Finally, the costumes for all members of the
cast are specified in some detail in the costume specifications (*chuanguan*) appended
to the manuscript. These formal differences parallel those seen between other play
texts for which there is both a Yuan edition and a text copied by Zhao Qimei from
the archives of the Imperial Palace. Stephen West has suggested that they point to
a significant difference in composition between Yuan commercial troupes and an
imperial troupe: that is, that an imperial troupe would consist of an all-star cast,
each of whom "would demand a certain amount of stage time."[17] However, in *Bowang*

shao tun these alterations did not result in an evenhanded focus on all the characters. Instead, the Ming edition merely broadened the play's almost exclusive focus on
Zhuge to one in which Zhuge shares the spotlight with Zhang. Formal disparities
alone cannot account for all the differences in emphasis between the two editions of
Bowang shao tun; they can also be at least partially attributed to the specific context
in which the Ming edition of the play was produced, that is, the Three Kingdoms
story cycle as it appeared on the Ming imperial stage.

THE MING EDITION OF *BOWANG SHAO TUN*—
HISTORICAL AND POLITICAL CONTEXTS

From what we can tell from extant texts and records, the Three Kingdoms story
cycle was well represented in Ming court performance. In his discussion on portrayals of the founding of the Han dynasty in early drama, Wilt Idema has noted a
high survival rate of Yuan and Ming play texts on the Three Kingdoms story cycle.[18]
Idema finds an "extraordinary predilection" of the Ming court for *zaju* on the Three
Kingdoms cycle, implying that these plays must have been seen as supporting the
imperial agenda, just as the plays on the Early Han might have challenged it. The
formal and textual ties between imperially staged Three Kingdoms plays suggest
that aspects of the story cycle that promote loyalty to the throne were highlighted
as the story was adapted to suit the needs of the imperium.

In colophons appended to the text Zhao Qimei specifically labeled eight of the
plays on Three Kingdoms themes in his collection as archival editions (*neifuben*).
One formal attribute that all eight plays share is that costume specifications are also
appended to the text. An additional four play texts on Three Kingdoms themes
from Zhao's collection can be added to this group, as they also share this attribute.[19] While the formal attributes of this group, of twelve plays are also common
to "Archival editions" of plays not connected to the story cycle in Zhao's collection, a
comparison of the nature of these attributes in the group of Three Kingdoms plays
reveals a consistent interpretation of the story cycle. Zhuge wears a "rolling cloud
cap" a "red cloud crane Daoist robe," and carries a feather fan in all four plays in
which he appears, identifying him as a Daoist sage.[20] Zhang wears a black robe, has
"fierce whiskers," and carries a jointed whip in all eleven plays in which he appears.[21]
Zhang's appearance in these plays—particularly his "fierce whiskers"—seems to
support his characterization as "hot-tempered" and "rude," both terms that are regularly used to describe him in the play texts.[22] Such consistency in costume and
accoutrements would render any character from the Sanguo cycle recognizable as
soon as he stepped on stage, and since costumes suggest character traits, their visual
aspect would encourage the audience to expect specific patterns of behavior.[23]

The texts of these twelve plays reinforce this high degree of visual continuity
from play to play with verbal continuity—that is, through repeated conventionalized references to incidents within the story cycle. In *Bowang shao tun* Liu Bei introduces himself and his two sworn brothers by describing their oath of brotherhood

in the Peach Garden. "We butchered a white horse in sacrifice to heaven, and killed a black ox in sacrifice to earth. We don't seek to be born on the same day, we only wish on that very day to die."[24] This description, using precisely the same phrases, appears in at least three other plays within this group.[25]

This unified vision usually functioned to promote loyalty to the throne. The majority of these plays feature a plot where Liu Bei and his men are portrayed as faithful subjects who uphold imperial authority. In eight of these twelve plays references to the emperor are raised above the rest of the text. I have argued elsewhere that this practice is a textual mark of a process seen within the plays themselves, whereby the potentially subversive ambitions of Liu Bei and his sworn brothers are subjugated to the interests of the emperor.[26] Zhang, who appears in eleven of these twelve plays, is the most lawless and insubordinate of the three brothers; his submission to the authority of the throne is key to reestablishing order, and is an important component of most of the plays in which he appears.

Bowang shao tun is one of only two play texts in this group of twelve that although labeled "Archival editions" in their colophons, do not have references to the emperor raised within the text. Indeed, in this play loyalty to the throne is never mentioned. However, this play does make use of these expectations concerning Zhang's rebelliousness and his eventual submission to Zhuge's authority to shape Zhuge into a self-controlled and controlling figure more clearly concerned with issues of righteousness than he appears in the earlier Yuan edition. In essence, Zhuge takes the place of the emperor; thus, the text's focus on the clash of wills between Zhang and Zhuge affirms Zhuge's authority not only through the dialogue of the text, but also by virtue of the conventionalized pattern their conflict represents.

THE YUAN EDITION AND
THE MING MANUSCRIPT COMPARED

The rest of this essay will examine how the vision of the story cycle—particularly the slant it provides on Zhuge and Zhang's relationship—differs in the Yuan and Ming play texts. I will focus on acts 1 and 2, as they represent two pivotal moments in Zhuge's early career—Liu Bei's third visit to his thatched hut, and Zhuge's deployment of Liu's troops in his first confrontation with Cao Cao. Finally, I will conclude with some speculations concerning what this comparison might tell us about the ideals of masculinity that these differences in characterizations reflect.

The assignment of lines in the Yuan and the Ming texts differs strikingly; in the Yuan play text attention is directed almost solely on Zhuge; in the Ming play text he shares the limelight with Liu Bei and his men, especially Zhang. This change in focus supports a different interpretation of Zhuge's character and motivations: in the Yuan edition Zhuge is both more ambitious and more practical in achieving his goals; whereas in the Ming manuscript he is closer to the paragon he became in the novel. While the Yuan edition begins with an introductory monologue by Zhuge, the Ming text begins with a scene featuring Liu, Guan, and Zhang. Examination of these introductory scenes reveals that, in the Yuan text, Zhuge freely reveals his emotions—particularly his personal ambition—whereas in the Ming manuscript Zhuge is a more enigmatic and reserved character. This shift was accompanied by increased attention on the volatile Zhang, and on the subplot in which Zhuge asserts his authority over Zhang.

The introductory scene in the Ming manuscript, which has no corollary in the Yuan edition, performs three functions. First, it establishes this play as part of the complex of court-sponsored Three Kingdoms plays. Liu, Guan, and Zhang appear in their standard attire, and introduce their brotherhood with a standard speech describing the Peach Garden Pledge. Second, attention is focused on Liu's strong desire to enlist Zhuge in his cause—he not only discourses at length about Zhuge's high repute, but also remains determined to visit Zhuge a third time in the face of fierce opposition from Zhang. Finally, this scene emphasizes the potential for future conflict between Zhang and Zhuge. Zhang first refuses to accompany his two brothers on their third visit, maintaining that the glowing recommendations of Zhuge must be overrated. His brothers leave without him, but at the very end of this scene he decides to follow them and vows to "have no qualms about burning that thatched hut down to the ground" if this time they do not succeed in seeing Zhuge.[27] Thus, in addition to clearly signaling this play's alliance with other Three Kingdoms plays performed on the imperial stage, the scene introduces Zhuge as a hermit-sage who must be wooed, and at the same time foreshadows the coming conflict between Zhang and Zhuge.

The differences in approach to Zhuge's character become even clearer once he appears. This occurs in the second scene of the Ming manuscript, which corresponds to the first scene in the Yuan edition. In both texts Zhuge expresses his reluctance to join the Liu cause. In contrast to the novel, where Zhuge is away during Liu's first two visits, Zhuge states that he "has not granted an audience" to Liu Bei.[28] In both texts Zhuge attributes his reluctance to see Liu to the fact that the times are unsettled and dangerous; however, the two texts differ on the feelings he expresses about this refusal. While in the Ming manuscript he ends his monologue with an exclamation about how peaceful and happy his life as a recluse is, in the Yuan edition he wonders when his time to go out in the world will come. Thus, the Yuan edition focuses on Zhuge's ambition, whereas the Ming manuscript focuses more on his lofty ideals—a characterization of Zhuge that has already been introduced in this text's first scene.

A stronger focus on the personal ambition of Zhuge remains consistent through the first act of the Yuan edition. In this edition, the calculated quality of Zhuge's refusal to see Liu Bei is clear from the outset. The stage directions call for "a surprised gesture" before Zhuge sings a line announcing Liu's arrival, but this is followed by "a reconsidering gesture" and a request for his servant boy to "stop rolling out the mat, and shut the cottage door."[29] Neither of these stage directions is given in the Ming manuscript, and the servant boy is requested to "quickly roll out the mat for me, and leave the cottage door half shut."[30] Thus, in the Ming text Zhuge greets Liu's visit with equanimity; while the Yuan text reveals Zhuge's mixed emotions; his initial surprise and subsequent reconsideration suggest that his indifference is feigned. These stage directions, preceded as they are by Zhuge's arias on his frustrated ambitions, lay bare Zhuge's purposeful manipulation of Liu.

Similarly, in the Yuan edition the reason Zhuge finally agrees to Liu's entreaties is more clearly tied to his own personal ambition then to his desire to see the country governed justly. In a song missing from the Ming manuscript he sings: "It is a shame that you will only be an emperor for three years," and the following stage directions call for him "to make a gesture of not going."[31] He abruptly relents after Liu Bei's newborn son is carried on stage: "[*Violently surprised gesture*] Servant boy, prepare to go, *this* one will be an emperor for forty years."[32] In the Ming edition both the strong emotion and the clear implications of concern for his future are absent. Instead, Zhuge states more obliquely: "I see that Lord Xuande [i.e. Liu Bei] has given rise to a joyful air, and a prosperous air is developing, therefore I will go down the mountain."[33]

In the Ming text Zhang's belligerent comments punctuate the audience between Zhuge and Liu. From the opening scene of the play, Zhang's hostility to Zhuge is much more apparent in the Ming text. This can partly be attributed to this text's fleshing out of the parts of all the supporting characters—Zhang's provocations are more apparent because they were fully recorded. However, there are other changes in the text that also call attention to Zhang's challenges to Zhuge's ability and authority. Songs that appear in the Yuan edition focusing on Liu's other men, such as a song describing Zhao Yun and Liu Feng in act 1, and songs praising Zhao Yun, Mi Zhu, and Mi Fang and four songs praising Guan Yu in act 3 of the Yuan edition are missing in the Ming manuscript. Further, words were altered in songs, and details added in dialogues that heighten the force of Zhang's hostility. At the same time, Zhuge's response appears more measured and dispassionate. For example, changes in the song "Zui Zhongtian" and its surrounding dialogue in act 1 sharpen the focus on Zhang and his hostility, as well as Zhuge's control. In the Yuan edition Zhuge characterizes both Guan Yu and Zhang as having an air of the "five hegemons"; in the Ming manuscript that description is reserved for Zhang alone. Zhuge accuses Zhang of being "lacking in principles and without modesty, having no respect and without a sense of what's right" in the Yuan edition. In the Ming text Zhuge begins the lines with the phrase "You say."[34] This alteration changes the line from one where Zhuge is expressing resentment of Zhang to one where he dispassionately repeats Zhang's assessment of him, all the while refusing to react to Zhang's taunts.

The significance of this difference in emphasis becomes more apparent in a comparison of act 2 of the two play texts. The Ming manuscript further elaborates Zhang's conflict with Zhuge. This conflict was apparent in the Yuan edition, but fewer details were provided, and those that were provided indicate that the conflict was more mutual than it appears in the Ming text. In the Yuan edition the sequence of songs where Zhuge is giving instructions to Liu Bei's men is punctuated by stage directions for Zhang to speak, and for him to be shouted down. Zhuge tells him: "Stand aside, we don't need you."[35] The Ming text enlarges upon this fairly simple interaction, as can be seen in this exchange when Zhang challenges Zhuge's orders to Zhao Yun:

> [*Zhang:*] I said that country bumpkin doesn't know how to deploy troops. Who ever heard of wanting to lose and not wanting to win in a fight? Zhao Yun, come over here. Wait until I go over there. [Mimes seeing Zhuge.]
>
> [*Zhuge:*] What is it, Zhang Fei?
>
> [*Zhang:*] I will go to Bowang and engage in battle.
>
> [*Zhuge:*] Zhang Fei, is your spear quick?
>
> [*Zhang:*] My spear is quick!
>
> [*Zhuge:*] Is your horse well fed?
>
> [*Zhang:*] My horse is well fed!
>
> [*Zhuge:*] Do you dare to kill?
>
> [*Zhang:*] I dare to kill!
>
> [*Zhuge:*] I can't use you. Get out.
>
> [*Zhang:*] This bumpkin! If he doesn't just infuriate me to death![36]

This confrontation epitomizes the characterizations of these two figures—that is, Zhang as a rash fighting man, and Zhuge as the cool and collected strategist.[37] In this scene Zhuge is clearly baiting Zhang by playing on Zhang's desire for action. Thus, both Zhuge's directions to Liu's men and his manipulation of Zhang emphasize his ability to control others. In the Yuan edition Zhuge is more emotionally invested in his conflict with, and eventual triumph over, Zhang; in the Ming text Zhuge exerts control over both his emotions and Zhang alike.

CONCLUSION

In the Yuan edition Zhuge expresses an array of emotions including frustration and ambition, anger and triumph. His motives for joining Liu Bei's cause are practical; he sees in Liu's son an opportunity to realize his ambitions. The Zhuge of the Ming text is less forthcoming about his motives, and seemingly more idealistic—in short, more like the Zhuge we know from the novel. As for the two texts' depictions of Zhang, the differences are less in Zhang's qualities—he is rude and rash in both editions—than in the amount of attention he is accorded. However, the increased focus on Zhang in the Ming text does not necessarily indicate an endorsement of

the qualities Zhang represents; rather, the opposite. Zhang's dramatic characterization is merely a convenient aid in this text's remolding of Zhuge's character, and
actually signals a move away from the freewheeling, martial heroic ethic of the *Pinghua* to the more orthodox Confucian ethics of the novel. It is a move away from
a masculine ideal of the warrior—whether conventional military or magical—and
toward that of the scholar-statesman.

In the Ming edition of *Bowang shao tun* the character of Zhang serves many
functions. First and most importantly, his insurgency and eventual suppression validates Zhuge's abilities as strategist. Second, the trope of Zhang's initial rebelliousness and final submission was an essential part of the plots of many of the Three
Kingdoms plays performed on the imperial stage, and perhaps something the audience at court had come to expect. The focus on this trope within this edition of the
play signals its incorporation into the imperial corpus. At the same time, the edition's insertion of Zhuge into the position usually occupied by the emperor validates
Zhuge's authority. Third and finally, the contrast in this edition between Zhang and
Zhuge highlights the command Zhuge exhibits over both others and himself.

Thus, Zhang's role here foreshadows his decreasing importance within the
story cycle, as it became more and more a vehicle for orthodox values. The competi-
tion in this play between Zhuge and Zhang—and particularly Zhuge's eventual
triumph—reflects a negotiation of values that was taking place as the novel recon-
figured popular and literary material accreted over a millennium for a literate Ming
audience. However, while the novel's characterization of these two figures proved
definitive in some respects, it by no means precluded different audiences from
seeing within the novel somewhat divergent meanings.[38] A certain sympathy for
Zhang, or at least a fascination with the clash between his style of masculinity and
that of Zhuge, can be detected from the fact that the scenes from acts 2 and 3 of
Bowang shao tun were incorporated into a series of stage adaptations from the Ming
though the Republican era.[39] The battle of wills between these two male figures
was repeatedly reenacted, even though the outcome always remained the same.

NOTES

1. For the Yuan edition I have consulted *Jiaoding Yuankan zaju sanshizhong*, ed. Qian
Zheng (Taibei: Shijie Shuju, 1962), 379–409; and *Xinjiao Yuankan zaju sanshizhong*, ed.
Qinjun Xu (Beijing: Zhonghua shuju, 1980), 729–750. For a facsimile edition of the Yuan
edition, see *Quan Yuan zaju sanbian*, ed. Jialuo Yang, vol. 6 (Taibei: Shijie shuju, 1973). For
a facsimile edition of the Ming manuscript see *Quan Yuan zaju sanbian*, vol. 1; for a modern
typeset edition, see *Guben Yuan Ming zaju*, ed. Jilie Wang, vol. 8 (Shanghai: Shangwu Yinshuguan, 1938).

2. Shigeki Takahashi makes this point in his detailed comparison of the play to the *Pinghua* and the novel, "Shokatsu Ryoo *Hakuboo shuuten* no kosatsu—*Sankoku heiwa* to Sankoku zatsugeki," *Chugoku koten kenkyu* 20 (1975): 158–171.

3. Takahashi (ibid., 167) states that while Zhuge constitutes the main thread of the plot, Zhang Fei is also an important strand, and notes that this dual focus distinguishes the play from narrative accounts of the same events.

4. For more details on this shift, see Tamaki Ogawa, "*Sanguo yanyi* de yanbian, trans. Hu Tianmin," *Sanguo yanyi xuekan* 1 (1985): 323–34; see also Kimberly Besio, "Zhang Fei in Yuan Vernacular Literature: Legend, Heroism and History in the Reproduction of the Three Kingdoms Story Cycle," *Journal of Sung-Yuan Studies* 27 (1997): 63–98. As the essays by Roberts, Tung, Cheung, and Yu in the present volume discuss, the contradictions between various Confucian values are a major preoccupation of the novel.

5. For a discussion of Zhuge's status shortly after his death, see Eric Henry, "Chu-ko Liang in The Eyes of His Contemporaries," *Harvard Journal of Asiatic Studies* 52, no. 2 (December 1992): 589–612.

6. Hoyt Tillman, "Zhongguo lishi yishi zhong de Zhuge Liang," in *Zhou Qin Han Tang kaogu yu wenhua guoji xueshu huiyi lunwenji* (Xi'an: Xibeidaxue xuebao bianjibu, 1988), 133–46; and Tillman, "One Significant Rise in Chu-ko Liang's Popularity: An Impact of the 1127 Jurchen Conquest," *Hanxue yanjiu* 14, no. 2 (Dec. 1996): 1–35. See also his essay in the preceding chapter.

7. Henry, "Chu-ko- Liang," 608, 603–4.

8. Weisi Ye and Xin Mao, *Sanguo yanyi chuangzuo lun* (Jiangsu: Jiangsu renmin chubanshe, 1984), 31; Yuqian Gu, "Yuan zaju Sanguo xi ticai tanyuan," *Yangzhou Daxue xuebao*, no. 1 (1999): 28–31.

9. See, for example, Zhensheng Qiu and Mingtao Liu, "Wangu yunxiao yi yu mao," in *Sanguo yanyi lunwen ji*, ed. Henan Sheng Shehui kexue yuan wenxue yanjiu suo (Zhengzhou: Zhengzhou guji chubanshe, 1985), 101–18; and Yiguo Liu, "Tan *Sanguo zhi tongsu yanyi* zhong Zhuge Liang xingxiang de xingcheng he suzao," in *Sanguo yanyi yanjiu ji*, ed, Editorial Section of *Journal of Social Research* and the Literature Institute of the Sichuan Academy of Social Sciences (Sichuan: Sichuan sheng shehui kexue yuan chubanshe 1983), 197–210.

10. Chen Shou, *Sanguo zhi* (Beijing: Zhonghua shuju, 1959), 944.

11. On Zhang's importance in the *Pinghua* see Zhensheng Qiu, *Sanguo yanyi zongheng tan* (Beijing: Beijing Daxue chubanshe, 1995), 34; and Ye and Mao, *Sanguo yanyi chuangzuo lun*, 30; it has also been noted in passing in the following studies: Zhouchang Chen, "*Sanguo zhi tongsu yanyi xingcheng guocheng lunlue*," in ed, Editorial Section of *Journal of Social Research* and the Literature Institute of the Sichuan Academy of Social Sciences, *Sanguo yanyi yanjiu ji*, 306–25; and Zhenduo Zheng "*Sanguo yanyi* de yanhua," *Xiaoshuo yuebao*, 13, no. 10 (October 1929): 1543–78. For discussions of Zhang's prominence in *zaju* from the Yuan and early Ming periods, see Chunxiang Li, "Yuandai de Sanguo xi ji qi dui *Sanguo yanyi* de yingxiang," in ed, Editorial Section of *Journal of Social Research* and the Literature Institute of the Sichuan Academy of Social Sciences, *Sanguo yanyi yanjiu ji*, 343–60; and Kimberly Besio, "The Disposition of Defiance: Zhang Fei as a Comic Hero of Yuan *Zaju*" (PhD diss., University of California, Berkeley, 1992). See also Ogawa, "*Sanguo Yanyi* de yanbian;"

and Zhaoxin Zhou, "Yuan Ming shidai Sanguo gushi de duo zhong xingtai," in *Sanguo Yanyi zongkao*, ed. Zhaoxin Zhou (Beijing: Beijing Daxue chubanshe, 1995), 301–46.

12. Zhou, "Yuan Ming shidai Sanguo gushi de duo zhong xingtai," 330; Besio, "Disposition of Defiance."

13. Twenty-eight of the thirty extant Yuan texts are of this type. Both Stephen West and Wilt Idema, following the suggestion of Moon Kyung Kim (Kin Bunkyoo 金文京), have argued that these twenty-eight texts are role texts—that is, that these texts provide all the information the lead singer would need to perform his or her part. See West, "Text and Ideology: Ming Editors and Northern Drama," in *Ming Qing xiqu guoji yantao hui lunwen ji* ed. Wei Hua and Ailing Wang (Taipei: Zhongyang yanjiuyuan, 1998), 237–83; and Idema, "Some Aspects of *Pai-yueh-t'ing*: Script and Performance," in *Proceedings of International Conference on Kuan Han-Ch'ing*, ed. Yongyi Zeng (Taipei: Xingzhengyuan wenhua jianshe weiyuanhui, 1994), 3–23 .

14. This number, while smaller than the sixty-eight that Wilt Idema has noted for the *zheng dan* of the play *Baiyue ting* 拜月停, is still quite large. Cf. Idema, "Some Aspects," 75.

15. Of the thirty extant Yuan editions, sixteen have Ming counterparts to which we can compare them. Among this group of sixteen plays, the majority of the Yuan editions have more songs than their Ming counterparts. However, the Ming manuscript edition of *Bowang shao tun* has the highest number of missing songs of any of these pairs. For a complete list, see West, "Text and Ideology," 252. This suggests that perhaps the play underwent a more drastic change in emphasis than usual as it was adapted for the Ming Imperial stage; only two other plays have numbers similar to *Bowang shao tun*. The Yuan edition of *Kanqian nu* 看錢奴 has twenty more songs than its Ming counterpart, and the Yuan edition of *Xue Rengui* 薛仁貴 has nineteen more songs than its Ming counterpart. For a discussion on the extensive revisions to the Yuan edition of *Xue Rengui* and the ideological implications of these revisions, see Wilt Idema, "The Remaking of an Unfilial Hero: Some Notes on the Earliest Dramatic Adaptations of 'The Story of Hueh Jen-Kuei,'" in *As the Twig is Bent . . . Essays in Honour of Frits Vos*, ed. Erika De Poorter (Amsterdam: J.C. Gieben, 1990), 83–111.

16. West, "Text and Ideology," 249.

17. Ibid., 251.

18. Wilt Idema, "The Founding of the Han Dynasty in Early Drama: The Autocratic Suppression of Popular Debunking," in *Thought and Law in Qin and Han China: Studies Presented to Anthony Hulsewe on the Occasion of His Eightieth Birthday*, ed. Wilt Idema and Erik Zurcher (Leiden: E. J. Brill, 1990), 181–207.

19. One more formal attribute seen in a majority of this larger group of twelve plays is that when a reference to the emperor (*sheng* = 聖 or *huang* = 皇) occurs, the remainder of the line remains blank and the reference is raised to above the margin of the next line of the text.

20. In addition to *Bowang shao tun* Zhuge Liang appears in *Pang lüe si jun* 龐掠四郡, *Wu ma po Cao* 五馬破曹, *Nu zhan Guanping* 怒斬關平, and *Taiping yan* 太平宴. These four plays are included in Jilie Wang, ed., *Guben Yuan Ming zaju*, vols. 17, 18, & 31 (Shanghai: Hanfen lou, 1941). For a comparison of Zhuge's costume in the novel, in these plays and in the *Pinghua*, see Liangxiao Tan, "Zhuge Liang fushi lun kao," *Shehui kexue yanjiu*, 1994, no. 5 (1994): 93–97.

21. In addition to *Bowang shao tun* and the four plays listed in note 20, Zhang also appears in *Xiangyang hui* 襄陽會, *San zhan Lu Bu* 三戰呂布, *Huanghe lou* 黃鶴樓, *Dandao pi sikou* 單刀劈四寇, *Danzhan Lu Bu* 單戰呂布, and *Shiliu yuan* 石榴園, in Wang, *Guben Yuan Ming zaju* vols. 4, 6, 7, 16, and 17.

22. For example, in act 1 of the Ming manuscript of *Bowang shao tun* Liu Bei refers to Zhang's "hot-tempered quality" in the first scene; in subsequent scenes Guan Yu and Liu frequently admonish Zhang to "stop being so hot-tempered." Zhuge also sings of how appropriate Zhang's nickname of "rude Zhang Fei" seems.

23. For more on theatrical conventions regarding costume and props, and their depiction in New Year's prints, see Catherine Pagani's discussion in the next chapter.

24. *Bowang shao tun*, 1a, in Wang, *Guben* vol. 8.

25. See *San zhan Lü Bu*, 4b, in Wang, *Guben Yuan Ming zaju*, vol. 6; *Dan zhan Lü Bu*, 7b, in *Guben Yuan Ming zaju*, vol. 16, and *Shiliu yuan*, 3a, in Wang, *Guben Yuan Ming zaju*, vol. 17.

26. Besio, "Zhang Fei in Yuan Vernacular Literature," 92. That *Bowang shao tun* is not marked in this manner might reflect that the Ming edition was a reworking of an earlier edition that was only partially assimilable into the Imperial agenda. The only other play that is labeled an "archival edition" and does not have references to the Emperor raised within the text is the play *Huanghe lou*, which has been attributed by modern scholars to the Yuan playwright Zhu Kai.

27. *Bowang shaotun* 1a, Wang *Guben Yuan Ming zaju*, vol. 8.

28. In this detail the play texts follow the Yuan narrative *Sanguozhi pinghua* reproduced in facsimile in *Quanxiang pinghua wuzhong* (Shanghai: Gudian wenxue, 1955). See page 417, where Zhuge clearly instructs his servant boy to tell Liu Bei that he is not at home.

29. Zheng, *Jiaoding Yuankan zaju sanshizhong*, 397.

30. *Bowang shaotun*, 2a, in *Guben Yuan Ming zaju*, vol. 8.

31. Zheng, *Jiaoding Yuankan zaju sanshizhong*, 400. The song is set to the tune of "Houting Hua."

32. Ibid.

33. 4a, Wang, *Guben Yuan Ming zaju*, vol. 8; see also Zhaoxin Zhou, "Yuan Ming shidai Sanguo gushi de duo zhong xingtai," 325–27; he notes that a similar scene occurs in act 7 of the *chuanqi* play *Liu Xuande san gu caolu* 劉玄德三顧草廬 and asserts that the novel's version of the third meeting (where Zhuge focuses on the righteousness of the cause) elevates Zhuge's thinking.

34. Zheng, *Jiaoding Yuankan zaju sanshizhong*, 399; 3b, *Guben*, vol. 8,.

35. Zheng, *Jiaoding Yuankan zaju sanshizhong*, 401.

36. *Bowang shaotun*, 7a, Wang, *Guben Yuan Ming zaju*, vol. 8; this exchange sets a pattern that is repeated three more times, as Zhuge conveys his orders to Liu Feng, Mi Lan and Mi Fang, and Guan Yu, respectively. In their final interchange Zhuge picks up the pace, and underlines the repetitiveness by posing all three questions at once.

37. Yingde Guo, "Qian tan Yuan zaju Sanguo xi de yishu tezheng," in Editorial section of *Journal of Social Science Research* and the Literature Institute of the Sichuan Academy of

Social Science, ed, *Sanguo yanyi yanjiu ji,* 136, also remarks upon the effectiveness of this scene in establishing the characters of Zhang and Zhuge when he cites this incident as an example of repetition. He considers repetition one of four artistic means of characterization used in Chinese drama.

38. For more on this issue see Anne E. McLaren, "Ming Audiences and Vernacular Hermeneutics: The Uses of *The Romance of the Three Kingdoms,*" *T'oung Pao* 81 (1995): 51–80.

39. Zhaoxin Zhou , "Yuan Ming shidai Sanguo gushi de duo zhong xingtai," 328–329 asserts that not only were the scenes in *Bowang shaotun* incorporated into scenes 12–16 of the *chuanqi Caolu ji,* but also the conflict between Zhuge and Zhang was further expanded and deepened. This conflict was also represented in the Qing *zhezi xi* "Fu jing 負荊" (excerpted from the play *Sanguo Ji* 三國記); see the Qing collection *Zhui baiqiu* edited by Wanhua zhu ren 玩花主人(Beijing: Zhonghua Shuju, 1955), 15–19.

7

The Theme of *Three Kingdoms* in Chinese Popular Woodblock Prints

CATHERINE PAGANI

Chen Shou's (233–297) *Chronicle of the Three Kingdoms* (*Sanguo zhi*), the third-century record of events involving the political and military conflicts between the rival kingdoms of Wu, Shu, and Wei from AD 168 to 265, has maintained a strong and enduring presence in Chinese culture, inspiring one of China's most influential novels, the fourteenth-century *Three Kingdoms* (*Sanguo zhi yanyi*) by Luo Guanzhong (c. 1330–c. 1400) and providing a story line for countless regional operas. So timeless is the *Three Kingdoms* story that it has found a place in both Chinese traditional arts and the modern media of television and computer games.

Themes from *Three Kingdoms* were a popular subject for the mass-produced woodblock-printed New Year pictures (*nianhua*) that were enjoyed by all levels of Chinese society. These colorful and dramatic images, which could communicate to literate and nonliterate equally, were designed to entertain as well as educate: their decorativeness made them ideal household adornments during New Year festivities, while their wide range of subject matter familiarized the viewer with traditional tales and legends while reaffirming cultural values. While the design and printing techniques reveal differences in the regional styles (and to some degree the socioeconomic level of the purchaser), *nianhua* in general show a consistency across Chinese culture touching on themes that were immediately appealing to and understood by the general population.

In this way, *nianhua* functioned much in the same way as another art form designed to reach a broad audience: regional theater. Chinese theater combines singing, music, and acting, and for this reason is often referred to as "opera" in the

West. The most sophisticated and highly regarded form of theater is Beijing opera (*jingju*), performed by professionals. Elizabeth Wichmann-Walzak discusses a contemporary *jingju* play on a topic related to *Three Kingdoms* in the next chapter. In addition to *jingju*, there are nearly two hundred different regional operas that reflect local customs and local dialects and are performed by different ranks of troupes.[1] However, while there are some variations in the areas of styles of singing and costume, all are part of a single art form, and overall are remarkably similar in the social codes of behavior and cultural attitudes they express in their narrative content.[2] Theater performances provided the population with a visual and oral means for transmitting historical information and cultural values,[3] and like the prints, did not depend on the written word to convey its ideas (*nianhua* had the further advantage of not being dependent on regional dialect).

This study examines the theme of the *Three Kingdoms* in the woodblock-printed New Year prints of the late nineteenth and early twentieth centuries. The many dramatic events found in the story offered ideal subject matter for the colorful and striking *nianhua*. As many of these prints employed theatrical conventions of stage settings, costumes, and makeup in their design, this study will also consider the influence that regional theater had as an important source for *nianhua* imagery.

Exploring this dialogue between the visual arts (in this case *nianhua*) and the performing arts (theater) offers one means of broadly understanding how ideas and values were disseminated within traditional Chinese culture in late imperial China and the importance of the theatrical versions of stories (as opposed to their literary counterparts) to the transmission of such ideas. But *nianhua* and theater have an even closer connection: *nianhua* functioned within the larger world of the performing arts by reiterating the same themes that were designed to encourage the Confucian morality central to Chinese culture. Moreover, an examination of the connections between prints and plays brings to light the important role that *nianhua* can serve as non-verbal, visual evidence in providing a more complete understanding of regional theater. Here the *Three Kingdoms* story offers a link between *nianhua* and theater: its underlying messages extolling themes of social values had a broad appeal, while the story's dramatic events made for theatrical performances that captivated the senses and prints that delighted the eye.

Woodblock-printed New Year pictures likely first appeared in the twelfth century, and by the late Ming dynasty (1368–1644), a number of important production centers emerged, fueled by the growing desire for items to adorn the interiors of homes. The most famous were those at Yangliuqing in the western suburbs of Tianjin in the north and in the area of Taohuawu in Suzhou in the south, both of which were known for the fineness of their prints. Production at these workshops reached its height in the Qing dynasty (1644–1911).[4] These prints showed a strong influence from classical Chinese painting and it has been said "their refinement of composition, technique and colouring . . . makes them comparable to the best Chinese genre paintings."[5] In fact, the classification of subjects in these prints followed that of painting.[6] Eighteenth- and nineteenth-century *nianhua* from Tao-huawu and Yangliuqing give testimony to the high quality of work that could be achieved with carved wood, ink, color, and paper.

The improvements in woodblock-printing technology in the late Ming dynasty gave way to decreased prices for *nianhua*, making them within reach of a larger proportion of the population. The resulting increased demand for *nianhua* encouraged the establishment of more print shops, both small family-run affairs as well as larger village industries; by the mid-Qing dynasty, print shops could be found in rural towns and villages throughout China.[7] Some regions developed reputations for the quality of their work and would sell their *nianhua* to outlying markets. However, it is important to note that the quality of the design and printing varied considerably among *nianhua*: the prints from Taohuawu, for example, that were influenced (and in some cases, also designed) by literati artists in the Jiangnan region were quite distinct from those produced in a small family-run shop in a rural village. By the late nineteenth century, *nianhua* had reached its widest audience. While lithography nearly ended the craft in the main production centers, the low-level technology of woodblock printing ensured its popularity in rural areas.[8]

Overall, *nianhua* themes may be grouped into four broad categories: auspicious messages, which include flowers, fruits, and other images that carry symbolic meanings for good fortune; genre scenes of daily life, including festivities both public and private, such as the annual dragon boat festival and wedding processions; landscape scenes; and literary subjects, which take their imagery from folk tales, legends, myths, and regional operas. This last category is of interest here. Prints on literary themes represent a sizable proportion of New Year pictures.[9]

There are inherent limitations in working with *nianhua*. Although produced in great numbers, particularly in the late nineteenth and early twentieth centuries, *nianhua* were regarded as a disposable art form, and therefore only a fraction survives. Prints could serve both elite and nonelite equally and thus it is often difficult to tell the intended audience for particular prints. Moreover, New Year pictures are rarely dated and for most prints the location of production is unknown: there were hundreds of print shops in operation from the mid-Qing onward, few prints carry maker's marks, and the prints were made from commonly found everyday materials that were not particular to any one area. In addition, prints were a highly portable art form and could be circulated over a wide geographical area. Thus, although these observations are general owing to the absence of attributable, datable material, they do demonstrate the historical significance of these prints, which far transcends their artistic and decorative value.[10]

The *Three Kingdoms* was an ideal theme for *nianhua*. The strong and lively narrative combined with beloved and detested characters, both male and female, created subjects that had immediate visual appeal. However, while the number of subjects for *nianhua* was potentially limitless, in practice only a few episodes appear to have been popular. A look at a representative sampling of prints produced three prominent themes, here listed in order in which they occur in the novel: "The Capture and

Liberation of Cao Cao"; "The Slopes of Changban"; and "The Betrothal (or Union) of the Dragon and Phoenix" (i.e. Liu Bei and Lady Sun) / "Returning to Jingzhou." Less-common subjects in prints include "Giving Chengdu to Liu Bei," "The Strategy of the Empty Fortress," and "Inspiring the Fighting Will of Huang Zhong."[11]

THEME ONE: THE CAPTURE AND LIBERATION OF CAO CAO

This episode highlights Cao Cao as a "paragon of wicked conduct"[12] and summarizes popular opinion concerning Cao Cao's character. Here the wily Cao Cao flees after a failed (and at the time unsuspected) assassination attempt on Dong Zhuo, the chief minister, who himself has been described in the *Sanguo* as "arrogant beyond reason" and known for his misuse of power.[13] The magistrate Chen Gong, who imprisons Cao overnight, later captures Cao. Tricked into thinking that Cao is loyal and upright, Chen frees Cao, and the two travel to the home of Lü Boshe, Cao's "uncle": a sworn-brother of Cao's father. After Lü leaves to get some wine for dinner, Cao and Chen hear the sound of a knife being sharpened. Fearing that they are about to be killed, they instead attack, murdering the entire household of eight men and women. It is then that they realize that the knife was meant for the slaughter of a pig for the evening meal. Horrified, Chen says to Cao, "You have made a huge mistake and we have slain honest folk."[14] Leaving the house, the two men encounter Lü returning home and kill him as well. Cao Cao replies coldly, "I would rather betray the world than let the world betray me."[15] Peri pessu Cao Cao would harm others before others could harm him.[16] Chen realizes that he has misread Cao's character and thinks to himself, "I took him for a true man and left all to follow him, but he is cruel as a wolf."[17]

The *nianhua* entitled "The Capture and Liberation of Cao (Zhuofang Cao)" shows a typical representation of this incident and is simple in its composition (figure 1). Three figures stand before a table. On the left, in a yellow robe, is Lü Boshe, holding in his hand a kettle while he receives his guests. On the right are Cao Cao and Chen Gong. This particular print employs several theatrical conventions in its depiction of the characters: Cao and Chen, for example, hold in their hands a tasseled baton, indicating that they have just arrived by horse. The use of such imagery is discussed in greater depth below.

THEME TWO: "THE SLOPES OF CHANGBAN"

This tragic episode focuses on personal sacrifice, loyalty, and devotion to duty. In a battle between the rival kingdoms of Wei and Shu, Cao Cao of Wei pursues Liu Bei of Shu. In the intensity of the conflict, Zhao Yun, the famous general of Shu, loses track of Lady Mi (Mi Furen), Liu Bei's wife, and her young son A Dou, the heir to the kingdom of Shu, who were entrusted into Zhao's care. Risking his life, Zhao searches for the missing family, declaring, "I will seek the lost ones in heaven or hell, through good or evil, and if I find them not I will die in the desert."[18]

Figure 1. The Capture and Liberation of Cao Cao

Eventually, Zhao locates the badly wounded Lady Mi near a half-dried well. Fearing that Zhao would not be able to save both her son and herself, Lady Mi commits suicide by throwing herself into the well. Included in the narrative is a poem praising Lady Mi's sacrifice:

> The warrior relies upon the strength of his charger,
> Afoot, how could he bear to safety his young prince?
> Brave mother! who died to preserve the son of her husband's line;
> Heroine was she, bold and decisive![19]

Zhao then covers her body so that it does not suffer further insult. Loosening his armor, Zhao then straps A Dou to his body. On the road back to Liu Bei, Zhao Yun is forced to fight (successfully) a number of adversaries: he "slew of Cao's captains half a hundred, all men of renown."[20] A Dou is delivered safely to his father. Interestingly, Liu Bei later chastised Zhao Yun for taking such extreme measures to rescue the boy. Throwing the boy to the ground, Liu angrily said, "To preserve that suckling I very nearly lost a great captain."[21]

The incident, as depicted in the popular print shown in figure 2, is set within a hilled landscape; its main characters engage in lively action as the kingdoms of Wei and Shu are arrayed for battle. At the center of the picture are Liu Bei (left) and Zhang Fei of Shu. At the right, deep in the hills and protected by a canopy, is Cao Cao of Wei. At the bottom-left corner, Zhao Yun offers a hand to the wounded Lady Mi, who holds A Dou on her lap. The well appears in front of her. Behind the trio is Zhang He in his pursuit of Zhao Yun. This scene is powerfully rendered with a minimum of bright color.

THEME THREE: THE BETROTHAL (OR UNION) OF THE DRAGON AND PHOENIX/RETURNING TO JINGZHOU

In a story of fidelity and devotion, Liu Bei marries the sister of his enemy, Sun Quan, ruler of the Eastern Wu kingdom. The arranged marriage was an attempt by the schemer Zhou Yu, Sun's advisor, to lure Liu Bei away from Jingzhou and keep him captive so that the city would eventually be handed over to his rival. At first Liu was reluctant to consider marriage so soon after the death of his wife, however advantageous it could be to him. Liu eventually consents to the union and spends the next year living with his wife's family. At this time, Zhao Yun reminds Liu of his obligations in Jingzhou. Liu is faced with a Confucian dilemma: he is torn between his conflicting obligations to his kingdom and to his wife, who decides to leave willingly with her husband. The couple sneaks away. Angered by this move, Sun Quan sends his generals Ding Feng, and Xu Sheng and their troops to prevent the couple's return to Jingzhou. Lady Sun (Sun Furen), remaining true to her husband, helps to extricate them from danger by confronting the soldiers. "Are you turned traitors?" she says as she reprimands them. The soldiers decide against arguing with

Figure 2. The Slopes of Chang Banpo

Lady Sun, and eventually the couple, accompanied by their escort, Zhao Yun, is allowed to pass the roadblock.

The woodblock print in figure 3 focuses on the marriage of Liu Bei and Lady Sun. Inside the house Lady Sun wears her red wedding gown and is accompanied by four female attendants carrying swords. Liu Bei was quite taken aback by the weaponry found in the bridal apartments. He was told by the housekeeper, "Do not be frightened, O honorable one. My lady has always had a taste for warlike things and her maids have all been taught fencing as a pastime."[22] With that, the attendants were ordered to remove their swords when they were at work, so not to disturb Liu Bei. Liu Bei stands outside the apartment, dressed in the robes of an emperor, symbolizing his right to rule and fitting the description of him as having "the air of an emperor and a look like the sun."[23] The poem on the print reads:

> Sparkling swords now light the wedding chamber,
> He who is famous for his loyalty is wed.
> The shadows of candles play on the scarlet walls, the bridegroom is half-drunk,
> Together they rejoice on the nuptial bed, seeing Jingzhou in their dreams.

In a second print on this theme, entitled *Returning to Jingzhou* (figure 4), the couple is shown traveling through a landscape on their way to Jingzhou. A large number of warriors are charging toward Liu Bei and his entourage (located in the center of the print): Ding Feng and Xu Sheng are on the bottom left, and Zhou Yu, Sun Quan's advisor, is on the right. Lady Sun sits in a carriage protected by Zhao Yun, his sword raised. At the upper left is Zhuge Liang (labeled here as Kongming), and at the upper center is Zhang Fei, coming to the rescue. Small Chinese characters on the print identify the other figures in the scene.

Certainly, prints such as these were popular owing to their vivid coloring and energetic rendering of the stories. They also focused on themes such a loyalty and friendship that resonated with the public and glorified traditional Confucian standards while vilifying inappropriate behavior. But this may be said of much of the *Three Kingdoms* tale. What distinguished these episodes in the novel from others in inspiring woodblock-printed pictures? This question might be answered by looking at another issue: how did the larger, nonliterate population become familiar with these tales? It appears that the stories in *Three Kingdoms* were already brought into the public consciousness through theatrical performances that focused on these themes.

Three of the four *Three Kingdoms* prints previously discussed use theater conventions, suggesting not only theater's pervasiveness and popularity but also its role in bringing certain parts of the *Three Kingdoms* story into the public consciousness. Theater performances would also have provided the context for an image that would allow for a full understanding and enjoyment of a *Three Kingdoms* print.

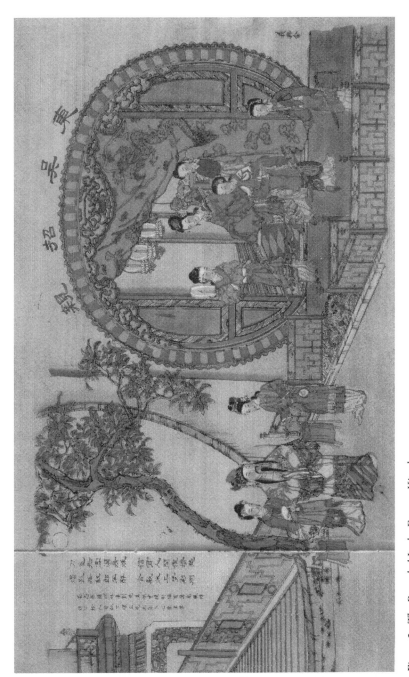

Figure 3. The Betrothal In the Eastern Kingdom

Figure 4. Returning to Jingzhou

Even though *nianhua* had the advantage of transcending the limitations of language in their use of visual clues, they did require that the viewer have some prior familiarity with the tale. Thus, to the informed viewer, the image of Zhao Yun with a child strapped to his chest, would immediately bring to mind the incident at the slopes of Changban, and with it the strong Confucian messages of a mother's sacrifice for her son's safety (for the greater good of the kingdom) and the loyalty of a warrior to his general.

From at least the Tang dynasty (618–906), the *Three Kingdoms* tale was a major subject for storytellers,[24] and its heroes have been an important part of Chinese drama from the Yuan dynasty (1279–1368).[25] In addition to full-length treatments, there were numerous other dramas based on the *Three Kingdoms*.[26] This story was "the ultimate source for hundreds of the spine-tingling and ear-splitting scripts of the modern Chinese 'opera'"[27] that were influenced by both the novel and these earlier dramatic precursors.

This connection to theater is clearly visible in the *nianhua, The Union of the Dragon and Phoenix/Returning to Jingzhou* (figure 5), the story of the joining in marriage of Liu Bei and Lady Sun, which makes use of symbolism found in stage productions. Here, the general Liu Bei, shown at the right, holds a baton of tassels, the theatrical symbol for a horse. With him are his wife and her attendant, who holds two flags with a wheel on each one, representing a chariot. Lady Sun stands behind the attendant and holds the ends of the flagpoles, symbolizing her seated position inside the chariot. As the group makes their way to Jingzhou, three male military leaders dressed for combat and maintaining static poses signifying their battle-readiness approach them. These men likely are Zhao Yun (the group's loyal escort), Zhuge Liang, and Zhang Fei, who arrive in time to rescue the couple from Ding Feng and Xu Sheng. Zhao Yun's youth is depicted by his natural makeup, while Liu Bei's long beard signifies his age (Liu Bei is described as "fifty and grizzled" in the novel).[28] Liu Bei, as in previous prints, is dressed in the robes of an emperor. The sets of flags attached to the shoulders of the military leaders indicate their status as generals.

Even a simple folk *nianhua*, such as the example produced in Wuqiang, Hebei, contains basic elements to show its origins in the theater (figure 6). Liu Bei, standing on the left side of the print, holds his tasseled baton; Lady Sun and her attendant both hold a pair of flags with wheels. As in the previous *nianhua*, Zhao Yun is placed at the center, holding a weapon in one hand and a tasseled baton in the other. His costume has a tiger head at the waist, indicating his military status.[29] Theatrical makeup is evident on all of the figures; furthermore, they face forward as if playing to an audience.

The *nianhua* entitled *Dangyang [County], Slopes of Changban* (figure 7) is more obviously connected to theatrical performances as the figures are placed as they might appear on stage. The six men, with four flags at their shoulders, are military leaders in the midst of battle. At the center is Zhao Yun saving the young A Dou. The blue cloud emanating from A Dou's head encloses a dragon, a reference to the boy as the heir to the dragon throne. On either side of Zhao Yun are

Figure 5. The Union of the Dragon and the Phoenix. Returning to Jingzhou

Figure 6. Returning to Jingzhou

Figure 7. The Slopes of Chang Banpo in the County of Dangyang

two Wei generals, Zhang He (left) and Cao Hong (right), both with painted faces. The placement of the characters in this scene is strongly suggestive of theater. All face forward and are situated at different levels corresponding to their placement on the stage. Their static poses lack the spontaneous energy characteristic of the same episode set within a landscape (figure 2).

The *nianhua* entitled *Zhao Zilong [Zhao Yun] Single-handedly Saves His Master* (Figure 8) successfully combines the energy of the landscape print and theatrical elements to produce a lively composition. In a manner similar to the *Dangyang County* print, this fine print from Yangliuqing also places Zhao Yun in the center of the print and with a nearly identical pose: his raised right arm holds a sword and his left a spear. A Dou is strapped to his chest, and rising from A Dou's head is a cloud with a dragon. Five warriors attack Zhao Yun, and two have painted-face makeup. In neither print do we find the unfortunate Lady Mi and the well, as the focus instead is on Zhao Yun, his bravery, and, above all, his single-minded loyalty to his ruler and to the heir to the throne.

However, not all of the identifications of the characters in the prints are straightforward. Returning to the *nianhua The Capture and Liberation of Cao Cao* (figure 1), the identification of the two figures in dark robes, Cao Cao and Chen Gong, remains tentative. The first figure, in the middle of the print, wears pale face makeup, a two-tiered cap, and a long dark-blue robe. This is quite possibly Cao Cao. Arlington, in his documentation of opera in Beijing in the early twentieth century, describes a particular headpiece, known as a *xiang diao guan*, worn by actors in the role of the "infamous traitor" Cao Cao, that resembles the hat shown here.[30] The blue robe suggests a dishonest statesman, again in keeping with the identification of the figure as Cao Cao.[31] However, Arlington also notes that Cao Cao is usually shown with a painted face in styles that can vary considerably. One type is pale white with dark makeup around the eyes and thin eyebrows: "the white face of evil and treacherous men."[32] This style of face painting appears to coincide with the figure tentatively identified as Chen Gong by his green robe, an indicator of a statesman who has earned military honors.[33]

Even in prints where the characters are identified by name, the face painting and the robes can show wide variations. While it is possible that these variations are arbitrary or result from artistic license, it is equally likely that they are indicative of regional and temporal variations in theatrical productions. In this way, these prints serve another function beyond their value to entertain and educate: they are tangible representations of performances where little or no traditional documentation (and here I am referring to the written word) exists. Reflecting popular taste, these *nianhua* are valuable pieces of evidence in their own right, and can shed further light on our understanding of Chinese theater.

Theater in China had a wide appeal, owing to what Barbara Ward has called the "totality" of the experience provided,[34] which could resonate on several levels within each viewer while at the same time touching all social strata that comprised the audience. The use of familiar symbolism added layers of meaning to a performance

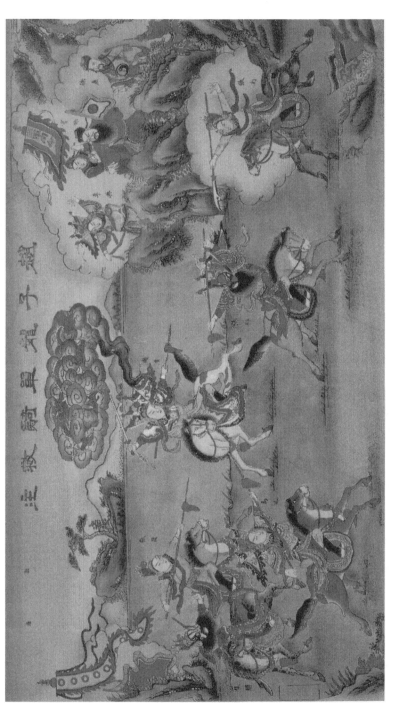

Figure 8. Zhao Zilong Singlehandedly Saves His Young Master

so that the audience would not only be entertained but also be presented with moral ideals. As Lin Yutang wrote of his own experiences: "[B]esides popularizing history and music among the people, [theater] has an equally important cultural function in providing the people with all their moral notions of good and evil. Practically all the standardized Chinese notions of loyal ministers and filial sons and brave warriors and faithful wives and chaste maidens and intriguing maid-servants are reflected in the current Chinese plays. Represented in the form of stories with human characters, whom they hate or love as the case may be, they sink deep into their moral consciousness."[35]

Thus, while theater performances presented well-known historical, legendary, and fictional tales, they simultaneously reinforced Confucian conceptions of moral goodness and moral badness central to Chinese culture. These dramas had a strong effect, for as Ward writes, "[B]y presenting these values *on the stage*, represented in human form by characters with whom the audiences could identify or from whom they dissociated themselves, the operas almost certainly achieved an impact greater than that of either the spoken or the written word."[36]

In both its literary and theatrical forms, *Three Kingdoms* highlights human social values such as righteousness, friendship, loyalty, brotherhood, generosity, and self-sacrifice, and denounces craftiness and cunning, narrow-mindedness, and disloyalty. For the mass population, in particular those attending a theatrical performance, this rather simplified reading of a complex tale would have been all that was needed: the audience was not interested in penetrating intellectual engagement in order to enjoy the story.[37] In the popular imagination, *Three Kingdoms* characters became the personification of human virtues and vices; for example, Zhuge Liang embodied wisdom and resourcefulness; Liu Bei, generosity and kindheartedness; Guan Yu, loyalty; Zhou Yu, narrow-mindedness; and Cao Cao, wiliness and cunning.[38] Presented in the theater, these characteristics were further highlighted through costume and makeup.

The *Three Kingdoms* prints examined here are products of an interest in theater, emphasizing its importance in Chinese culture and reveal a strong link between two different art forms that reached broadly across social strata. *Nianhua* reinforced ideas presented in theater on the historical past (whether actual or fictionalized), the values of society, and the distinctions between proper and improper conduct. And like theater, woodblock prints contributed to the cultural climate of town and village life. *Nianhua* and theater thus were not independent art forms but functioned together, presenting the same tales and promoting the same cultural ideals. This connection is particularly evident in prints depicting scenes based on *The Romance of the Three Kingdoms*, a popular subject for both theater and *nianhua*. The story, with its intense human drama and theme of moral retribution, contained all the elements necessary for broad appeal.

But with all the complexities of the tale and the endless variety of themes for prints, only a few scenes appeared in *nianhua*. One possible explanation for this lies in a closer examination of the theater-*nianhua* connection. The majority of extant prints studied here employed theater conventions, such a makeup and costuming, symbolic attributes, and dramatic poses in the depiction of their subjects. These *nianhua* were designed to capture a single moment on the stage. Research shows that these prints do correspond to known plays based on the *Three Kingdoms* theme. Liu Bei's marriage was depicted in the Yuan *zaju Duel of Wits Across the River* (*Ge jiang dou zhi*).[39] The play *The Pavilion of the Yellow Crane*, another drama from the Yuan-Ming period, is also depicted in *nianhua* (figure 9).[40] This scene takes place after Cao Cao was defeated at Red Cliff. Zhou Yu invites Liu Bei to a feast in the pavilion of the Yellow Crane, where he plans on killing Liu. The scene is depicted in theatrical fashion with Zhou Yu in the center with the advisor Lu Su to the left. On the right are Liu Bei, in the robes of an emperor, and Zhao Yun, his flags indicating his rank of general. A second example involves the play, *The Strategy of the Empty Fortress*, which was still being performed into the twentieth century.[41] A woodblock print shows Zhuge Liang's defense of the town and fortress of Xicheng (figure 10). Hearing of an attack by the army of Wei and knowing that his own troops are limited, he devises a strategy. The gates of the fortress are left open and Zhuge Liang sits on the watch-tower and plays the *qin*. The enemy decides that this must be an ambush and leaves the town. Zhuge Liang is depicted here atop the fortress, playing the *qin*. Three warriors from the kingdom of Wei approach on horseback. It is expected that further research along these lines will reveal that popular themes in *nianhua*, such as "The Capture and Liberation of Cao Cao" and "The Slopes of Changban," were connected to popular plays performed in the late Qing period.

Whether made in rural or urban centers, *nianhua* were a commercial enterprise, and their production must have been fueled in some way by public demand. Con-sumers may have wished to acquire prints of favorite or current theatrical produc-tions. It stands to reason that the prevalence of theater-inspired scenes is tangible evidence of the popularity of the theater in general and of certain *Three Kingdoms* plays in particular. Further examination of the production and provenance of the prints may also reveal regional preferences or changes over time in popular demand for certain stories, thereby providing additional insight into the history of Chinese popular theater.

But prints and theater may have shared yet another connection. In addition to serving as a souvenir of a performance or story for the general audience, *nian-hua* may have acted as a different kind of visual record for those whose interest in theater ran deeper. The *nianhua The Capture and Liberation of Cao Cao*, produced in the Dailianzeng workshop in Yangliuqing (figure 1), contains handwritten anno-tations concerning the specific costuming of each character, mentioning the type and color of robes and headwear as well as any accessories held in the hand. Other prints show similar marginalia.[42]

These issues bring to mind several questions worthy of investigation: Was there a direct correlation between theatergoers and purchasers of theater-inspired *nianhua*? Did the depictions found in *nianhua* correspond to regional perfor-mances? Did the depictions remain relatively constant over time and geographical

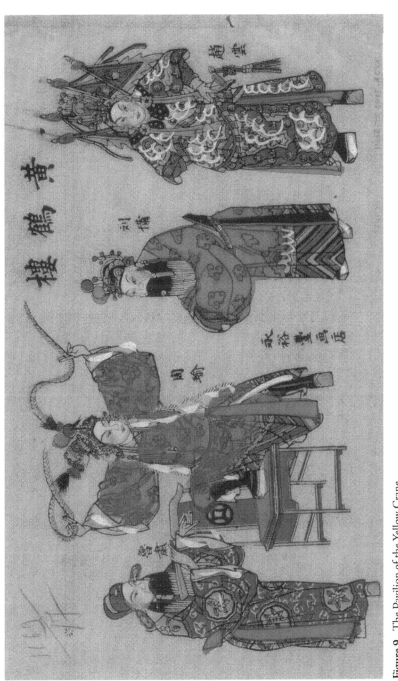

Figure 9. The Pavilion of the Yellow Crane

Figure 10. The Strategy of the Empty Fortress

area? How do the *Three Kingdoms* prints compare with *nianhua* depicting other theatrical themes? To what degree was the production of the prints determined by local theater? And what were the sources for *nianhua* imagery? Did artists view the performances firsthand? These are not simple questions to answer, largely owing to a lack of extant material culture as well as absence of information on the provenance, date, patronage, and use of the prints. However, these prints are valuable visual documents, and the examination of a wider sampling can shed light on the interplay between theater and *nianhua* and the dissemination of ideas across Chinese culture. More than appealing pictures associated with New Year celebrations that depict Confucian exemplars of loyalty and paragons of wickedness, *Three Kingdoms nianhua* are dramatic and colorful representations of popular taste in traditional China.

NOTES

1. See Issei Tanaka, "The Social and Historical Context of Ming-Ch'ing Local Drama," in *Popular Culture in Late Imperial China*, ed. David Johnson, Andrew J. Nathan, and Evelyn S. Rawski (Berkeley and Los Angeles: University of California Press, 1985), 143–60.

2. Barbara E. Ward, "Regional Operas and Their Audiences," in Johnson, Nathan, and Rawski, *Popular Culture in Late Imperial China*, 173.

3. James Hayes, "Specialists and Written Materials in the Village World," in Johnson, Nathan, and Rawski, *Popular Culture in Late Imperial China*, 107.

4. Bomin Wang, *Zhongguo banhuashi* [*History of Chinese Printed Illustration*] (Shanghai: Shanghai renmin meishu chubanshe, 1981), 169–70.

5. Maria Rudova, *Chinese Popular Prints* (Leningrad: Aurora Publishers, 1988), 8.

6. Refer to the lists provided by Hua Li, *Chinese Woodcuts* (Beijing: Foreign Languages Press, 1995), 85, 90.

7. The number of print shops active in the Qing dynasty are countless. At Yangliuqing, near Tianjin, for example, some of the famous print (and painting) shops included Dailianzeng and Qijianlong, the two largest, as well as Aizhuzhai, Gaoqingyun, Meili, Rongchang, Shengxing, Wanshunheng, Xianzhang, Zengshun, and Zhenchudai; at Taohuawu in Suzhou, famous shops were Chensisheng, Laowenyilanji, Lufushun, Lujiashun, Luyunlin, Moxiangzhai, Shenwenya, Wangrongxing, Weihongtai, Wenhezhai, Wujinzeng, Zhangwenju, Zhangxingju, and Zhuchaji. Throughout China, many towns were active in print production. The most prominent among them included, by province, Anhui: Fuyang, Jieshou, Linquan, Jieshou, Su county and Taihe; Fujian: Fu'an, Fuding, Quanzhou, and Zhangzhou; Hebei: Daming, Handan, and Wuqiang; Henan: Kaifeng and Zhuxianzhen; Hunan: Huangpi, Jun County, Shaoyang, Tantou, Wuhan, and Xiaogan; Guangdong: Anbu, Chenghai, Foshan, and Xinghui; Guangxi: Dongxing, Guilin, Nanning, and Quanzhou; Shaanxi: Chang'an, Fengxiang hanzhong, Pucheng and Shenmu; Shandong: Dongchang,

Gaomi, Pingdu and Yangjiabu; Shanxi: Datong, Linfeng and Yuncheng; Sichuan: Chengdu, Jiajiang, Jianyang, and Mianzhu; and Yunnan: Baqu, Baoshan, Lijiang and Nanjian. This list was compiled from Bomin Wang and Songnian Bo, *Chinese New Year Prints* (Beijing: Cultural Relics Publishing House, 1995); and Lüsheng Pan and Jialu Tang, *Nianhua* [*New Year pictures*] (Shanghai: Shanghai renmin yishu chubanshe chubanxing, n.d.).

8. This was a time-consuming activity that involved not only carving the woodblocks and printing them, but also making the paper by hand. See Hanzhong Zuo, ed., *Minjian jianzhi mubanhua* [*Folk Papercuts and Woodblock Prints*] (Changsha: Hunan meishu chubanshe, 1995), 37–42.

9. Rudova, *Chinese Popular Prints*, n.p.

10. The *nianhua* examined in this study come from several published sources. The most valuable has been the catalog from the Hermitage Museum in St. Petersburg, which features nearly two hundred images from the museum's comprehensive collection of more than three thousand Chinese popular prints representing over one hundred printing shops. Fifteen prints on the *Sanguo* theme are included in the catalog, and date to the late nineteenth and early twentieth centuries. Many are from Yangliuqing, a production center known for the fineness of its work. In addition to the Hermitage *nianhua*, popular prints from various production centers appear in several Chinese publications. The majority of these *Sanguo* prints were made in the southern Chinese area of Taohuawu in Suzhou, well known for its *nianhua*. These may be found in Bomin Wang and Songnian Bo, *Chinese New Year Prints*.

11. These titles were taken from the prints themselves.

12. C. H. Brewitt-Taylor, introduction to *Romance of the Three Kingdoms*, by Lo Kuan-chung, trans. Brewitt-Taylor (Rutland, VT: Charles E. Tuttle, 1959), ix.

13. Lo Kuan-chung, *Romance of the Three Kingdoms*, 36, 38.

14. Ibid., 42.

15. Ibid.

16. Winston L. Y. Yang, "The Literary Transformation of Historical Figures in the *San-kuo chih yen-i*: A Study of the Use of the *San-kuo chih* as a Source of the *San-kuo chih yen-i*," in *Critical Essays on Chinese Fiction*, ed. Winston L.Y. Yang and Curtis P. Adkins (Hong Kong: Chinese University Press, 1980) 59, discusses this incident in the novel as an illustration of how, in presenting Cao Cao unfavorably, Luo Guanzhong added an incident not documented in the official history.

17. Lo Kuan-chung, *Romance of the Three Kingdoms*, 42.

18. Ibid., 435.

19. Ibid., 437.

20. Ibid., 438.

21. Ibid., 440.

22. Ibid., 569.

23. Ibid., 565.

24. C. T. Hsia, *The Classic Chinese Novel* (New York: Columbia University Press, 1968), 35.

25. William Dolby, "Yuan Drama," in *Chinese Theater*, ed. Colin Mackerras (Honolulu: University of Hawaii Press, 1983), 43.

26. Andrew Plaks writes that there were curiously few documented full-length dramatic treatments of the story in the sixteenth century when many editions of the 1522 *Sanguo yanyi* text were published. See Andrew H. Plaks, *The Four Masterworks of the Ming Novel* (Princeton, NJ: Princeton University Press, 1987), 371. For a list of the extant and nonextant dramatic texts on the *Sanguo* theme, refer to Plaks, *Four Masterworks*, 370–71n. 35 and L. C. Arlington, *The Chinese Drama from Earliest Times until Now* (Shanghai: Benjamin Bloom, 1930), 129, 170, 172.

27. Brewitt-Taylor, introduction, vi.

28. Lo Kuan-chung, *Romance in the Three Kingdoms*, 562.

29. Other theatrical conventions are mentioned in Jack Chen, *The Chinese Theatre* (London: Dennis Dobson, 1948).

30. Arlington, *Chinese Drama*, 93, and plate. 58, fig. 83.

31. Vladimir Kalvodova-Sis and Joseph Vanis, *Chinese Theatre*, trans. Iris Unwin (London: Spring Books, n.d.), 24.

32. Arlington, *Chinese Drama*, 108–9, fig. 118.

33. Kalvodova and Vanis, *Chinese Theatre*, 24.

34. Barbara E. Ward, "Not Merely Players: Drama, Art and Ritual in Traditional China," *Man*, n.s., 14 (1979): 23.

35. Yutang Lin, *My Country and My People* (New York: Halcyon House, 1938), 266.

36. Ward, "Regional Operas," 183–84 (emphasis in the original).

37. Robert E. Hegel, "Distinguishing Levels of Audiences for Ming-Ch'ing Vernacular Literature," in Johnson, Nathan, and Rawski, *Popular Culture in Late Imperial China*, 140.

38. These standard characterizations are offered in several sources, among them Yang, "Literary Transformation," 49, 57, 61.

39. Plaks, *Four Masterworks*, 370–71, lists this play in his list compiled from a variety of sources including Fu Xihua, *Yuandai zaju quanmu* (Beijing: Zuojia, 1957).

40. Plaks, *Four Masterworks*, 370–71.

41. Arlington provides a synopsis of this play (*Chinese Drama*, 170).

42. Rudova, *Chinese Popular Prints*, figure 131, illustrates a *nianhua* consisting of scenes from two different plays or stories. This print also contains handwritten markings detailing the kind and color of clothing for the figures depicted.

8

Three Kingdoms at the Dawn of the Twenty-First Century

The Shanghai *Jingju* Company's *Cao Cao and Yang Xiu*

ELIZABETH WICHMANN-WALCZAK

Theatrical versions of *Three Kingdoms* events are among the most vivid and pervasive in popular Chinese culture. Arguably, even today *Three Kingdoms* characters are "perhaps better known through stage-performances than by actual reading."[1] The Shanghai *Jingju* Company's *Cao Cao and Yang Xiu*, originally mounted in 1988 and significantly revised and restaged in 1995, is one of the most recent of these theatrical versions.[2] It is also one of the most successful. I believe that *Cao Cao and Yang Xiu* is one of the finest pieces of theater created in the twentieth century anywhere in the world, and that it is certainly one of the finest *jingju* in existence today. Others agree with me. In 1988, it was named an Outstanding New *Jingju* Play (*Youxiu jingju xin jumu*) at the Ministry of Culture's (national) Festival of New *Jingju* Plays; in 1989 it received the National *Xiqu* Institute Award; and in 1995, *Cao Cao and Yang Xiu* was awarded the grand prize at the National Festival of *Jingju* Art, in essence recognizing it as the finest *jingju* created since the Cultural Revolution. At the symposium held by the Chinese Theater Artists Association in celebration of that recognition, scholars and artists praised the production as "simultaneously providing a window into history and a clear image of contemporary problems," and as the finest play ever created about Cao Cao.[3] And *Cao Cao and Yang Xiu*'s audience reception matches this extraordinary critical acclaim—it continues to fill houses whenever it is performed. The success of this play and its production at the Shanghai *Jingju* Company throw intriguing light on twenty-first-century theatrical possibilities for both *Three Kingdoms* material and the *jingju* theatrical form.

111

Cao Cao and Yang Xiu is based on characters and incidents in chapter 72 of the Mao Zonggang edition of Luo Guanzhong's novel *Three Kingdoms* (*Sanguozhi tongsu yanyi*.) In the latter part of that chapter, Cao is camped at Xiegu, unable to advance and unwilling to retreat. Asked to provide the night's password while gazing into a bowl of chicken soup and considering this untenable military situation, Cao says "chicken tendons (*jilei*)." When Yang learns of this password, he interprets it as meaning that Cao has decided to retreat—as he explains to Xiahou Dun, it is a shame to waste chicken tendons, but they are tasteless; hence, there being no advantage to maintaining the present situation, it is best to retreat. Yang and Xiahou ready their men to do so, Yang saying that he wants to avoid rush and confusion later. When this preparation for retreat comes to Cao's attention, he is furious and has Yang beheaded for destroying the morale of the soldiers. The novelist then explains that Yang Xiu is an officer whose intellectual brilliance is both useful and threatening to Cao Cao, and that Yang himself is inclined to show off unnecessarily and inappropriately. Yang has easily been able to divine the meaning of riddles Cao has created involving the composition of written-characters. Yang has provided intellectual assistance to one of Cao's sons while appearing to plot against the other. And Yang has let Cao know that Cao can keep no secrets from him—that while others may believe Cao was truly asleep when he killed an attendant who placed a cover over him, Yang knows that in fact Cao was awake and acted intentionally. Cao has therefore been looking for the right opportunity to get rid of Yang, and Yang's apparent prognostication of retreat serves this purpose for him. In the end, however, Cao is wounded and finally does retreat. Two other minor incidents in the chapter, not actually connected with the story of Yang Xiu, are featured in the play as well: Cao Cao sends a written declaration of war to which Zhuge Liang replies that they will fight the next day, and Zhang Fei and Wei Yan are sent along two different routes to cut off Cao's supplies.

This simple story, taking about as much space in the novel itself as it has just done in this essay, is brought alive for contemporary audiences in the *jingju Cao Cao and Yang Xiu*, in a way that both provokes deep thought and provides intense aesthetic enjoyment. While the basic plot is the same, significant alterations and additions have been made. A central premise of the *jingju* is that Cao Cao is actively searching for worthy men of ability to serve his cause, and has intentionally sought out Yang Xiu, who at his own request is put in charge of providing provisions and horses for Cao's armies. Yang is very successful, and within half a year merchants from the enemy areas of Xiongnu, Western Shu, and Dongwu bring horses and grain to the capital to sell to him. Kong Wendai, a younger officer whom Cao distrusts because he has killed Kong's father, has traveled to those areas and done the groundwork for Yang. Hearing that Kong has just returned from enemy territory, and without learning the reason for his travel, Cao kills him as a traitor and is about to kill Yang when the merchants arrive and he realizes his error. Yang is devastated to learn that Kong is dead, and does not believe Cao's explanation—that Kong returned and reported to him late at night, and Cao killed him unintentionally in his sleep. Cao claims that this "night-dream killing disease" is an old illness of his. Cao then arranges a great memorial for Kong, and spends the night alone in the memorial hall. Cao's favorite concubine enters the hall and covers him with a cloak, and Cao is horrified to learn that she has done so at Yang's suggestion. Aware that Yang doubts him and convinced that he must make Yang accept the fiction of the "night-dream killing disease" in order to continue with his policy of seeking worthy men of ability, Cao persuades his concubine to kill herself, tells the court that he killed her in the throes of his illness, and then weds Yang to their daughter. However, Yang soon infuriates Cao again by insisting that they should retreat from Xiegu. Zhuge Liang responds to Cao's written declaration of war with a series of riddles involving the composition of written characters, and Yang compounds his offense by interpreting the riddles before Cao does, and allowing Cao to pay the agreed-upon forfeit—Cao serves as Yang's horse boy in a desperate circumambulation of the camp in the snow. When Yang hears that Cao has chosen "chicken tendons" as the password for the night, he prepares for retreat and sends men to counter an expected attempt to cut off their supply lines. Cao learns of this and has Yang arrested and brought to the execution ground; then news comes that Zhuge Liang has tried to cut the supply lines but has been foiled by Yang's preparations. Just as Cao is considering letting Yang off once more, the assembled generals jointly urge that he be reprieved. Cao and Yang then talk alone, but have reached no agreement when they are interrupted by news that Zhuge Liang's armies are approaching. Yang cries out to Cao to retreat, and Cao responds by ordering him beheaded.

Though literally scores of artists and experts were involved in the creation of *Cao Cao and Yang Xiu*, three artists stand out as absolutely key. The initial creation process involved its own "three kingdoms": that of Yaxian Chen the playwright, Ke Ma the director, and Changrong Shang the creator and performer of the character Cao Cao. Together they reworked and gave life to the script initially written by Chen.[4]

Creating a new *Three Kingdoms* play is a formidable task—the extreme familiarity of the major characters makes reinterpretation a risky business in terms of audience acceptance. To quote one of the first major translators of *Three Kingdoms jingju* plays into English, most plays have "religiously adhered to the spirit of Lo Kuan-chung's [Luo Guanzhong's] great novel . . . the wit of K'ung-ming [Kongming] confounds Chou Yu [Zhou Yu]; Chao Tzu-lung [Zhao Zilong] is . . . brave . . . , Liu Pei [Liu Bei] . . . timid and perplexed, and Chang Fei [Zhang Fei] . . . tempestuous. The characters are as consistent as those of Dickens."[5] For *Cao Cao and Yang Xiu*, it is clearly the character of Cao who poses the greatest challenge in these terms—the traditional Cao Cao is well known, indeed: "sly, tough, cruel, wanton, cold-blooded, unscrupulous, ruthless, pompous, sententious, and sentimental . . . he is an unmitigated villain. Yet his rascality appeals to the imagination . . . [and] this is mainly due to the art which Chinese actors have lavished on him for generations, polishing the role, from facial make-up to the most trivial tricks of speech, until it attained the acme of perfected villainy."[6]

Previous attempts to create a new Cao Cao have not been particularly success-ful—for instance, Changrong Shang characterizes Guo Moruo's Cao as "too good to be believable—he's not really Cao Cao at all."[7]

Chen, Ma, and Shang set out to create "real men" for their production, "not the traditional historical images, but three-dimensional characters" with complex inter-nal lines of thought and consistent character development.[8] Ma's detailed work with Chen in revising the script provided the basis for this approach to character: "The original script had an excellent skeleton of ideas, but the lines of each charac-ter's development were unclear—what was said first, second, etc. didn't work well for the characters."[9] As part of their work on character development, Ma and Shang used improvisation extensively in early rehearsals, and Shang spent a great deal of time reading Cao's original writings, especially his poetry. Shang believes strongly that "to create a three-dimensional character, you must capture the real, internal feeling of the time and place, and must use both internal and external skill (*neigong he waigong*)."[10] Shang prefers to begin with the internal aspects, and likes the *huaju* ("spoken drama," a form descended from Western-style realism as imported into China in the early twentieth century) method of writing one's own biography of the character one is creating. After extensive internal work on Cao Cao, Shang moved on to the next major phase for a *hualian* (painted-face role) actor—he "changed his face" by designing a new *lianpu* (face design) for Cao.[11] As the costume designer for the 1995 version of the production described it, "Shang Changrong insisted that he *goulian* (draw a face) for Cao Cao—as a *hualian* actor, one of his specialties (*tedian*) is *goulian*. But he created a new face. He changed the base color, adding yellow and red to the [traditionally matte] white, making it more like flesh; he used the tradi-tional [narrow triangular] eyes but made them somewhat larger and more open; and he greatly enlarged the traditional red patch [indicating masculine courage] on the forehead."[12] The resultant appearance keeps him completely recognizable as Cao Cao, and yet transcends the conventional image—the effect is very much like "seeing inside" the traditional face to the real man. And indeed, that is one of the major effects of Shang's total performance.[13]

Work was similarly detailed on the other characters and aspects of the script. Ma felt that the character of Yang Xiu as originally written by Chen "was too virtu-ous—a bit naive, a bit formulaic."[14] For instance, Yang originally sent Cao's favorite concubine into the memorial hall to cover him with a cloak simply out of a desire to comfort Cao; in the final version, Yang is intentionally testing the veracity of Cao's claim to a "night-dream killing disease," making both his own and Cao Cao's motivation considerably more complex and thematically related. Ma reasoned that if the characters were equally real, audience members would be able to identify with them equally well. And this was a major goal of the production. Even the curtain call was carefully planned, with this goal and its thematic implications in mind. Rather than simply having the actors clap with the audience, Ma wanted a curtain call that would allow the audience further, intimate contact with the characters in a more contemporary context. Shang believed that contemporary popular music would help achieve this effect, and asked a friend's college-student son to recommend some pieces. He suggested China's anthem for the recent United Nations World Peace Year, a song featuring the refrain "*Women dou dao yiqi lai*/We are all coming together." At the end of the play, after Cao says "Behead him!" and the executioner raises his blade, the lights black out—then the anthem begins to play, the lights come back up brightly, and Cao and Yang smile, shake hands with one another, and come forward to shake hands with members of the audience. I have seen this curtain call last for up to half an hour, as audience members push forward to greet Cao and Yang, and the actors who embody them.

The finely drawn, three-dimensional characters are just one reason for the overwhelmingly positive response to *Cao Cao and Yang Xiu*. Certainly the sumptuous set and costume designs were also a factor for both versions of the production that I have seen, those of 1988 and 1995; for the latter they were extremely innovative as well. But three aspects of *Cao Cao and Yang Xiu*, shared by both versions, were fundamental to the success of the production: music, themes, and aesthetic/entertainment appeal.

Music is the expressive core of *Cao Cao and Yang Xiu*. The atmospheric music is lush; it is provided by an expanded orchestra that includes not only a full traditional *jingju* orchestra with a complete *luogu* ("gongs and drums") section and a full complement of *jinghu* and *erhu* (small and mid-sized two-string spike fiddles), as well as plucked (*yueqin* and *pipa*) and wind (*suona* and *dizi*) instruments, but also numerous additional Chinese instruments including *banhu* (another type of two-stringed spike fiddle), *guzheng* and *guqin* (ancient plucked instruments somewhat similar to the zither), *pengling* ("bump bells") and *bangzi* clappers, and Western instruments including violins and violas, a cello, a bass viol, a synthesizer, clarinets, flutes, and percussion instruments. The featured instruments in the atmospheric music are the *guzheng* and *guqin*, creating a haunting classical flavor and providing an exceptional setting for the vocal music itself. According to the company head, Zhongcheng Li, in creating vocal music (*changqiang*) for new *jingju* plays a respect for tradition is critical—whereas scenery and costumes can be extremely innovative, following historical and purely imaginative impulses, vocal music must stay within the parameters of *jingju* so that the result will, in fact, be *jingju*.[15] Creative changes to traditional vocal music vocabulary in *Cao Cao and Yang Xiu* are therefore made sparingly, primarily for special character interpretation or "a bit of contemporary feel (*shidai gan*)." Nonetheless, the atmospheric and vocal music share an innovative quality, which I have come to call "contemporary Chinese emotionalism," and reveal creative musical approaches developed during and after the Cultural Revolution. The vocal music as a whole is also faster and tighter (*jincou*) than in traditional plays, although Li does not consider this a creative act. As he puts it, "this is practical, because the audience's life is faster, and they think faster. In the future, they may want things slower, instead."[16]

One common creative practice in *jingju*, especially in the early years of *jingju*'s development and during the Cultural Revolution period, was the adaptation of musical materials from outside the *jingju* form to *jingju* vocal music. In *Cao Cao and Yang Xiu*, such adaptation occurs at the initial introduction of one of the major characters: Cao's favorite concubine, Qian Niang. She first appears singing a short, extremely lyrical passage, expressing her anxiety for him—although Yang Xiu has been working for half a year, no provisions or battle horses have yet reached the capital, and Cao is extremely concerned. As the composer Yiming Gao explains, the passage is composed in a *qupai*, or preexisting melodic form from the classical *kunqu* theater.[17] The *qupai* is "Hu Jia Shi Ba Pai (foreign reed-whistle eighteen beat)" and is very close to the thematic source material for the atmospheric music and the play as a whole. However, Gao has also used "a little Shanghai popular music of the 1930s and 1940s," especially in the second line of the third couplet, for the phrase "Mengde yan gai (Mengde's color changes)." The composition is designed to present Cao's favorite concubine as a special and attractive woman, revealing her as a refined, dignified, and warmhearted character while musically establishing the connection between Qian Niang and the main plotline and themes of the play.

The adaptation of musical materials from three different sources outside *jingju* is used to portray the three merchants from enemy territories. The merchants are presented as comic characters, and are placed in circumstances that are clearly related to late twentieth- and early twenty-first century economic developments, adding to the humor of the scene. In the action preceding this short musical passage, Yang Xiu proves an expert if not very truthful bargainer, explaining to the merchants that although prices for their goods were high six months ago when Kong Wendai urged them to bring grain and battle horses to the Han capital for sale, major changes in the market have now "unfortunately" reduced those prices to a fraction of what they once were. The merchants then express their frustrations in song, based on musical sources from Sichuan for the rice merchant from Western Shu (termed *chuandiao* by the composer, Gao), from the *pinghua* and *tanci* ballad (*quyi*) forms of Jiangsu—especially Suzhou—for the rice merchant from Dongwu (termed *pingtandiao* by Gao), and from Mongolia for the Xiongnu horse merchant (termed *xibeidiao* or *mengguger* by Gao).[18] The passage generally "brings down the house" with laughter, as the audience simultaneously delights in seeing the three uniquely distinct "outlanders" bested by the clever Yang Xiu, and sympathizes with the plight of the merchants as portrayed by three very appealing *chou* (comic male) actors.

Such examples not withstanding, most of the striking vocal music in *Cao Cao and Yang Xiu* is firmly grounded in traditional *jingju* musical vocabulary and techniques, innovatively and expressively applied. One exemplary passage begins after Cao Cao's favorite concubine has told him that it was Yang Xiu who sent her to cover him as he slept, and builds to the moment when Qian Niang takes Cao's sword and cuts her own throat. The passage is sung entirely in *erhuang* mode. Traditionally, Cao Cao rarely if ever sings in *erhuang*—as Changrong Shang explains, having him do so here creates a substantially deeper and more thoughtful character.[19] The full aria builds in traditional fashion, from mid-range metrical types (*banshi*) that are slower and more controlled, to increasingly faster metrical types, and ultimately to the fastest, with breaks in the building meter expressed through metrical types such as shaking meter (*yaoban*) and broad meter (*kuanban*), indicating exterior calm and interior tension, and through the free-metered "stopping of the heart" of dispersed meter (*sanban*), expressive of overwhelming emotion.[20] But some of the metrical types used in this progression are far from standard. For instance, Cao initially expresses his realization of Yang's intent, and his grief at what he believes this must mean for his beloved concubine, in a passage of *handiao*. This metrical type was originally sung only by performers of female roles (*dan*), and was adapted for the *hualian* role for Shengrong Qiu's work in the classic *Orphan of the House of Zhao* (*Zhao shi gu er*)—it facilitates exceptionally lyrical emotion expression, especially for the *hualian* performer.[21] And in this passage, sparing but highly effective adaptation is made of musical materials from outside the *jingju* form, as well. Most striking is the use of harmony, which occurs briefly but very movingly toward the end of the passage, in a sung *kutou* (section of stylized weeping) in which Cao and Qian Niang cry out to one another in their grief.

Cao Cao and Yang Xiu was created with a particular audience in mind. Since the mid-1980s, the Shanghai *Jingju* Company has been creating new plays for at least three specific, targeted groups of people: school-age audiences, popular urban audiences, and intellectual urban audiences.[22] *Cao Cao and Yang Xiu* is intended for urban intellectuals. A substantial proportion of urban intellectuals are considerably more familiar with Western music and the music of film and television than they are with the musical language of *jingju*. The strongly orchestral atmospheric music and the contemporary musical source material work alongside with and function almost as a musical "translation" of the traditional *jingju* musical vocabulary and techniques of the production. A major aim of the production is to build an appreciation for the traditional music and larger, long-term audiences for all *jingju* plays.

The highly philosophical and daringly political themes of *Cao Cao and Yang Xiu* are also crafted with urban intellectual audiences in mind. The director, Ke Ma, believes that for this audience, and for the future of *jingju* as a whole, *jingju* must become a theater of thought and ideas, in which individual character and the human condition are explored and expressed. From the first time that he read Yaxian Chen's script, Ma believed that it could be the catalyst for a new, "thinking" *jingju*.[23] Certainly *Cao Cao and Yang Xiu* has provoked considerable thought concerning its themes and import. Changrong Shang has said that the central theme of *Cao Cao and Yang Xiu* is "perpetual human conflict (*ren de yongheng maodun*)," and critics have stressed messages such as: "[O]ne who cannot transcend self and the concerns of self is doomed to tragedy."[24] In directing the play, Ma's stated aim was to show both sides of Cao and Yang, and the reasons for the failure of their cooperation. He sees that failure as the embodiment of what he terms "the principal Chinese weakness—one Chinese alone is great, but two will argue and destroy each other," and believes that *Cao Cao and Yang Xiu* is the finest expression of this problematic dynamic since Lu Xun's *True Story of Ah Q* (*Ah Q zheng zhuan*).[25] Some of these ideas are in fact shared with the audience directly, via the printed programs distributed by the Shanghai *Jingju* Company at performances of *Cao Cao and Yang Xiu*: they explain that "the twofold moral character of Cao and Yang, at once lofty and petty, makes them ultimately incapable of working together for the common good."[26]

As Moss Roberts describes in the afterword to his masterful translation of *Three Kingdoms*, during the 1980s Chinese scholars attempted to identify a single main theme in that novel.[27] Of those that he lists, two seem most related to *Cao Cao and Yang Xiu*. "The cruelties and injustices of feudal (i.e., dynastic) government" certainly are echoed in the play. And "the theme of ideal liege finding ideal minister, their rise to power, and their tragic end" is confronted, and humanized—in *Cao Cao and Yang Xiu*, there are no ideal rulers or ministers, only brilliant but flawed seekers of power, and power does indeed bring tragedy. The concepts of virtue (*de*) and the Mandate of Heaven (*Tianming*), however, probably bring the greatest illumination to the thematic import of *Cao Cao and Yang Xiu*. Speaking of Liu Bei, Roberts states these concepts and their relationship very succinctly: "Xuande has his own leadership qualities: his natural charisma or magnetism, called *de* in Chinese and translated 'virtue.' The force of his persona attracts and holds the allegiance of his associates, his armies, and the populations he governs. He wins men's hearts. Xuande's virtue is the higher reason why he deserves to rule. . . . The Mandate of Heaven 'finds' a man of virtue who establishes a new dynasty."[28] Cao Cao has been seeking worthy (*xian*) men, a status related to virtue, and has chosen Yang Xiu to serve him because of Yang's ability. But Yang's growing popularity with Cao's generals and soldiers becomes increasingly worrisome to Cao. And when Cao's generals all plead with Cao on the execution ground to spare Yang and each offers to serve as his guarantor, they in fact seal his fate. As Cao, "greatly startled," sings:

> Nor- ma-lly praise for Cao end-le- ssly flows,
> *Ping ri li yi   pian song yang dui Cao mou,*
> Now it   seems all   rea- lly goes to Yang Xiu!
> *Que yuan lai   zhong wang suo gui shi Yang Xiu!*[29]

Cao may fear more than a simple attempt to usurp his power—he may fear the arrival of the far greater power of the Mandate of Heaven, drawn to Yang Xiu by Yang's worth and virtue as shown in the allegiance he receives from the generals. Viewed in this light, the relationship between Cao Cao and his brilliant minister Yang Xiu can be seen as paralleling those between rulers and their ministers at times of national crisis throughout Chinese history—including the one between Mao Zedong and Peng Dehuai just before the Great Leap Forward, and, although the play was written just before the events occurred, the relationship between Deng Xiaoping and Zhao Ziyang in the late spring of 1989. Commenting upon the present through reference to the past is a long-standing tradition in Chinese theater.

But in this case, the play in fact resonates with the plight of strong leaders and strong ministers throughout time and the world.

The themes of *Cao Cao and Yang Xiu* are further clarified for the audience through the use of theatrical devices that also greatly increase the entertainment value of the production. Chief among these is the character "Seeker of Worthy Men," who functions in many ways like a Brechtian narrator, conversing directly with the audience. The Seeker opens and closes the play, as well as most scenes within it. He first appears beating a gong and announcing that Cao Cao is seeking worthy men who wish to pursue great careers—he expresses the apparently sincere belief that the only reason Cao was defeated recently at Red Cliff was that he lacked a Zhou Yu or a Zhuge Liang. Later, after Cao kills Kong, the Seeker's call for worthy men takes on a darker cast. And since Cao killed Kong without investigating the reasons for his travels to enemy territory, when the Seeker then lauds Cao for having the wisdom of Judge Bao—for clearly investigating every detail, rewarding good and punishing evil, and transcending Yao and Shun—the irony fairly drips. At other times, though, the Seeker seems to sympathize with Cao. For instance, when Cao weeps and strikes his head abjectly after confessing to Yang that he has killed Kong, and seems to be putting himself in Yang's hands, the Seeker expresses the belief that Cao indeed seeks worthy men with a true heart. Similarly, after Yang Xiu has bested Cao at solving Zhuge Liang's riddle, has allowed Cao to serve as his horse boy, and has again urged Cao to retreat from Xiegu, the Seeker opines that "Yang Xiu this fellow, is really a pain (*taoyan*)—do people with great ability have to be such great pains?" He then pauses, however, and continues in a different vein: "But let me take that back—if there weren't pains like this, that would really be a pain!" Through humor and empathy, the Seeker leads the audience to genuinely look at the conflict between Yang and Cao from both sides. And the perpetual, reoccurring nature of their conflict is underscored by the development of the Seeker's character in the course of the play. While only a few years is encompassed by the action of the plot, the Seeker ages dramatically. Initially a beardless young man with jet black hair, he appears at the end of the play as a white-bearded old man with shaky legs, calling once again for worthy men who wish to pursue great careers and help Cao avoid defeats like the most recent one at Xiegu.

Entertainment value is without a doubt an important facet of *Cao Cao and Yang Xiu*. Traditionally, the four performance skills of *jingju* are placed in the following, descending order: song, speech, acting, dance/martial arts. But as Changrong Shang put it, "[I]n this play, the order of importance is acting, speech, song, dance/martial arts."[30] He Shu, who created the role of Yang Xiu for the 1995 production, put it a different way; in his view, "[T]he time of just listening to theater (*ting xi*) is over—audiences now also want to see, and what they see must look good (*hao kan*), must feature acting (*biaoyan weizhu*)."[31] The final scene of the play, in which Cao Cao invites Yang Xiu to have a heart-to-heart talk (*tan xin*), exemplifies this emphasis on acting and speech. Alone together at the top of a flight of stone stairs, silhouetted against the same glowing full moon that oversaw their initial meeting, Cao and Yang reveal to one another the depth of their mutual admiration, and the extent of their intractable natures. Their short, emotion-laden, parallel colloquial phrases build to rich, shared laughter—which then breaks down into simultaneous, forlorn sobs. Although not a word is sung, profound emotions are expressed—and it looks very, very good.

Through the story of Cao Cao and Yang Xiu's ultimate inability to work together for the common good, this *jingju* speaks poignantly to a much broader spectrum of the human condition. A tragedy of failure in political cooperation, its creation is actually a triumph in artistic cooperation. *Cao Cao and Yang Xiu* departs in intriguing and meaningful ways from traditional theatrical images of *Three Kingdoms* characters and events. It is quite possibly closer to much older literary and historical views of those characters and their actions, and is very clearly much closer to twenty-first-century audiences, as well. Chen, Ma, Shang, and their colleagues have given a priceless gift to audiences in China, and indeed throughout the world.

NOTES

1. Brewitt-Taylor, quoted in L. C. Arlington and Harold Acton, *Famous Chinese Plays* (New York: Russell and Russell, 1937), 353.

2. In 1988, I was extremely privileged to observe a portion of the original rehearsal process for the Shanghai *Jingju* Company's *Cao Cao and Yang Xiu*, and to attend the premiere. Since then I have observed the entire rehearsal process for the 1995 revised restaging of the play, and have attended over three dozen performances. Under a grant from the Committee for Scholarly Communication with China, I spent October–December 1995 and March–May 1996 with the Shanghai *Jingju* Company, primarily in Shanghai but also on tour to Tianjin and Beijing. Information in this paper is derived primarily from research conducted during that time, including: interviews with artists, administrators, and scholars; observation of rehearsals and performances; and programs and unpublished manuscripts in the company's archive. Additional later interviews have been conducted both in person and by mail and telephone. Earlier research with the Shanghai *Jingju* Company (July–September 1987 and December 1987), funded by a Fujio Matsuda Fellowship, informs this study as well. See Elizabeth Wichmann, "Tradition and Innovation in Contemporary Beijing Opera Performance," *Drama Review* 34, no. 1. (Spring 1990): 146–178.

3. Zhongguo Xiju Jia Xiehui (Chinese Theater Artists Association), "*Cao Cao yu Yang Xiu* de biaoyan yishu" (*Cao Cao and Yang Xiu's* Performance Art), a symposium held December 7, 1995; citations are from notes taken by Elizabeth Wichmann-Walczak.

4. The history of the initial creation process is a bit like an episode from *Three Kingdoms* itself. As Changrong Shang relates it (December 3, 1995), in autumn 1987 he found both the weather and the state of *jingju* stagnant and stultifying. The head of the Shanxi

Jingju Troupe in X'ian, Shang was distressed that the troupe was performing only old plays, and with old performance methods—there were no good new plays to be had. He had experienced what he describes as two small successes with new plays in 1979 and 1984, and wanted a big one now—he wanted to "throw a huge rock into a stagnant pool." A friend of his, Meiqiang Shi, had seen Chen's new script in published form, and recommended it to Shang. Shang who read it, thought it could be a good play, and exchanged letters with the playwright. Chen was delighted that someone was interested in producing it. According to the *jingju* historian Dongsheng Hu (a scholar of *jingju* history and retired chair of the Department of *Jingju* History at the Beijing Xiqu Research Institute [Beijing Xiqu Yanjiu Suo]), the script had previously been offered to *jingju* companies in Beijing, but they had refused it, presumably because of its political sensitivity (1995). Shang felt that Xi'an was not the place to mount the production—that the troupe and its audiences were too restricted. So he wrote to his friend Mengyun Wang and then secretly took the train to Shanghai, where Wang introduced him to the leaders of the Shanghai *Jingju* Company, Bomin Ma and Zhongcheng Li. They met with him the second day Shang was in Shanghai, read the script that night, and the next day agreed to stage it. Zigui Li was to work with Chen on revising the script, while Shang and the Shanghai leaders worked on borrowing Shang from Shanxi. Then Li's wife became ill, and Ke Ma stepped in as director. Ma felt that the play required extensive revision to be actable—he sent Chen a fifty-page explanation of the changes needed—and the two began working on the script in May. Rehearsals began in July. Shang returned to Shanghai, lived in the company's dormitory, rehearsed all day, and practiced singing, laughing, and crying at night with his tape recorder. As he puts it, "I'm sure the neighbors thought they had a madman staying at the Shanghai *Jingju* Company." The December performances won the Ministry of Culture's "Outstanding New *Jingju*" designation.

5. Arlington and Acton, *Famous Chinese Plays*, 251.

6. Ibid., 151.

7. Changrong Shang, interview by Elizabeth Wichmann-Walczak, Shanghai, May 2, 1996.

8. Ke Ma, interviews by Elizabeth Wichmann-Walczak, Shanghai, November 3; 1995, Beijing, December 2 and 6, 1995.

9. Ibid., December 6, 1995.

10. Changrong Shang, Interview by Elizabeth Wichmann-Walczak, Beijing, 3 December 1995.

11. Changrong Shang, Interview by Elizabeth Wichmann-Walczak, Beijing, November 30, 1995.

12. Lijun Ong, (costume designer with the Shanghai *Jingju* Company), interview by Elizabeth Wichmann-Walczak, Beijing, November 26, 1995.

13. Notes from Zhongguo Xiju Jia Xiehui (Chinese Theater Artists Association), "*Cao Cao yu Yang Xiu* de biaoyan yishu" (*Cao Cao and Yang Xiu*'s performance art), 1995.

14. Ke Ma, interview, December 6, 1995.

15. Zhongcheng Li, interview by Elizabeth Wichmann-Walczak, Shanghai, May 8, 1996.

16. Ibid.

17. Yiming Gao, interview by Elizabeth Wichmann-Walczak, Beijing, December 3, 1995.

18. Ibid.

19. Changrong Shang, interview, May 2, 1996.

20. For description and analysis of traditional *jingju* vocal music practices, see Elizabeth Wichmann, *Listening to Theater: The Aural Dimension of Beijing Opera* (Honolulu: University of Hawaii Press, 1991).

21. Yiming Gao, December 3, 1995.

22. See Elizabeth Wichmann-Walczak, "'Reform' at the Shanghai *Jingju* Company and Its Impact on Creative Authority and Repertory," *Drama Review* 44, no. 4 (Winter 2000): 96–119.

23. Ke Ma, November 3, 1995.

24. Notes from Zhongguo Xiju Jia Xiehui (Chinese Theater Artists Association), "Cao Cao yu Yang Xiu de Biaoyan Yishu" (*Cao Cao and Yang Xiu*'s performance art), 1995.

25. Ke Ma, December 6, 1995.

26. Shanghai *Jingju* Yuan, "*Jingju* zou xiang qingnian: Shanghai *Jingju* yuan xunhui zhanyan" (*Jingju* Moves Toward the Youth: Shanghai *Jingju* Company's touring exhibition performances), *Beijing zhanyan shuoming shu*, performance program/playbill for Beijing tour, November 1995.

27. Moss Roberts, trans., *Three Kingdoms, A Historical Novel*, attributed to Luo Guanzhong, abridged ed. (Berkeley and Los Angeles: University of California Press, 1999), 414.

28. Ibid., 418.

29. Yaxian Chen, *Cao Cao yu Yang Xiu*, Shanghai *Jingju* Company's August 2 revised manuscript, 1995 (revised from original 1987 version), 22.

30. Changrong Shang, interview, May 2, 1996.

31. Shu He, interview by Elizabeth Wichmann-Walczak, Shanghai, November 30, 1995.

IV

Three Kingdoms in Contemporary East Asia

9

From *Three Kingdoms* the Novel to *Three Kingdoms* the Television Series

Gains, Losses, and Implications

JUNHAO HONG

INTRODUCTION

Over the last several decades, the revolutionary advancement of communication technology has not only promoted the formation and dissemination of popular culture, but has also made traditional and high cultures more dependent on these effective new communication technologies for diffusion, inheritance, and even survival. In such a process, traditional and high cultures enter various levels of the society with an ever-larger scale and at an ever-faster speed. However, some of the attributes of traditional and high cultures are also inevitably more or less assimilated to the attributes of popular culture, thus losing some of their uniqueness.

The production and broadcast of the eighty-four-episode television series *Three Kingdoms* (*Sanguo yanyi*), along with the production and broadcast of several other television megaseries adapted from Chinese classical novels, represent a global trend that has also been occurring in China. Traditional Chinese culture now relies on new communication technologies to be disseminated. While Chinese traditional and high cultures are being promulgated with the help of new communication technologies, they are also experiencing a quiet and almost imperceptible evolution.

Compared to the huge body of study on popular culture in Western countries, research in this field is rare in China. Using the television series *Three Kingdoms* as a case in point, this article attempts to examine how Chinese traditional and high cultures have been diffused in recent years, and what gains and losses result from the process of diffusing traditional and high cultures via new communication technologies. In addition, this paper also tries to analyze the implications of these gains and losses. This study suggests that, regardless of whether it is good or bad, in China television is becoming the main channel to convey traditional and high cultures and has an enormous impact on the evolution of both their format and content.

FROM *THREE KINGDOMS* THE NOVEL TO *THREE KINGDOMS* THE TELEVISION SERIES

The novel *Three Kingdoms* is one of China's "four Ming masterpieces of the classical novel," and one of the favorite traditional novels of the Chinese people. The novel was written over one thousand years after the Three Kingdoms period. It created a unique tapestry of characters—heroes and villains alike—from the hundreds of warlords and statesmen of the era and brilliantly and vividly portrayed the various historical events and scenes. The depiction encompassed battles and stratagems, political power-mongering, and an emphasis on traditional Chinese or Confucian themes, such as loyalty, filial piety, honor, humility, and self-sacrifice. It has been called one of the milestones of the Chinese historical, classical, and traditional novels.[1]

The novel has 120 chapters, but throughout these chapters the story never flags. Its richness and longevity represents a first in classical Chinese literature. Moreover, it has greatly influenced East Asian thought and life. Since it was written, there have been more than forty translations, including into Japanese, Korean, English, Russian, French, German, and Polish.[2]

However, in the last several decades the novel *Three Kingdoms*, sharing the fate of Chinese classical literature and traditional culture in general, has faced an awkward situation: fewer people have bought and read it. This has represented a trend. Traditional and high cultures were in a disadvantageous position compared to popular culture, which is greatly benefited by being diffused mainly by new communication technologies, such as television, computer, and digital technology.

Before the television series *Three Kingdoms*, television producers in China had already been enthusiastic about adapting classical masterpieces and broadcasting them to hundreds of millions of viewers. Prior to the production of the series *Three Kingdoms* in the early 1990s, a number of other well known classical novels had been adapted for television, such as *A Dream of Red Mansions* (*Honglou meng*), *Journey to the West* (*Xiyou ji*), *Strange Stories from A Chinese Studio* (*Liaozhai zhiyi*), and *Outlaws of the Marsh* (*Shuihu zhuan*). All these dramas had received high ratings.

The decision to adapt the novel *Three Kingdoms* into a television series was made by the Chinese central government. Claiming the novel *Three Kingdoms* as one of the nation's historical treasures, the central government did not allow any foreign or overseas involvement with the huge production project. Nor did they allow any local television stations or independent production companies to be involved, despite the fact that some foreign broadcasting companies had expressed strong interest in coproducing the series *Three Kingdoms* with China's television stations and that some Chinese independent production companies had spent years preparing to produce such a series. The central government ordered China Central Television (CCTV), the nation's official and only national television network, to produce and distribute the series *Three Kingdoms*.[3] Fulin Wang, a Chinese television director renowned worldwide, became the general director of the series. Before the series *Three Kingdoms*, he had directed the influential television series *A Dream of Red Mansions*. The production of the epic megaseries *Three Kingdoms*, consisting of eighty-four one-hour episodes, lasted four years. The production costs set a record in China's television history. The total production costs were 170 million Chinese yuan (about 20 million U.S. dollars).[4]

According to data obtained from CCTV and the General Bureau of Radio, Film and Television of China during my research trip to China, *Three Kingdoms* has recorded a number of other "mosts" in the history of China's television drama production: the largest number of people involved in the production (altogether, 400,000 performers, and a production crew of a few hundred members who traveled more than 10,000 kilometers); the biggest number of reruns (it has been broadcast a total of 120 times at various television stations, excluding broadcasts in foreign countries); the biggest audience (a total of 1.2 billion of people across the world have watched the series); the highest ratings among all Chinese entertainment programs (on average the rating was around 60 percent); the largest number of videotapes sold (five million); and finally, it has been exported to the largest number of foreign countries and areas (a total of 12 countries and areas). Broadcasting rights for outside the Chinese mainland were sold for 2 million U.S. dollars, which was also the most expensive price ever for a television production from mainland China.

The public received the television series *Three Kingdoms* with unprecedented enthusiasm. As soon as the TV series *Three Kingdoms* was broadcast in 1994, it immediately attracted an audience far beyond just the literate audience. Between late 1994 and early 1995, China Central Television and many provincial and regional television stations broadcast the series during prime time. The TV *Three Kingdoms* immediately became the most popular topic of conversation for hundreds of millions of people.[5] A poll conducted among the television audiences in Beijing showed that 53.2 percent of the respondents watched every episode of the series and 88.3 percent watched at least some part of *Three Kingdoms*. Only 11.7 percent of television viewers reported that they had not seen it.[6]

THE GAINS AND THE LOSSES

As one might expect from its broad viewer base, responses to the series were both positive and negative. In the view of many experts, and the general audience, although the series has some regrettable aspects it should be acknowledged as one of the few such productions to have achieved great success.[7]

In addition to the accomplishments discussed above, the television version of *Three Kingdoms* has also set several records in the literary and artistic aspects of China's television drama production as well: it is much more faithful to the original classical novel than other television adaptations from classical novels; the performance of the actors and actresses in the televised *Three Kingdoms* seem much more real than those in other television series involving historical themes; the background sets, props, and costumes used in *Three Kingdoms* look close to those of that historical time; and the overall atmosphere created by the series gives the audiences a much more historical feeling than that of other television series adapted from classical masterpieces.[8] Unlike many other TV dramas, including some recently produced TV dramas either on historical themes or adapted from classical works, *Three Kingdoms* is rendered in a serious fashion with great care being taken to ensure its fidelity to the original literary work. Details of conversations, settings, costumes, formalities, events, and characters accord with the particular historical period. One of the most important achievements is that the television version successfully highlights the dramatic plots and stories of the novel *Three Kingdoms* and takes advantage of television—a new communication technology—to maximize the impacts of those plots and stories. At the same time, it also successfully simplifies the narrative parts of the novel and reduces or eliminates those parts not closely related to the theme. In general, it successfully strikes a balance between the depiction of the major military and political confrontations and the characterization of the events and people.[9]

The television version holds to the essential structure of the novel, offering a panoramic scenario of that time. It tries to be as close to the original classical novel as it can, but is not mechanically bound to the novel. Unlike other TV series that were based on classical novels, *Three Kingdoms* is a full adaptation. It is replete with of historical atmosphere, and the awe-inspiring battle scenes are artistically presented. Ancient warfare incorporated numerous different land and water battles. In order to film a number of major battles and make them look real, the producers spent huge sums of money. For example, a division of the Chinese army—4,000 soldiers—and another 10,000 people were involved in the shooting of the Battle of Guandu, a key military event in the story, and 30,000 costumes and 70,000 theatrical props were used, providing the viewers with the chance to see a lifelike smoke-and-fire-filled battlefield.[10] The shooting of this battle alone cost 400,000 Chinese yuan, an amount of money that would have been sufficient by itself to produce a midsize television series.

Criticism of the series has centered on four points: It is argued that *Three Kingdoms* does not sufficiently deliver the most important theme of the original novel to the viewers; that it does not provide the audiences with a systematic description of the society of that time; that it is strong in depicting the "superficial" aspects of the story but weak in exposing the things underneath the surface; and that sometimes it offers overly simplified or even distorted versions of historical events. Some critics have commented that the narration is too simple to be stirring and that the quality of each part is uneven. And in its focus on the major military and political confrontations of the time, it somewhat fails to provide a sufficient characterization of the leading figures in the drama.[11] For example, the series depicts Cao Cao as sinister and ruthless, but it does not devote sufficient effort to revealing another characteristic of Cao Cao's—such as his strategic talent and his daring. Although the series does successfully depict Liu Bei as a kindhearted and civilian-oriented person, it does not sufficiently present his other talents, such as his strong leadership and tactical abilities. Finally, the series depicts Zhuge Liang as an intelligent military commander, but pays little attention to his other attributes.

There are also concerns about the style, the approach toward adaptation, the use of language, and the production skills of the television series. The series is strong in providing a "realistic flavor" but is weak in presenting the romantic style and legendary color of the original novel. The television version pays too much attention to reflecting the "historical reality" but neglects one of the novel's unique characteristics—that is, its romantic style and legendary color, which is one of the most important reasons for it to be considered one of the four most influential classical novels in China. In some critics' view, one of the greatest successes of the novel *Three Kingdoms* is its perfect mixture of a realistic approach and a romantic style.[12]

It is also said that, in order to attract viewers and receive the large market share and high ratings that translate into huge advertising revenues and profits, the television version of *Three Kingdoms* unfortunately follows the patterns of most television programs, both in China and other countries, by purposely emphasizing or expanding plots or stories that can meet the "tastes" of television viewers. Moreover, the television series even adds things that have no basis in the novel simply to satisfy the "needs" of modern television audiences. There are overemphasized love stories, artificial-looking martial-arts-based fighting scenes, and luxurious ancient dancing and singing shows. Sometimes, these scenes are added at the price of "distorting the spirit of the original work."[13] For instance, the love story of Lü Bu and Diao Chan is depicted in the minutest detail. Also, the personal life of Cao Cao is barely mentioned in the novel, but it becomes a colorful love story in the television series. Furthermore, a number of episodes devote a large portion of their time to presenting exotic ancient Chinese rituals and protocols in an attempt to pique the viewers' curiosity, and to keep them watching the program.

The language used in the television series is half classical and half modern. While some people say that the parallel use of modern and classical languages makes the show naturally authentic and classically elegant, others argue that the classical lines make the drama hard to understand and less enjoyable. The latter comment that not only some adults, but also many young viewers, still have difficulties in understanding the classical Chinese language, particularly in its oral form. Moreover, the use of the classical language ruins the "realistic feeling" of the series.[14]

Regarding this issue, the producers of the TV *Three Kingdoms* actually faced a dilemma. The principal goal of the producers was to make the series as close to the classical novel and the historical reality as possible. Therefore, in the hope of providing the audience with historical atmosphere, the producers tried to maintain the artistic style, background sets, props, costumes, rituals and protocols, and language as close to those of that historical period as possible while still being acceptable to the majority. Totally using the classical language was not an option, because the majority of the audience would have problems in understanding it; nor was totally using the modern language acceptable, because the historical feeling would be substantially reduced. Thus, using a combination of a half-classical language and a half-modern language seemed to be the only option. In that way, it could be understood by the audience and yet provide a historical feeling as well. Even though the combination of a half-classical language and a half-modern language was not the type of language used by the people during the Three Kingdoms period, it could nevertheless enhance the historical flavor of the television series. In fact, the use of a half-classical language and a half-modern language does not cause too much trouble for the audience. According to a survey, most of the young viewers and peasants not only could easily comprehend the language, but many even said that they learned a lot of classical Chinese words and grammatical structures, which they might not have learned otherwise.[15]

In some critics' opinion, the martial-arts skills of the actors were questionable in quite a few of the fighting scenes, especially those ones on horseback.[16] But detailed depictions of those fighting scenes and martial-arts were not supposed to be the focus of the series; rather, the focus is placed on the strategic plans and plots of *Three Kingdoms*. In other words, the emphasis of the series was on a macrodepiction of the novel rather than on a microdepiction of every fighting scene and each display of martial arts. In many cases, the producers purposely simplified the depiction of fighting scenes and martial arts performances, and instead stressed the depiction of those plots that could more effectively highlight the themes of the original novel. And in fact, the fighting scenes and displays of martial arts are not that weak. Some television audiences judge *Three Kingdoms* by the standard of martial-arts or military movies, and forget that the series *Three Kingdoms* is not merely a martial-arts or military movie. As the producers claimed, the television version of the novel is an epic, not a mediocre kung fu show. Its main purpose is to depict the rich and complicated story arising from the intertwined political and military relationships among the three kingdoms. Too much emphasis on fighting scenes and martial arts, such as using up-to-date special effects and fancy martial artists for the stunts, would have only reduced the realistic feeling of the series, for that type of martial arts is usually exaggerated. They are enjoyable, but artificial.[17] Therefore, while the depiction of fighting scenes and martial arts is necessary, only an appropriate use of special effects and sophisticated martial arts could properly enhance the artistic quality of this series, because the story is based on many heroic figures that are well known to hundreds of millions of people mainly or entirely for their legendary martial-arts abilities.[18]

A key issue regarding the successes and failures of the series is that the novel *Three Kingdoms* is not just an average novel; it represents a culture. Based on the historical story of the Three Kingdoms period, it contains many important political, military, cultural, economic, and social attributes and thus manifests a synthetic set of values and social norms. The "Three Kingdoms culture" represented in the novel *Three Kingdoms* is one of China's most important and influential traditional cultures. On the macro level, it has had a profound impact on the formation of China's unique political, military, and economic characteristics, and at the micro level, it has also had a profound impact on the evolution of Chinese philosophy, literature, art, historiography, and even technological innovation.[19] The Chinese traditional and high cultures represented by the novel *Three Kingdoms* have played a critical role in the formation and development of the spiritual life and national characteristics of the Chinese, and these spiritual traits and national characteristics have been widely spread to many parts of the world.

To a certain degree, some of the criticisms of the TV *Three Kingdoms* arose from familiarity with the story of *Three Kingdoms;* the novel's plots and characters are deeply rooted in the Chinese psyche. Therefore, each viewer could have his or her own preferred version of the depiction of the whole story, or the depiction of some specific plot or some particular characters. There are certainly gaps between the audiences' preferred versions and the director's version. In fact, while the television series may have some aspects that do not fully reflect the quality of the original novel, it does have quite a few aspects that obviously surpass the original novel, such as the vivid and effective depiction of the various battlefields and the superb performances of the leading figures. Therefore, many people feel that the television series *Three Kingdoms* is better than any other television series based on a classical novel. Another factor involved is the commercialization of China's television. The pervasiveness of commercial television programs, including most television dramas, has somewhat "trained" or changed the tastes of the audiences. It has generally lowered their artistic standards, and helped to create their stereotypes about the nature of "good" television programs.

IMPLICATIONS

Among the four masterpieces of the Chinese classical novel, the novel *Three Kingdoms* is the most influential due to the novel's scale of diffusion and readership size. But as mentioned, over the last several decades the audience of the novel *Three Kingdoms*, like those of all classical works, has markedly dwindled in size. Therefore, one of the purposes for producing the television series *Three Kingdoms* was to "popularize the classical masterpieces" and to "inherit the magnificent Chinese traditional culture."[20]

In a country such as China that has over 200 million television sets, a program in prime time would easily reach one billion viewers. By the mid-1990s, there were a total of 230 million television sets in China, surpassing the number of 200 million television sets in the United States and becoming the country with the most television sets in the world.[21] Thanks to the spread of television sets in China, the television series *Three Kingdoms* and the rich Chinese traditional culture contained within it reached hundreds of millions of viewers—men and women, old and young, urban inhabitants and rural inhabitants, well-educated and less-educated people, intellectuals and workers, farmers, herdsmen and soldiers, people of the majority Han nationality and people of ethnic minority groups, lovers of traditional and high Chinese cultures and those who couldn't care less about them.

One of the important social implications of this unprecedented diffusion of Three Kingdoms culture is that it provides a new set of role models and idols for the Chinese people. Role models in Chinese society are constantly changing over time. From the 1950s and to the 1980s, the Chinese Communist Party decided the role models and heroes for the people and society. They used all kinds of educational, cultural, and ideological vehicles to promote these models. Up until the 1980s, role models were always closely mingled with politics. They were designated according to the political and ideological needs of the party. Role models thus included figures such as Lei Feng, an exemplary soldier of the Chinese People's Liberation Army who devoted himself to serving the public and helping the needy, and Jiao Yulu, a party secretary who dedicated himself to the improvement of Lankao County in central China's Henan Province in the early 1960s.[22] However, beginning in the 1980s this mechanism became less and less workable; the media became more open and diversified, and began to play an ever-larger role in establishing popular heroes. With the broadcasting of *Three Kingdoms* and other newly produced television dramas based on historical themes or adaptations from classical novels, Chinese society has rediscovered role models from the past. Many people now enjoy discussing eminent historical figures, such as the revered Guan Yu, who is noted for his bravery and loyalty, and celebrated as the most outstanding general of the Three Kingdoms period, and Zhuge Liang, a supremely intelligent commander and scholar respected by both officials and commoners alike. To a certain degree, the development of new media technologies has accelerated the emergence of those role models and idols for the Chinese people and society. The people now have more paragons on which to model themselves and in whom to find spiritual strength. Especially in colleges and universities, students like to have more options for selecting role models for themselves instead of being "assigned" the role models and idols by the party and government. Many of the leading figures in the *Three Kingdoms* series have become heroes because of their honesty and loyalty to each other, which represents one of the most important traits of the Confucianism-rooted Chinese traditional and high cultures.

In addition, the production and broadcasting of the *Three Kingdoms* series has also initiated a "Three Kingdoms wave" that promotes various aspects of Chinese traditional and high cultures. The places mentioned in the Three Kingdoms story have become favorite spots of both domestic and foreign tourists; Three Kingdoms-related souvenirs and cultural products have become popular items in the market; and computer games based on Three Kingdoms figures have become favorites among teenagers. Object, a Beijing-based software company, made *The Battle of the Red Cliffs*, which follows characters from the *Three Kingdoms* series and is its best-selling game for the personal computer. *The Battle of the Red Cliffs* was also released in Taiwan, Hong Kong, South East Asia, and North America. According to the company, in just three months 25,000 units of *The Battle of the Red Cliffs* were sold in the United States alone. This success led the company to decide to specialize in role-playing games based on Chinese historical themes.[23] Soft-World, Taiwan's largest games software company, is the maker of *Romance of the Three Kingdoms*, and it has already developed the Three Kingdoms game at three centers in Beijing, Shanghai, and Guangzhou, China's three largest cultural and commercial cities. With the big success of *Romance of the Three Kingdoms*, the company's president predicted that, within three years most of his company's games will be based on Chinese stories or Chinese topics.[24]

Probably the most important "cultural" contribution of the television series of *Three Kingdoms* is the resurgence of interest in the classical novel *Three Kingdoms* itself, which in turn has fueled an enthusiasm for reading and studying the Chinese classics.[25] The broadcast of the *Three Kingdoms* greatly increased the public's interest in reading the novel *Three Kingdoms* and, as a result, sales of the classical novel *Three Kingdoms* were substantially increased. For a period of time, many bookstores throughout China sold out their stocks of the novel. Meantime, the sale of *lianhuanhua* books—Chinese comic books—of *Three Kingdoms* also boomed. The reprinted series of *Romance of the Three Kingdoms lianhuanhua* books sold at least 100,000,000 sets.[26] Some viewers even held exhibitions and parties based on the novel, and a great many schools adopted part of the novel into their textbooks. Moreover, some newly opened stores and companies were named after the novel. The television series also brought Three Kingdoms cultures and Chinese traditional and high culture to the world on a much larger scale, and with unprecedented speed. The television drama sold very well abroad. Apart from television broadcasts and videotape sales in Hong Kong, Taiwan, Singapore, Macao and Japan, videotapes also sold very well in Thailand, Korea, and Malaysia. In addition, videotapes or cable television broadcasts of *Three Kingdoms* were available in Europe, North America, and Australia.[27]

The television series *Three Kingdoms* not only transmits and diffuses Three Kingdoms culture, but also further enriches and supplements Three Kingdoms culture. Because of the broadcasting of the series, Chinese traditional culture is no longer just "historical stuff" but has become "modern stuff" as well. In other words, the series has not only revived Chinese traditional culture as represented in the novel *Three Kingdoms*, but also has given it fresh blood. Thus, traditional and high cultures can be felt in people's thinking and actions, and can be seen everywhere among the people, influencing many people's everyday lives.

THE THEORETICAL SIGNIFICANCE
OF THE TELEVISION SERIES

The success of *Three Kingdoms* on television demonstrates that television is becoming the primary medium for massively and effectively diffusing and popularizing traditional culture in China. Television is the most powerful method to transmit and convey traditional culture, reflecting a global phenomenon that has already been seen in most industrialized countries.

As Neuman observes, as a worldwide trend, television has had an immense influence on traditional culture.[28] For many people, watching television has replaced reading books, especially reading classical books.[29] A technical but crucial reason for this phenomenon is that, confronted by conventions and expressions unfamiliar to modern audiences, it is hard for later generations to understand classical writings from many centuries ago. Also, "communication in writing relies on the formal meanings of words and requires a much greater number of words than oral speech to convey the same idea," because "it is addressed to an absent person who rarely has in mind the same subject as the writer."[30] Television language is much more easily understood, even if the content it conveys is not contemporary, for the language it uses is much closer to the oral form. Therefore, watching television requires less engagement than reading, and consequently it is more popular among children, the old, the poor, and particularly the less educated, who are the majority in most societies.[31]

This trend has been occurring throughout many regions across the world. In the past several decades, the BBC has been acting as the main provider of traditional and high cultures. For example, many Shakespearean dramas have been shot as films and presented on television. They have attracted audience from varying levels of society, and have generated considerable speculation about Shakespeare and British classical literature and traditional culture.[32] Japanese television has also often produced and broadcast shows based on classical masterpieces that imply strong traditional cultural identities.[33] Television is thus considered a vital instrument for conveying cultural heritage in a manner that meets the needs of the lower classes, "elevating" and "educating" people, and striving for cultural identity and unity; in other words, it is a vital instrument to "propagate high culture."[34] In many other developed countries, television is also a dominant institution in promoting culture and identity, including diffusing and popularizing traditional and high cultures.

Theoretically speaking, the idea that of necessity television has become the main conveyer of traditional and high cultures can be traced back to the works of Harold Adams Innis, a pioneer communication scholar who proposed that in any given period a new communication medium that better copes with the problems of communicating knowledge eventually will replace the old one and become dominant.[35] Based on Innis's ideas, another renowned communications scholar, Marshall McLuhan, further suggested that, because television offers a shared experience and enables the homogenization of cultural consumption, it would have a strong impact on the linear, segmented print medium.[36] To Chandra Mukerji and Michael Schudson, thanks to the unique role of television in society, it is obvious that television can and should be seen as the primary manifestation of culture.[37] Barry D. Ricco indicates more specifically that television will inevitably be the main conveyer of cultural values and representations in contemporary society.[38] Peter Goodall shares Ricco's view, and further believes that in modern society television will not only be the generator and bearer of culture, but also the single most important purveyor of culture.[39]

In China, it is also through television, specifically through the production and broadcasting of the television series *Three Kingdoms*, that the classical novel *Three Kingdoms*, Three Kingdoms culture, and Chinese traditional and high cultures have been diffused, popularized, and promoted to a wide audience and in a most effective way. The promotion of the *Three Kingdoms* story has led, either directly or indirectly, to the popularization of Chinese traditional art, literature, drama, and history. Also, the production of the series *Three Kingdoms* massively spread the classical novel *Three Kingdoms*, Three Kingdoms culture, and Chinese traditional and high cultures to the world. *Three Kingdoms* videotapes have been sold across the world, ranging from Asian countries, European countries, and North and South American countries, to Oceanic countries, becoming the television series in China that has sold the most copies of videotapes.[40] The musical cassettes of the theme songs of the series have been played everywhere, both at home and abroad.

However, along with the profound influences of the television series on culture and society, there are also concerns about its negative impacts. A macro-level concern is that "traditional Three Kingdoms culture" is evolving into a "popular Three Kingdoms culture," and a micro-level concern is that the pervasive influence of the televised *Three Kingdoms* would turn out to be a potential obstacle for the diffusion and spread of the original classical novel *Three Kingdoms*. The fast and massive spread of Three Kingdoms culture via new communication technology has overtly or covertly changed many of the elements of traditional Three Kingdoms culture and has transformed traditional Three Kingdoms culture into pop culture. Further, although the sales volume of the novel *Three Kingdoms* did witness a huge increase due to the broadcasting of the television series, in the long run the sales volume of the novel *Three Kingdoms* may decrease because future generations would tend to know the story of the Three Kingdoms from the television rather than from the literature. In other words, more and more people in the future may just want to watch the television version. Because the television series can never be the same as the novel *Three Kingdoms*, it cannot fully deliver the richness and integrity of "traditional Three Kingdoms culture" to the people. Accordingly, while the production and broadcasting of *Three Kingdoms* has promoted the classical novel and Chinese traditional culture, it may also have also deprived the novel of its position in Chinese culture and society, and thus may have become an obstacle for the future popularization and inheritance of Chinese traditional culture.[41]

Moreover, another concern far beyond cultural and artistic caveats has emerged: concern about the impact of the violence of the television series *Three Kingdoms* on people, especially on young people. Although violence has been generally regarded as harmful to young people, it has invariably appeared on television in China, where children have almost free access to such programs. The number of scenes in television programs featuring violence has steadily grown in the past decade, and according to a research report by the Chinese Academy of Social Sciences, the televised *Three Kingdoms* not only features typical violence but also has the most violent scenes. Many children have developed an interest in television dramas featuring violence. As the loyal fans of the series, they have been strongly influenced by its violent scenes. A survey on urban children in the 1990s showed that 58 percent of those surveyed enjoyed watching stimulating TV programs featuring detectives, warfare, and kung fu, and 31 percent liked watching feature movies that targeted adults, especially those with high audience ratings, such as *Three Kingdoms*.[42] The repeated broadcasting of the television *Three Kingdoms* on various television stations has therefore aroused widespread social concern about violence in TV programs and its ever-increasing influence on children and young people in China.

Nevertheless, despite the negative impact the series *Three Kingdoms* may have, it is successfully replacing the old art forms and is becoming the main purveyor of Chinese traditional and high cultures. In one sense, the television series *Three Kingdoms* has created a successful way of delivering and diffusing works from traditional and high culture with a popular culture approach.

CONCLUSION

When the televised version of *Three Kingdoms* was produced and broadcast, there as some speculation about a political motive behind its production and broadcasting. It concerned one of the stories about the confrontation between Zhuge Liang, the prime minister in the Shu kingdom, and Sima Yi, a general from the Wei kingdom, who is known for his knowledge of military strategy. In the view of some observers, the confrontation between Zhuge Liang and Sima Yi is being played out again across the Taiwan Strait. Starring in the role of Zhuge Liang is Chen Shui-bian, the Taiwanese president, and in the less glamorous role of Sima Yi is the Chinese president, Jiang Zemin. When it comes to the issue of Taiwan, Jiang Zemin has been playing the same sort of wait-and-see strategy that Sima Yi deployed so successfully against Zhuge Liang.[43] But these speculations are just speculations and do not have a basis. The production and broadcasting of dramas such as *Three Kingdoms* are basically the result of the changing sociopolitical and cultural environment in China, and various factors have contributed to the "birth" of such television dramas, including political considerations, economic incentives, cultural motivations, and audience demand.

First, producing such dramas is much more politically safe than producing dramas on other themes and genres. This type of television drama seems to satisfy all levels of Chinese society, including the party and government, who view television dramas as a new form of national culture. Therefore, producers of such drama not only do not need to worry about their programs being censored or "killed" by the party and government, but often receive financial support and guidance from the party and government.[44] Second, it is much more economically safe to produce such dramas than to produce television dramas on other themes and genres. The classical epic novels are the best known and most-loved literary works in China. Television drama writers are enthusiastic about translating them onto the screen, because these television adaptations are sure to generate a great reaction.[45] For the same reason, television drama producers and distributors anticipate that these adaptations will also have a big potential for exportation overseas, and various story-based products can be manufactured as toys and souvenirs. Third, it is also much more culturally safe to produce such dramas than to produce dramas on other themes and genres. In the early stages of the development of Chinese television, television dramas were produced under the framework of a planned economy, and mainly in state-run studios. The drama as a cultural commodity for the purpose of entertainment was ignored. Over the past two decades however, television dramas have incorporated multifaceted aesthetic styles, diverse themes and genres, and marked improvements in production quality. But the swift growth of television drama production in recent years has also faced many new problems and challenges. The increasing commercialization of the television industry as a whole and drama production in particular has led more and more television drama makers to tend to produce vague romances, superficial kungfu dramas, and local versions of the imported, third-class-and-below, cheap Western detective series. As a result, Chinese television dramas in recent years have deteriorated into formulaic love stories of petty urban people. Glamorous actors, beautiful actresses, colorful settings, exotic locations, posh sedans and residences, unrealistic affluence, and sometimes even decadent lifestyles, rather than strong characters and story lines, usually decide the market success of a television drama today.[46] Accordingly, the adaptations of Chinese classics of indigenous Chinese culture are highly favored by both the producers and the audiences, and the production of those television dramas has become a new opportunity for success. All of these factors have made the production of television dramas on historical themes and genres or adaptations from classical masterpieces much less risky than the production of other types of dramas.

Certainly, adapting a masterpiece of the classical novel into a television series is a sophisticated and systematic project of gigantic proportions. The successful adaptation of the novel *Three Kingdoms* to the series *Three Kingdoms* relied on both those who were engaged in the production and those who consumed the product. In the conversion from the novel *Three Kingdoms* to the series *Three Kingdoms*, there were both gains and losses, and the gains and the losses both deserve fair acknowledgment and objective examination. First, the combination of new communication technology and traditional and high cultures greatly promotes the diffusion of traditional and high cultures. Second, in recent years television in China has also become the wholesale distributor of forms, images, and contents of mainstream culture, including both popular culture and traditional and high cultures just as it is in many developed countries. Third, the combination of new communication technology with traditional and high cultures greatly helps Chinese traditional and high cultures spread to the world, thus greatly promoting cultural exchange and catalyzing cultural globalization. And finally, in the process of diffusing traditional and high cultures through new communication technology, Chinese traditional and high cultures also lose some of their unique elements or integrity, yet some new elements are also added—namely, elements of popular culture. So, Chinese traditional and high cultures are also experiencing a process of assimilation into popular culture. Despite some criticisms of the television series *Three Kingdoms* for being superficial, story- and plot-based rather than figure- and characterization-based, and overly focused on the sensory and the visual, the television series *Three Kingdoms* has disseminated the Three Kingdoms story and Three Kingdoms culture on an unprecedented scale. Also, the series greatly promotes the public's interest in classical Chinese literature and traditional Chinese culture previously "abandoned" by them. Furthermore, the television series *Three Kingdoms* successfully widens future prospects for the combination of traditional and high cultures with mass media and popular culture.

Television itself is already part of culture now, preserving the universal logic of culture and manifestly open to and contributing to change. As Roger Silverstone sees it, involvement with television is "an involvement with a type of communication which in its compression and redefinition of historical, geographical, social and cosmic experience identifies a coherence, a continuity and a commonness in culture."[47] Therefore, from an optimistic perspective, television will not destroy the continuity of culture—popular culture and traditional and high cultures as well—but will contribute to its development and prosperity. However, from a pessimistic perspective, old-fashioned art forms, such as novels and operas, have been losing their advantage in massively and effectively conveying and transmitting traditional and high cultures. Their survival faces serious challenges due to unfair technological limits and obsolescence. What is most problematic is that they cannot attract the younger generation as they did their parents. As seen in many places, people rarely read classical novels, or watch opera. In China, because classical novels use ancient Chinese language that has too many classical words and usages unfamiliar to modern ordinary readers, only those with high education have the ability and interest in to read these novels. Moreover, busy lifestyles deprive many people, especially young people, of time and energy to read classical novels.[48]

The television series *Three Kingdoms* is both a small and a big phenomenon in China's culture and society. On the one hand, it is just one more television drama; but on the other hand, it has echoed a global trend—television is exerting various strong influences on every culture and society. For better or for worse, television in China has refashioned and reshaped the lives of hundreds of millions of people and is playing an ever-more important role in modern life. Chinese television has made large strides toward diffusing, popularizing, and preserving the country's thousand-year-long traditional and high cultures, and has made it more accessible to more people than ever before in Chinese history.

NOTES

The author gratefully acknowledges the assistance of Lina Mao in the writing of this essay.

1. Yuping Qian, *Zhongguo gudian wenxue* (Beijing: Beijing Education College Press, 1987).

2. Luning Wang, *Zhongguo gudian xiaoshuo zai haiwai* (Beijing: Kelin Press, 1988).

3. Bojun Shen, *Sanguo manhua* (Chengdu: Sichuan People's Press, 2000).

4. Yaming Tu,"Dianshi lianxu ju Sanguo Yanyi zhiwai de gushi," *Dazhong dianshi*, no. 8 (1994): 4–7.

5. Ling Wang, *Zhongguo wenxue mingzhu* (Tianjing: Tianjing People's Press, 1991).

6. J. Feng, "TV Series 'The Romance of Three Kingdoms' Wins Acclaim," *Beijing Review* March 27–April 2, 1995, 30.

7. Shen, *Sanguo manhua.*

8. Fanglin Zhao,"Bao Guo'an banyan Cao Cao de xu ru sheng," *Dazhong dianshi*, no. 3 (1995): 69. Dan Zhu,"Jiegou jianjie xingge shengdong," *Dazhong dianshi*, no. 1 (1995): 60. Fanying Feng, "Yibu meiyou chaoji mingxing de youxiu dianshiju," *Dazhong dianshi*, no. 1 (1995): 60. Xiawen Zhu, "Xingshen jiebei: Lun Bao Guo'an banyan de Cao Cao," *Dazhong dianshi*, no. 1 (1995): 70. Guanpeng Zhao, "Tang Guoqiang de jiechu biaoyan," *Dazhong dianshi*, no. 2 (1995): 69.

9. Wenbi Gao, "Dianshi Sanguo Yanyi shi yibu zui dhenggong de gudian mingzhu gaibianju," *Dazhong dianshi*, no. 4 (1995): 68. Yu Feng,"Ping Cao Cao de san xiao," *Dazhong dianshi*, no. 3 (1995): 69–70. Fan Rong,"Cao Cao, Yige Zhenshi de Fuza Renwu," *Dazhong dianshi*, no. 2 (1995): 68. Du Chen,"Cao Cao yu Liu Bei jiujing shei shi yingxiong?" *Dazhong dianshi*, no. 2 (1995): 69.

10. J. Feng,"The Romance of Three Kingdoms' Wins Acclaim," 30.

11. Wenbi Gao, "Zhizuo daxing dianshi lianju de kunnan" *Dazhong dianshi*, no. 1 (1995): 60. Yifan Jiang,"San xiang Sanguo," *Dazhong dianshi*, no. 1 (1995): 70.

12. Dan Zhu,"Shi Wei Xiang Yu Buxiang Zhijian," *Dazhong dianshi*, no. 4 (1995): 69.

13. Yong Hu, "Xiyi dianshi lianju Sanguo Yanyi de zhuti," *Dazhong dianshi*, no. 5 (1995): 16. Ren Sha,"Guodu fancha zaocheng wuzhen," *Dazhong dianshi*, no. 2 (1995): 71.

14. Jianying Yang,"Zuihao neng shiyong geng tongsu yidong de yuyan," *Dazhong dianshi*, no. 1 (1995): 61. Liu Xinxin,"Zuihao you zimu," *Dazhong dianshi*, no. 3 (1995): 69.

15. Tu,"Sanguo Yanyi zhiwai de gushi," 4–7.

16. Xiong Xiao. "Tan Dianshi Lianxu ju Sangguo Yanyi de Wushu biaoyan," *Dazhong dianshi*, no. 1 (1995): 62; Haiying Zhao,"Leisheng da, yudian xiao: Sanguo Yanyi zhong de renwu," *Dazhong dianshi*, no. 1 (1995): 61.

17. Fang Wang,"Shi nian jian xin," *Dazhong dianshi*, no. 11 (1995): 4–6; and no. 12 (1995): 18–21.

18. Ling Liu,"Yingxiong renwu quefa yingxiong qizhi," *Dazhong dianshi*, no. 3 (1995): 70. Haiying Zhao,"Leisheng da, yudian xiao," 61.

19. Yuanyuan Ruan "Rang lishi zoujin women," *Dazhong dianshi*, no. 6 (1995): 20. Tu, "Sanguo Yanyi zhiwai de gushi," 4–7. Gao,"Dianshi Sanguo Yanyi."

20. Wang, "Shi nian jian xin."

21. Junhao Hong, *The Internationalization of Television in China: The Evolution of Ideology, Society, and Media Reform Since the Reform* (Westport, CT: Praeger, 1998).

22. "Chinese Society Has New Set of Role Models, New Kinds of Idols," *Xinhua News Agency*, 16 January 2003.

23. Anh-Thu Phan, "Developer To Put Growth Plans into Play; Firm Prepares for Move into Lucrative Online Market Showcasing Role-Playing Games with Chinese Historical Themes," *South China Morning Post*, January 18, 2002, 17.

24. Anh-Thu Phan, "China Seen as Market and Maker of Games," *South China Morning Post*, January 18, 2002, 12.

25. L. Zhu, "Real Life Stories Mirror Social Life," *China Daily*, January 11, 2002.

26. H. Zhong, "Battle of the Books," *China Daily*, July 19, 2002.

27. J. Feng, "'The Romance of Three Kingdoms' Wins Acclaim," 30.

28. W. Russell Neuman, "Television and American Culture: The Mass Medium and the Pluralist Audience," *Public Opinion Quarterly* 46 (1982): 471–87.

29. Larry Woiwode, "Television: The Cyclops That Eats Books," *USA Today* March 1, 1993, 84. Chris Arthur, "The Telefaithful," *Contemporary Review* 268, no. 1563 (1996): 194–204.

30. Lev Semenovich Vygotskii, *Thought and Language* (Cambridge, MA-: MIT Press, 1962) 142.

31. Todd Gitlin, "Flat and Happy," *The Wilson Quarterly* 17, no. 4 (1993): 47–49.

32. Mark Thornton Burnett and Ramona Wray, *Shakespeare, Film, Fin de Siècle* (New York-St. Martin's Press, 2000).

33. Eiko Ikegami, "A Sociological Theory of Publics: Identity and Culture as Emergent Properties in Networks," *Social Research* 67, no. 4 (Winter 2000): 989.

34. Hilde Van den Bulck, "Public Service Television and National Identity as a Project of Modernity: The Example of Flemish," *Media, Culture & Society* 23 (2001): 61.

35. Harold Adams Innis, *The Bias of Communication* (Toronto: Toronto University Press, 1951).

36. Marshall McLuhan, *Gutenberg Galaxy*, (Toronto: University of Toronto Press, 1962).

37. Chandra Mukerji and Michael Schudson, "Popular Culture," *Annual Review of Sociology* 12 (1986): 47–66.

38. Barry D. Ricco, "Popular Culture and High Culture: Dwight MacDonald, His Critics and the Ideal of Cultural Hierarchy in Modern America," *Journal of American Culture* 16, no. 4 (1993): 7–18.

39. Peter Goodall, *High Culture, Popular Culture: The Long Debate* (St. Leonards, Australia: Allen & Unwin, 1995).

40. Tu, "Sanguo Yanyi zhiwai de gushi," 4–7.

41. Zhifang Yang, "Gudian zuopin de younan," *Dazhong dianshi*, no. 3 (1995): 70.

42. He Sheng, "Regulating Media Violence," *China Daily*, February 22, 2002.

43. "China's Softly, Softly Bid to Woo Taipei," *Australian Financial Review* 4 (December 2001): 11.

44. L. Zhu, "Real Life Stories."

45. J. Bo, "TV Producer's Career Sees Dramatic Rise," *China Daily*, January 15, 2003.

46. L. Zhu, "Real Life Stories."

47. Roger Silverstone, *The Message of Television: Myth and Narrative in Contemporary Culture* (London: Heinemann Educational, 1981).

48. Douglas Gomery, "As the Dial Turns," *Wilson Quarterly* 17, no. 4 (1993): 41–46.

10

The Reception and the Place of *Three Kingdoms* in South Korea

JINHEE KIM

The most valuable aspect of reception studies is that it recognizes the centrality of the reader; the reader is not a passive participant but is as active as the author in maintaining identity and differences within the very space of reading. However minor the transformations wrought by the reader, the reader exercises his or her own will to power, even if not always to subvert otherwise radical power relationships. Two German scholars have dominated traditional reader-oriented studies during the twentieth century. Wolfgang Iser, author of *The Act of Reading: A Theory of Aesthetic Response* (Baltimore: Johns Hopkins University Press, 1978), explores extensively the significance of individual responses while Hans Robert Jauss is interested in the examination of the relationship between literature and history as well as the history of reception. Jauss, as noted in his seminal publication *Toward an Aesthetic of Reception* (Minneapolis: University of Minnesota Press, 1982), views literature as an interaction between past and present, asserting that in the course of reading the reader will be able to integrate past meanings as part of present practices. To this uncomplicated but essential point of inquiry, Umberto Eco, one of the foremost semioticians in the Western Hemisphere, offers his theoretical response. "How" to read a work of literature, Eco argues, requires prior knowledge of how the work was produced, including knowledge about the author. When this prior knowledge is not available, readers fill in the conceptual lacunae as best as they can with the existing knowledge. In his theory of communication, Eco recognizes the importance of text-reader dynamics and asserts that it is from the reader that the meaningful reading arises when an act of communication provokes a response in public opinion, since "definitive verification will take place not within the ambit of the book but in that of the society that reads it."[1] Eco further claims that "we are not so interested in speculating about our world from the point of view of a novel, but are rather eager to do the opposite, to analyze the world of a novel from our point of view."[2] In accordance with Eco's model of reading, the crucial point in the text-reader relationship is the question of agency, of "who does the reading." In line with Jauss and Eco's vision, the starting point of this essay is to recognize the significance of the reader as cultural agent, since such a thesis promises to truly account for the experiences and identities of South Korean readers. Under the theoretical directions outlined above, I examine the reception of *Three Kingdoms* in South Korea, focusing on the text's historical trajectory as manifested in the framework of translation and adaptation. The essay will also discuss the cultural place of the novel in contemporary reception, particularly its relation with popular culture and imagination.

More than five hundred entries are found under *Sam guk chi* [*Three Kingdoms*] in the database of the National Library of Korea in Seoul. While the translations vary in length, original language, and poetic license, most of them are translations of Chinese texts, the oldest one extant dating all the way back to 1871.[3] Translating *Three Kingdoms* was particularly warmly embraced by the publishing industry in the twentieth century. There are nearly half a dozen translations that precede the 1945 liberation from Japan, although they are not readily available in bookstores. Those translators—Kôn-hûi Pak, Yu-sang Ko, Chu-wan Yi, and In-kwang Yi—undertook the project during the Japanese occupation, and were entirely dependent on Japanese texts.[4] For many decades following the 1945 liberation, Korean translators shunned Japanese texts, but lately Japanese-text-based translations have reemerged as South Korea eagerly rides the wave of globalization. Not only have Japanese household appliances and automobiles saturated the South Korean market, but also intellectual products including film, literature, and cartoons have become popular among South Korean consumers. New talents like Yang-uk Cho, Kye-sông Yi, and Yông Pak quickly have seized the opportunity to capitalize on the marketability of non-Chinese-text-based translations.[5]

During the Korean War (1950–53), not a single copy of *Three Kingdoms* saw a day in print, because most cultural activities, including publishing, came to a virtual stop. In the early postwar era (1955), Ûn-yông Kim's translation appeared, followed by the translations by Sông-hak Yi and Yông-hae Choê.[6] Tong-ni Kim—one of the most prominent writers of twentieth century—published his translation in 1964 with the help of two of his contemporaries, Sun-wôn Hwang and Yun-sôk Hô.[7] In 1967, a translation by the prominent novelist Chong-hwa Pak was printed.[8] In the 1970s, Chu-dong Yang, a leading literary scholar of the time, and the novelist Ki-hwan Pang tried their hands at translation, and a popular novelist, Pi-sôk Chông, followed suit in the following decade.[9] Translation of *Three Kingdoms* saw a steady growth in the 1990s and has continued to grow in the new millennium, spearheaded by the work of the novelist Hong-sin Kim.[10]

Adaptation, side by side with translation, has formed an important part of the long tradition of *Three Kingdoms* publication. Over the course of the past ten years or so, both seasoned and young talents, such as Wôn-jung Kim, Kyông-min Pak, Wôn-gi Chông, and Hang-kyu Yi, have demonstrated their literary flare by recasting the various elements of *Three Kingdoms*.[11] Further, more academically oriented endeavors concerning *Three Kingdoms* produced dictionaries and reference books.[12]

No invention has transformed the demographics of the readership of *Three Kingdoms* more dramatically than computer games. Before the Internet became a staple in South Korean households, the readership of *Three Kingdoms* was limited to adults, as the novel was considered inappropriate for young readers.[13] The birth of the Internet and its paraphernalia has attracted a great many young readers, shattering the old belief that only adults are mature enough to enjoy and comprehend the gist of *Three Kingdoms*. One can find numerous Internet sites, usually run by young readers, that provide free information to anyone interested in learning about a range of topics concerning the novel. Topics include textual aspects of the novel such as character, plot, geography, and Chinese idiom, and assorted curiosities ranging from weaponry, battle scenes, treasures, and maps, to battle strategies. The explosion of fan clubs through which anonymous readers share independent interpretations and findings on the novel has fostered a tremendous following among young readers. The new readership has helped transform the novel into a learning tool.[14] For example, audiocassette tapes built around the dialogues in the novel are popular among K-12 students of conversational Chinese.

Besides the advent of cyberspace, other developments attesting to the popularity and longevity of *Three Kingdoms* have loomed large on the horizon. First, the Sinologist Wôn-gi Chông, who gives guest lectures on public television on classical Chinese literature, has announced formally the establishment of The Institute for *Three Kingdoms* Studies. Second, the late comic-book writer U-yông Ko resurrected his *Sam guk chi*, by converting it to the latest digital technology. Ko, arguably one of the most influential, popular artists of the 1970s, launched his career with an adaptation of *Three Kingdoms*. As soon as Ko's cartoon serial started its run in *Sports Daily* [*Ilgan sûp'otsû*] in 1978, the newspaper doubled its circulation. The following year, when the serial was ready to be published as a book, Ko was ordered by the government to cut out nearly one hundred pages of his manuscript on the grounds that his *Sam guk chi* exploited violence and sex. Although Ko was later encouraged by his friends and colleagues to "rehabilitate" his *Sam guk chi*, he repeatedly rejected the suggestion by saying that the thought of the censored work turned his stomach. Twenty-one years later, Ko finally brought himself to open the big sack of papers in the corner of his studio. Once the knot was undone, Ko immersed himself in the project by attending to all the details in one frame after another. The product of this long, arduous period of restoration was the 2001 publication of a two disk CD-ROM.[16] A print version was published shortly afterward.

Unlike contemporary reception, tracing the historical trajectory of *Three Kingdoms* is wide open for debate; consequently, far more information is needed than what is available. Fragments of information, albeit inconclusive, cast light onto the cultural paths *Three Kingdoms* might have taken. The Chinese woodblock text of Chin Su, which dates back to 1670, is a critical piece, because it confirms the theory that Koreans had been introduced to *Three Kingdoms* at least two hundred years before the 1871 translation appeared.[16] Although it is difficult to establish a definitive account of the complex relationship between *Three Kingdoms* in translation and Chin Su's historical text, it is not as difficult to conclude that the arrival of *Three Kingdoms* in Korea should be located in an earlier time. Evidence documenting such an event is found in the 1569 entry in *The Annals of Chosôn Dynasty*.[17] The entry in question reads: "While conversing with his ministers on a banquet table, the king remarked: 'The hollering of Zhang Fei frightened ten thousand solders.' One of the ministers quickly responded: 'That phrase is a quotation from *Three Kingdoms*, isn't it, Your Highness? I heard the novel is widely circulating among the commoners although I have not had the opportunity to read it yet. How did you obtain a copy, Your Highness?'"

A quick glance at the entry, demonstrates that Sôncho (r. 1567–1608), the fourteenth king of Chosôn, was an avid reader of the novel. The popularity of *Three Kingdoms*, both at the royal court and among the common people, supports the theory that Chinese literature, at least the kind that is represented by *Three Kingdoms*, helped Koreans to develop an enormous appetite and a vibrant market for foreign literature. The entry also directs our attention to the strong probability that *Three Kingdoms* was translated into the vernacular script, since apparently the commoners had access to it. Thus, the readership of *Three Kingdoms* could have surpassed the bounds limited by the Chinese-oriented aristocrats.

Despite this apparent enthusiasm and fascination, the once favorable reception of *Three Kingdoms* was met with opposition. Following the ban on such popular Chinese novels as *Jin Ping Mei* (*The Plum in the Golden Vase*) and *Shuihu zhuan* (*The Water Margin*), which were blacklisted on the grounds that they promoted sex and adultery and taught the young people the evils of manipulation and violence, *Three Kingdoms* came under attack as well. The book allegedly corrupted the innocent by mixing fact with fiction. The guardians of the citizens, a class comprised of aristocrats and high-ranking officials, might have united to enact a ban on the novel. It is not entirely clear whether it was the purist campaign that succeeded in bringing the soaring popularity of *Three Kingdoms* down to the earth. If it did, then it must have been rather short-lived. In the years following the Seven-Year War with Japan (1592–99), *Three Kingdoms* was clearly reinstated among the commoners to the extent that even women and children could recite the novel line by line.[18] Furthermore, the content of the novel was frequently included in state or civil examinations in the ensuing years.

A few South Korean scholars have attempted to establish serious scholarship based on the historical and archaeological findings of *Three Kingdoms*.[19] Working under the rubric of differentiating fact from fiction, Wôn-jung Kim, a renowned Sinologist, claims that *Three Kingdoms* committed an egregious mistake in portraying Liu Bei as a hero and Cao Cao as a villain. Kim claims that the historical Cao Cao ruled his people with the pen, not with the sword and thus *Three Kingdoms* does injustice to the historical Cao Cao. On the allegedly erroneous depiction of Cao Cao as the coldhearted, bloodthirsty Machiavellian, Kim states: "Our Confucian scholars glorify Liu Bei as a supreme example for brotherhood. But Liu Bei once said: 'Brothers are like arms and legs, but wife and children are like clothes.' Liu Bei abandoned his family, not once but three times. In contrast, Cao Cao is a man who believed that man's success depended on hard work and talent. It is Cao Cao's philosophy that deserves our admiration, not otherwise. It is time to reevaluate such a disparaging view of Cao Cao."[20]

The formalist approach, which centers on disputing the traditional interpretation of the text, is now eclipsed by the notion that *Three Kingdoms* is a work of fiction. Accordingly, the focus of recent studies has shifted from an inquiry about the validity of interpretation to an inquiry about the cultural values of the text. In connection with this, the 1988 publication of *Sam guk chi* by Mun-yôl Yi, one of the most notable writers of our time, is very instructive. By far the most well known adaptation of *Three Kingdoms*, Yi's *Sam guk chi* has sold more than one million copies so far, and has been voted by high school students as the most essential book in preparing for the nationwide college entrance examinations.[21] This labor of love was completed after a long, meticulous process. Yi traveled to Taiwan to collect different versions of *Three Kingdoms*, which he accomplished with assistance from his Sinologist friends and colleagues. Back home, after a long deliberation, Yi decided to translate Mao Zonggang's version instead of Luo Guanzhong's in order to prevent duplicating the tenor and theme of previous translations. Although the skeleton of Mao's narrative structure is kept intact, Yi's *Sam guk chi* is not shy about adding many new features, such as poems and footnotes, that are not found in Mao's Chinese text. Such changes, Yi claims, were essential because he wanted to give his adaptation a modern flavor. Yi also devotes a large section in his book to the description of each protagonist, detailing the many stages of the characters' transformation into epic heroes. What is most notable about Yi's adaptation is his commentary, in which the author discusses a range of topics from history, philosophy, and science to military revolutions, successions to power, and the rationale for waging wars. On the purpose of his adaptation, Yi is as forthright as he is with his creative energy: "It took four years and four months of hard work to finish the manuscript. *Three Kingdoms* is a classic that will be read for many generations to come. I wanted to make certain that I do justice to the novel. If the young people in my country can experience the great joys of *Three Kingdoms* while reading my *Sam guk chi*, then I have accomplished my mission."[22]

Myông Choê, professor of political science at Seoul National University, recently challenged Yi's conviction that *Three Kingdoms* is a classic for all time. Scrutinizing the social impact of the novel, Choê states: "Lately, after observing the current presidential election, I have come to conclude that *Three Kingdoms* should be removed from the bookshelves of our libraries. The central character of *Three Kingdoms* is war, a war between power-mongers that manipulate everything in their power in order to destroy their enemies. Cao Cao is no warrior but a brute. Liu Bei is a shameless opportunist. Zhuge Liang is a master of deception. What can our youngsters learn from such a wicked book as *Three Kingdoms*? Who dare call it a classic?"[23]

It is not the first time that *Three Kingdoms* was considered to pose a threat to the innocent indigenous people and that the legitimacy of *Three Kingdoms* came under attack. As if repeating the sentiments of the controversy that erupted several centuries ago, Choê raises his voice to warn the public against its influence on the youth. To Professor Myông Choê's irascible criticism, the writer Mun-yôl Yi offers this response:

> The state of the current political landscape is, without doubt, comparable to the chaos depicted in *Three Kingdoms*. Professor Choê's claim that our politicians exploit the tactics of manipulation, conspiracy, and trickery to carry out their agenda has some truth. But this is not an adequate reason to ban *Three Kingdoms*. His claim that the novel sets a bad example to our teenagers is even more difficult to accept. Even if the poor conduct of our politicians shows undeniable similarity to that of the characters, the novel is not to blame, but rather our politicians, because they misread the novel. If we ban *Three Kingdoms*, following Professor Choê's advice, then it will find itself in the company of books produced by European masters: Homer and Shakespeare, to name a few. How, then, should we deal with literature giving explicit pictures of betrayal, deception, and murder that is committed none other than by one's own flesh and blood? What shall we do with such cruelty and immorality? [24]

The latest controversy surrounding *Three Kingdoms* is a sign that the necessary machinery of cultural dialogue is in place so that the public can participate in the debate leading to the formation of cultural values. Despite the controversy, Mun-yôl Yi has announced a plan to revise his *Sam guk chi* and include the episodes following the death of Cao Cao, which he left out in the previous publication. Yi's efforts to champion *Three Kingdoms* have been followed by others: the novelist Sôk-yông Hwang plans to offer extensive footnotes in his project and Sông-gi Cho has proposed to use only *hangûl*, the vernacular script, in his adaptation.[25]

Yi's view that *Three Kingdoms* is an embodiment of human triumph and existential struggle is echoed by that of the novelist Yông-kyu Pak, who focuses his research on uncovering the hidden messages in the novel:

The country that produces no heroes is a country no man respects. The age that produces no heroes is an age veiled with darkness. Where there are no heroes, there are no hopes. Those who have lost hope no longer dream. When there are no dreamers, the race of people is in danger of perishing as a whole. The terrain of twentieth-century Korean history is disfigured with failure, despair, and division. The sovereignty of our country was lost at the very beginning of the century, and we were oppressed for thirty-five years. And now, we are divided between North and South. We are living in a dark time. In darkness no flowers bloom, and no trees bear fruit. But heroes are born in difficult times. Like a lonesome flower in the thick woods, heroes will rise in the dark. It is now more than ever that we need heroes. Our nation needs heroes. If we cannot find heroes here and now, then we must invoke heroes from the past so that they will cast a light onto our path and renew our hope.[26]

Pak finds the political turbulence depicted in *Three Kingdoms* remarkably similar to the reality wrought by the uncertainties surrounding Korea's political institutions and the instability of its national security. It is precisely those pictures of chaos and destruction that Pak seems to behold as teachings that might apply to lives in the present. The long, convoluted plot and the scale of two hundred-some characters are those of an epic, and the sudden demise of heroes is a magnificent display of human struggle. Pak's view that his country is suffering from a vacuum of great men leads him to invoke the heroes of *Three Kingdoms*. In the universe of *Three Kingdoms*, readers can start to envision a future, which is empowered by independence and pride in both the domestic and the international realms. To Pak, *Three Kingdoms* is the ultimate signifier of political aspirations.

Notwithstanding their status as recipients of an influx of other cultures, a great number of South Korean readers, as shown above, have sustained an active role when they encounter a literary model that has crossed national, linguistic, and cultural barriers. As Umberto Eco claims, the readers of the receiving culture generate readings of their own independent of those of the originating culture. This view is echoed in Jauss's theory, which urges the historian of literary reception "to rethink constantly the works in the canon in light of how they have affected and are affected by current conditions and events."[27] Therefore, the crucial term in cultural reception proves, ultimately, to be that of specific human agency. Upon a more careful look at the reader, it becomes clear that the reader is both the producer and the consumer of a text. The thesis is particularly profitable in cross-cultural studies, because the indigenous readers read the text, however foreign, by using the information recognizable from their own cultural background. Seen in this way, South Korean readers, when engaging in the reception of *Three Kingdoms*, prove to be active participants in constructing worldviews, which are in turn deeply entrenched in their local—both cultural and historical—conditions.

NOTES

All the translations in this essay are mine. Romanization of Korean names, titles and words follow the McCune-Reischauer system.

1. Umberto Eco, *The Role of the Reader: Explorations in the Semiotics of Texts* (Bloomington: Indiana University Press, 1979), 241.

2. Ibid.

3. This is the oldest translation that is currently available for viewing in the National Library of Korea. Commonly referred to as the Yi Book after the translator's surname, the book is 33.5 cm long and 20.0 cm wide.

4. Kôn-hûi Pak, *Sam guk chi* (Seoul: Chosôn Sôkwan, 1913); Yu-sang Ko, *Sam guk chi* (Seoul: Pakmun Sôkwan, 1917); Chu-wan Yi, *Sam guk chi* (Seoul: Yôngp'ung Sôkwan, 1918); In-kwang Yi, *Sam guk chi* (Seoul: Pakmun Sôkwan, 1926).

5. Yang-uk Cho, *Sam guk chi* (Seoul: Chakka Chôngsin, 1997); Kye-sông Yi, *Sam guk chi* (Seoul: Sôul Munhwasa, 1999); Yông Pak, *Sam guk chi* (Seoul: Taehyôn, 2000).

6. Ûn-yông Kim, *Sam guk chi* (Seoul: Mun'unsa, 1955); Sông-hak Yi, *Sam guk chi* (Seoul: Sônjin Munhwasa, 1958); Yông-hae Choi, *Sam guk chi* (Seoul: Chông'ûmsa, 1959).

7. Tong-ni Kim, Sun-wôn Hwang, and Yun-sôk Hô, *Sam guk chi* (Seoul: Pak'yôngsa, 1964).

8. Pak's translation has enjoyed the fortune of several reprints, the last of which arrived in the bookstore in 1997.

9. Chu-dong Yang, *Sam guk chi* (Seoul: Chinsun Sôkwan, 1976); Ki-hwan Pang, *Sam guk chi* (Seoul: Samhûisa, 1977); Pi-sôk Chông, *Sam guk chi* (Seoul: Taehyôn Munhwasa, 1981).

10. Hong-sin Kim, *Sam guk chi* (Seoul: Daesan, 2000).

11. Kim, Won-jung. *The Correct Version of "The Romance of Three Kingdoms"* (in Korean) (Seoul: Sinwôn munhwasa, 1999); Kyông-min Pak, *Digital Sam guk chi* (in Korean) (Seoul: Asea Munhwasa, 2000); Wôn-gi Chông, *Sam guk chi for Manias* (in Korean) (Seoul: Ch'ôngyang, 2000); Hang-kyu Yi, *One Volume Sam guk chi* (in Korean) (Seoul: Tonghae, 2000).

12. *"Sam Guk Chi" Dictionary* (in Korean) (Seoul: Pôm'usa, 2000); *Who's Who in Sam Guk Chi* (in Korean) (Seoul: Tûlnyôk, 2000).

13. Incidentally, *chang'gi*, the chess game loosely based on the novel, is still very popular among older people.

14. Man-su Yi, *Let's Learn One Thousand Chinese Characters in Three Kingdoms* (in Korean) (Seoul: Uriduri, 2004); *Let's Learn English through the Comic Book: Three Kingdoms* (Seoul: Ijibuk, 2002).

15. Yông-tu Kang, *Yônhap News* (in Korean), October 17, 2002.

16. This nine-volume woodblock text of Chin Su is available for viewing in the National Library of Korea in Seoul.

17. *The Annals of Chosôn Dynasty* (*Chosôn Wangjo Sillok;* 조선왕조실록) is an official record of Chosôn dynasty (1392–1910), which recorded meticulously information concerning

the everyday lifestyle of the general public as well as of the residents in the royal court. Originally written in Chinese characters, *The Annals* has lately been translated into the vernacular *han'gûl.*

18. Although not a single copy of the sixteenth-century translation of *Three Kingdoms* has been found, it is strongly suspected that *Three Kingdoms* was translated into the vernacular Korean script, since women were able to read the novel. In the Chosôn dynasty, women and commoners were prohibited from learning Chinese script.

19. *Three Kingdoms* has found its place in North Korea as well. My research shows that there are at least two new translations of the novel, both published in 1991, and both titled *Sam Guk Yôn Ûi* (삼국연의). The copies can easily be obtained in the West.

20. Wôn-jung Kim, *Correct Version of "Three Kingdoms,"* 15.

21. The popularity of Mun-yôl Yi's adaptation led the cartoonist Hûi-jae Yi to devote six months of his time, eighteen hours a day, to giving the novel a new form. While transforming the novel into drawing, the cartoonist Yi studied traditional Chinese costumes by watching the Chinese video version of *The Romance.* Hûi-jae Yi's cartoon of the same title was published in 2002. Hûi-jae Yi, *The Comic Book: Three Kingdoms* (in Korean) (Seoul: Aiseum, 2002).

22. Mun-yôl Yi, *Three Kingdoms* (in Korean) (Seoul: Min'ûmsa, 2002).

23. Myông Choê, "'Say No' to *Three Kingdoms*" (in Korean) *Han'guk ilbo* (*Han'guk Daily*), November 16, 2002.

24. Mun-yôl Yi, "*Three Kingdoms* Is Worth Reading" (in Korean), *Han'guk ilbo* (*Han'guk Daily*), November 22, 2002.

25. The interest in *Three Kingdoms* has lately crossed over to the visual space. With sponsorship from the Sichuan Cultural Ministry in China, *Tong'a Ilbo* (*Tong'a Daily* 동아일보) brought an exhibition, which features approximately two hundred artifacts gathered from the museums in Sichuan Province. The exhibition is scheduled to stayed in Seoul from the end of 2002 through March 17, 2003.

26. Yông-kyu Pak, *Three Kingdoms* (in Korean) (Seoul: Min'ûmsa, 2002), 8.

27. Hans Robert Jauss, *Toward an Aesthetic of Reception,* trans. Timothy Bahti, introduced by Paul de Man (Minneapolis: University of Minnesota Press, 1982), 58.

11

Studies of *Three Kingdoms* in the New Century

Bojun Shen

Translated by Kimberly Besio

From the 1980s on, research on *Three Kingdoms* has made considerable progress. In fact, "*Three Kingdoms* studies" has become one of the most outstanding subfields within scholarship on the Chinese classical novel. In the short space of twenty years (1980–2000), the Chinese mainland has published approximately one hundred books and monographs on *Three Kingdoms* research (including essay collections)— twenty times more than the previous thirty years. Further, during that same period more than sixteen hundred scholarly articles have been published, equivalent to more than ten times the number of the preceding thirty years. Over all, during the last twenty years research has far exceeded that of any other historical period in both breadth and depth; new opinions have been raised on a whole series of questions, which in turn have led to new breakthroughs. At this, the beginning of the twenty-first century, how do we foster emergent trends in *Three Kingdoms* research, and how do we refine our analysis? These are questions that deserve the careful reflection of all scholars in this field. In this essay I briefly describe my thoughts on several questions worthy of attention.

RESEARCH ON EDITIONS

In studying a book one must first be clear on its editions; this is an elementary fact of academic research. If you wish to thoroughly and systematically investigate a work, then clarifying the origin and development of its editions is a necessary foundation. No matter who we are, if we lack information on editions, then the accuracy, scientific nature, and comprehensiveness of our scholarship will be limited. To raise a typical example, some people often use the phrase: "The empire, long divided must unite, long united must divide" to epitomize the main theme of the novel, and to analyze Luo Guanzhong's thought. Actually, this offhand and expedient manner of speaking, although convenient, is inaccurate. First of all, the basis for this phrase is the first sentence of the Mao (i.e., Qing) edition of *Three Kingdoms*: "Here begins our tale. The empire long divided must unite; long united must divide."[1] None of the Ming editions have this sentence, and thus it cannot capriciously be used to represent Luo Guanzhong's authorial intentions. Second, for Luo Guanzhong "division" and "unity" do not have equal importance. Even though the work does show the course from unity to division that took place during the final years of the Eastern Han, that is merely the beginning of the entire book, and is a narration of established historical fact. The "division" Luo describes does not reflect his major preoccupation. In fact, it reflects just the opposite: he finds that period of history bitterly painful. The author expended most of his ink on the focal point of his description—the difficult transition from "division" to "unity," and the great achievements that came out of the bitter struggle by the various heroes to reunify the empire. If one wants to fully grasp the ideological connotations of a work, one must understand the differences between the various editions. If we want to raise the standards of research as a whole, then we must establish its basis in edition studies.

Prior to the 1980s, research on the various editions of *Three Kingdoms* was fairly superficial. Some scholars were aware that in addition to Mao Lun and Mao Zonggang's annotated and revised edition (the "Mao edition"), which circulated during the Qing Kangxi era (1662–1723), there were also other important editions, such as the Ming dynasty Jiajing (1522) edition entitled *The Vernacular Romance of the Three Kingdoms* (*Sanguo zhi tongsu yanyi*, the "Jiajing edition" or the "TS"). However, they generally accepted the thesis set out in 1929 by Zhenduo Zheng in his famous essay, "The Evolution of the *Romance of the Three Kingdoms*." He claimed: "These various editions all must come from the same source; they all take the Jiajing edition as their prototype."[2] From this thesis developed the following common misunderstandings: (1) The Jiajing edition was closest to Luo Guanzhong's original, or was in fact written by Luo. (2) *Three Kingdoms* derived only from one filiation of editions. (3) Among the numerous editions of the *Three Kingdoms* only the Jiajing and Mao editions were worth paying attention to. Therefore, for a long time, when discussing *Three Kingdoms*, all the histories of Chinese literature or of the novel would for the most part focus on the Mao edition, mentioning the Jiajing edition in passing only, and almost disdaining to mention other editions such as the *Sanguo zhi zhuan* editions and the Li Zhuowu commentary edition. This situation hampered, to a certain degree, efforts to raise the overall level of *Three Kingdoms* scholarship.

During the first few years of the 1980s people began to pay attention to research on the Jiajing edition. However, their basic understanding concerning the origin and development of editions of *Three Kingdoms* was still essentially the same as before.

Thus, even though during this period new possibilities began to emerge, we still did not attain any major breakthroughs. However, from the mid-1980s, especially after January 1987 when the Society for the Study of *Three Kingdoms* held a meeting on editions of *Three Kingdoms*, specialists' knowledge on the origin and development of editions deepened greatly, and these specialists produced a series of valuable new observations. First, actually not all Ming editions took the Jiajing edition as their prototype; the various editions titled *Sanguo zhi zhuan* form their own textual system. Second, in terms of textual development, the ancestral edition of the various editions titled *Sanguo zhi zhuan* was likely to be closer to Luo Guanzhong's original work, or perhaps even was Luo Guanzhong's original work (of course, the different *zhi zhuan* editions all may have had some alterations added by the engravers.) Further, while the Jiajing edition has been revised and polished, it still has quite a few errors and omissions. Third, as far as form goes, the editions of *Three Kingdoms* can be divided into three filiations: the *zhi zhuan*; the *Vernacular Romance* (*tongsu yanyi*); and Mao Zonggang's *Sanguo zhi yanyi*. According to these new assessments, since the Jiajing was not the edition closest to Luo Guanzhong's original work—and thus was even less likely to be Luo's original work—it would be unreliable to base textual research determining when the book was written on this edition and its annotations.[3] These findings broadened people's perspectives and assaulted old modes of thinking, propelling development throughout *Three Kingdoms* studies.

However, even now research on the editions of *Three Kingdoms* is neither deep enough, nor systematic enough. Academics have not yet done much research on the various editions of the *zhi zhuan* filiation. Our knowledge remains relatively sketchy concerning how each filiation of editions relates to the others in terms of the evolution of the story cycle, or how much mutual assimilation there might have been between these filiations. Some rather large divergences continue to exist regarding our understanding of the contents of different editions. For example, scholarly opinion is still poles apart on whether the plotline concerning Guan Suo or Hua Guansuo found in some editions was a part of Luo's original work, or was added in the process of copying and engraving. If these questions are not resolved, they will directly influence research on the two larger questions of when the book came into existence and the original appearance of Luo's work. Research on these two larger questions will in turn affect our stance on a whole series of issues. Therefore, we must continue to build upon the base already established in edition studies, and apply our advances in this area to promote further innovation throughout our research on *Three Kingdoms*.

CREATIVE RESEARCH APPLICATIONS

From a macroscopic viewpoint, if researchers on *Three Kingdoms* hope to make headway in this new century, then we must expand our consideration, and employ our research methods more creatively. This matter is extraordinarily complex. Here I will limit my discussion to three main points.

The wider cultural context

Beginning in the late 1980s, as people conducted research on *Three Kingdoms* from a number of levels and angles, literary research expanded to include cultural research. This was not only a reflection of the contemporary "cultural studies craze" but also a necessary step if the field of *Three Kingdoms* studies was to advance in both depth and breadth.

A work that is both profound in composition and abundant in detail is not merely a literary phenomenon; it is also a cultural phenomenon. This is clearly the case with a monumental work such as *Three Kingdoms*, which has had such a strong and long lasting influence on the spiritual lives and national identity of the Chinese people. Looking at it from a purely literary perspective, its historical contributions to the genre, its rich and colorful plot, its magnificent and multifaceted characterizations, its vast and yet tightly organized structure, its bold and forceful artistic style qualify *Three Kingdoms* to be considered one of China's great classical novels. At the same time, *Three Kingdoms* is an encyclopedic work into which is distilled a rich cultural content, and which contains a multifarious cultural significance. Thus, research on *Three Kingdoms* can be carried out from a cultural angle, as well as from a purely literary angle. For example, to account for the enormous influence of *Three Kingdoms* within Chinese culture, Manzi He transcended purely literary analysis and added an explanation taking into account popular views of history. He has said that: "*Three Kingdoms* was truly China's first successful historical novel . . . however, that it enjoys such a deep and broad influence cannot be totally attributed to the artistic qualities of the novel itself, nor can we give Luo Guanzhong and Mao Zonggang all the credit for how widely the story cycle has spread and how deeply the characters have entered the people's hearts."[4] He points out that an even more important factor in the novel's enormous influence is that from the Southern Dynasties on, anyone wanting to understand history would pay special attention to the crucial historical juncture of the Three Kingdoms period; further, various artistic forms aided in the dissemination of the story cycle. This explanation of the novel's popularity is clearly more comprehensive and more profound than one based on the novel alone.

In addition, from the mid-1980s on, at the same time that we were making headway in literary research on *Three Kingdoms*, some scholars have also examined *Three Kingdoms* from the angle of practical applications such as personnel, strategy, management, and the art of leadership and have published a number of works on "applied research." That is, they have conducted research based on the assumption that *Three Kingdoms* crystallizes the ancient wisdom of the Chinese people, and thus may offer enlightenment on how to live our daily lives. This is entirely possible. Of course, this "applied research" does not constitute the main body of research on *Three Kingdoms*, much less the whole of *Three Kingdoms* research.

In this new century it is even more imperative that we conduct broad-ranging research against the wider backdrop of Chinese culture. Our studies should take at least three directions. The first is that we must continue to explore the special qualities and literary achievements of *Three Kingdoms*. The second is that we should consider the relationships between *Three Kingdoms* and Chinese culture, and mine the novel for its cultural content. The third is that we should continue to elucidate the vast influence *Three Kingdoms* has had on our national spirit and character. In this way we can broaden and enhance *Three Kingdoms* research.

NEW METHODS

As the history of academic research testifies, the renovation of research methods is important. The issue of research methods is not merely a matter of what kinds of tools one uses, but is also a philosophical issue that has implications for the orderliness of one's methodology and the depth of one's epistemology. Every historical advance in our research of classical novels has been related to a change in our research methods. The course of development in research on *Three Kingdoms* over the last twenty-one years proves this point. For example, quite a few scholars have given brilliant expositions on the characterization of Zhuge Liang. Among these works, two influential representatives are Zhensheng Qiu's essay "A Single Feather in an Empyrean of a Myriad Ages" and Xianghua Chen's monograph *Research on the History of Zhuge Liang's Characterization.*[5] Yet Jun Huang opened up an entirely new avenue of inquiry when he carried out an investigation based on the concept of motifs. Huang pointed out that Zhuge Liang struggled to perform what was considered impossible, and dared to compete with heaven, ultimately failing in the attempt. His spirit, and his final tragic outcome, was actually an enduring motif in our nation's literature including myths, legends, and fiction. The process whereby Zhuge Liang evolved from a historical figure into an artistic image must have been influenced and conditioned by our racial memory of ancient mythological tragic heroes—especially Kua Fu. "The extremely solemn and heroic struggle launched by such figures as Kua Fu and Zhuge Liang against nature and the mandate of heaven can only be continued from one generation to the next by passing on the torch."[6] This kind of exposition can provide some new insights. In the new century, as people's thinking takes yet another step away from old ideas, new literary theories and new research methods will unceasingly come to the fore. We ought to approach them with an open mind and an eye to the facts, and conscientiously differentiate, select, and assimilate them into our research in order to further our studies of *Three Kingdoms*.

NEW VIEWPOINTS

Academic research is a process of constant inquiry and seeking after the truth. This eternally requires the courage to break away from old ideas and point out new views. In the past twenty-one years, quite a few researchers have upheld the principle of "liberating thinking and seeking truth from facts" and have had the courage to think independently. They have questioned paradigms, expanded the ideas of previous scholars, raised new considerations, or opened up new fields of inquiry, and have thus made gratifying progress on a whole series of questions. For example, in the early 1980s some scholars made quite a stir when, basing themselves on European literary theories of narrative that posited a pattern of movement "from stereotypical models to individualized models," they pointed out that the characters in *Three Kingdoms* were brilliant examples of stereotypical models.[7] Some scholars disputed this, feeling that the concept of "stereotypical model" was not scientific. Shangsheng Liu then went a step further by proposing a new category. He felt that the characters in *Three Kingdoms* represent a high point in the art of stylization, and thus these stylized images became stereotypes.[8] This insight enhanced our understanding of the novel. In this new century we ought to maintain this boldly creative spirit, and strive for new accomplishments worthy of our time.

HISTORY OF THE FIELD

In the last twenty-one years it is certainly true that there have been quite a few excellent works within *Three Kingdoms* studies that evidence deep thinking, novel viewpoints, and original ideas. However, there have also been a relatively large number of no more than average pieces on hackneyed topics; they are superficial in content and lack new ideas. Some essays, one can tell at a glance, are just the same old rubbish, and the author, having no outstanding ideas of his own, cannot even begin to comment on the ideas of others. Similar situations are common in other fields of research. Of course, the reasons why mediocre work exists in such abundance are quite complex. Some research is mediocre because the level of analysis is not very high; some is mediocre because there isn't sufficient effort dedicated to the scholarship; and other work is pedestrian because the attitude toward scholarship is not rigorous enough (perhaps it was cobbled together at the last minute for the sake of a tenure or promotion review, or hastily done in order to secure an invitation to a scholarly conference, or written with only a smattering of knowledge about the subject). In addition to all these reasons for second-rate scholarship, there is one more important reason—a lack of understanding regarding the history of the field.

In any area of scholarship there will be a process of origination and development, and continual enrichment and refinement by gradual accretion. It is only when we have fully grasped the research achievements that have already been made that we can speak of development and creation; it is only by standing on the shoulders of those who have gone before us that we can see further than they did. Therefore, in researching any problem one must first confront its research history to understand how much and to what extent others have already done research, what viewpoints they have formulated, and what problems they have encountered. Only after such a course of action can one determine the starting point of one's own research, and select an appropriate angle from which to proceed.

This is established scholarly procedure. If one is not sufficiently familiar with the research history of a problem, or worse yet doesn't know anything about it, and works behind closed doors just relying on "impressions upon reading" then we will inevitably end up with the awkward situation of "the blind leading the blind."

If one does not know the history of the field, then choosing a thesis will be a capricious process. Often one will just research whatever happens to be "hot," or whatever is easy to put one's hand to; and this almost certainly leads to the creation of a tired old retread. Of course, this is not to say that one cannot do research on topics others have researched before. As long as one can come up with new materials, new viewpoints, or new methods to apply to an old topic, one can still write a perfectly fine essay. However, with an insufficient basis in thought and skill, an old topic can easily lead to old contents. Conversely, there are some valuable topics that have been neglected because researchers are ignorant about previous scholarship. For example, in the past ten years no more than a smattering of articles have appeared on the utilization of parallelism within the novel, or the use of poetry, rhymed prose, ballads, and proverbs. Further, while quite a few works mention in passing the unique qualities of the language in *Three Kingdoms*, only one or two articles have been written that really focus on this topic. This cannot but be considered a great deficiency.

If one's understanding of the history of the field is insufficient, there will inevitably be some limits to how much one can refine one's viewpoint, and the following three circumstances will be difficult to avoid. First, one's starting point will tend to be low; second, one's thinking will tend to be narrow; and third, one's ideas will tend to replicate those of others. For example, during the 1950s, under the influence of leftist thinking, some people simply denounced the ideological tendency toward "respecting Liu and devaluing Cao" in *Three Kingdoms* as "feudal orthodox ideology." Since the economic reforms of the 1980s this idea has been discussed anew, and a number of scholars have already pointed out that the reason why Luo Guanzhong "respected Liu" was not simply because Liu Bei was surnamed Liu. (Liu Biao and Liu Zhang were also surnamed Liu, and their family history was even more illustrious than Liu Bei's, however, they consistently met with derision. Thr emperors Huan and Ling of the Han were both surnamed Liu and they were even more roundly criticized.) Rather, this attitude was due to the fact that from the first the Liu Bei camp had the slogan "above serve the nation, below pacify the masses" and unstintingly devoted their efforts to reunifying the nation in order to restore the Han. Thus, from the Song and Yuan periods on, the greater populace admired them. The qualities of the leaders of the Liu camp—the benevolence of Liu Bei, the wisdom of Zhuge Liang, the righteousness of Guan Yu and others like him—are all in keeping with the morality of the masses. The reason why Luo Guanzhong "devalued Cao" was that Cao Cao acts as a stereotypical archcareerist, who often butchered the common people and ruined men of talent. Luo described in affirmative terms Cao's great enterprise of unifying the North and his unusual courage and resourcefulness, and thus did not just capriciously belittle Cao. From this we can see that Luo's tendency to "respect Liu and devalue Cao" was primarily a reflection of the attitude of the masses, which tended to adopt the standard of "support me and you're a prince, mistreat me and you're an enemy" when supporting or criticizing feudal governments and feudal statesmen. This viewpoint has already gained common acceptance in *Three Kingdoms* research circles. If today some researcher were still to use "feudal orthodox ideology" to explain the tendency in *Three Kingdoms* to "respect Liu and devalue Cao," then at best they would be repeating interpretations already discussed in the 1950s, and absolutely could not claim to have a "new viewpoint." One often sees some researchers spending a lot of energy writing an essay that they themselves feel is pretty innovative, but in reality does nothing but repeat opinions other people have long since already described. This occurs because they were not clear on the history and the present state of the field.

If one is unaware of previous scholarship, and also has spent insufficient energy conscientiously coming to grips with the source material, one's statements on facts will inevitably be inaccurate, and one can even make a fool of oneself over some fairly elementary questions. For example, for a fairly long period of time, people have mistakenly believed that *Three Kingdoms* "altogether describes over 400 individuals." During the last several years several comparatively authoritative histories of Chinese literature and of the Chinese novel have been published and most describe *Three Kingdoms* in this way. As early as 1984 I wrote an article pointing out that this description had its origins in the "*Sanguo zhi* zongliao," a chart that appears at the front of the Jiajing edition of *Three Kingdoms*. Actually, "*Sanguo zhi* zongliao" is arranged according to the history *Chronicle of the Three Kingdoms* (*Sanguo zhi*). A number of figures appear in it—such as Cao Cao's wives and most of his sons, Cao Pi's wives and most of his sons, as well as several famous literati such as Ruan Jie and Ji Kang—who do not appear in the novel. Conversely, some figures in *Three Kingdoms*, such as the Zhang brothers who led the Yellow Scarves uprising, "Master Still Water" Sima Hui, and Zhuge Liang's good friends Cui Zhouping, Shi Guangyuan, and Meng Gongwei, all cannot be found in the "*Sanguo zhi* zongliao." From this it is obvious that the "*Sanguo zhi* zongliao" is not a chart of the characters in the novel, and fundamentally cannot be used as a basis for calculating the number of individuals in the novel. According to an initial count of the Mao edition of *Three Kingdoms*, there are more than 980 named characters in the novel.[9] Unfortunately, some researchers have neither paid attention to my article nor have they rigorously checked their sources, and thus continue to pass on this outmoded and mistaken idea. This diminishes the scientific quality of their work. In view of this situation, in 1992 I wrote a second article further pointing out that the "*Sanguo zhi* zongliao" altogether listed 511 figures (after recently rechecking the numbers once again I realize that three figures were listed twice, thus the real number should be 508.) Past scholars had not counted carefully, and had only roughly calculated the number. I thus argued that even if we were basing the idea that "*Three Kingdoms* describes over 400 individuals" on the "*Sanguo zhi* zongliao" it is still not accurate.

Having made this comparison of the "Zongliao" and the novel, we can determine that the summary "*Three Kingdoms* describes over 400 individuals" is the product of sloppy scholarship, and is completely incorrect. Based on the number of entries in the characters section that I edited for the *Dictionary of Three Kingdoms* there are over 1200 individuals mentioned in the novel; among these over 1000 are given full names.[10] Among China's great novels it is truly the one with the most characters.[11] This originally was only a small issue, but due to inertia, it became a habitual error that has gone uncorrected for years. I hope that in the future researchers will call attention to this and not continue to pass on erroneous information.

In sum, these facts suggest that by valuing and strengthening research on the history of the field we will be able to improve the overall quality of research on *Three Kingdoms*. To this end we ought to yearly compile an index of works on *Three Kingdoms*, systematically collect and collate new sources, and write articles specializing on this topic, in order to point the way for future research.

DIGITALIZATION

Humanity is entering the digital information age. As computer technology and the Internet have flourished, "digitalization" has become a global trend, and has dramatically changed our lives, work, and scholarship. Against this backdrop, how we can use computer and Internet technology to open up and develop the field of *Three Kingdoms* studies has become an issue that we urgently need to confront and explore.

Up until now, digitalization and computer research has remained basically nonexistent in the area of *Three Kingdoms* studies. Certainly quite a few researchers have begun to use computers, but they only use them as writing and bibliographic tools in place of pens and note cards. And while quite a few researchers have started to "surf the Net," they primarily use the Internet to send and receive e-mails, and to inquire about and pass on some academic information. But due to the limitations of our knowledge, using computer and Internet technology to advance analytical research on *Three Kingdoms* is still in its formative and preliminary stages. Our efforts have been scattered on a whole range of research issues. Thus, not only has there been a lot of repetition in our efforts, but also our resources are often unavoidably incomplete. Accordingly, our ways of thinking have been parochial, and our results one-sided and random. At this, the threshold of a new century, the digitalization of *Three Kingdoms* scholarship—the use of computer and Internet technologies to carry out research in order to render our research more modern, consistent, and scientific—will certainly accelerate achievements within *Three Kingdoms* studies. There will be a relatively large number of breakthroughs on important questions. Consequently, *Three Kingdoms* studies will make a qualitative leap, effectively enhancing and advancing our research.

According to our current understanding, a *Three Kingdoms* studies digitalization project initially ought to include the following activities:

1. Digitalize editions of *Three Kingdoms*. As of now several compact disk versions of *Three Kingdoms* have been published, and the novel has already been put on several sites on the Internet. However, these compact disk and Web editions of *Three Kingdoms* are essentially based on the widely available typeset and punctuated Mao edition, and thus are only appropriate for a general reader. If we want to use computers to carry out in-depth and detailed academic research, then we must digitalize all the various editions of *Three Kingdoms*. This is a prerequisite for using computers to develop our research on *Three Kingdoms*. Only if we complete this fundamental project can we develop an array of research methods analyzing *Three Kingdoms*.

2. Use computers to carry out comparisons of editions. This will aid us in determining the process by which the novel formed, and the developmental relationship of the various editions.

3. Search for and examine texts and illustrations.

4. Compile and research commentaries.

5. Establish a database of linguistic resources for *Three Kingdoms*.

6. Establish databases, such as a character database, a database of official positions, a geographical database, and databases of battles, weapons, historical sites, researchers, articles, and books. All these databases could be Web-based.

The *Three Kingdoms* digitalization project would entail intersections with scientific research, and would require great knowledge on the part of scholars developing this research—both about computers and about the classic novel. *Three Kingdoms* specialists will need to collaborate with computer specialists. Such collaboration will be crucial for completion of this important project.

At the same time, since both the amount and difficulty of the work related to the *Thee Kingdoms* digitalization project will be enormous, we must unite all the people and institutions with an interest in this project both within China and internationally. We must pool our resources in every way, allocate tasks, work cooperatively, and unite to tackle key problems. We may then collectively share the resulting wealth of information.

ACADEMIC EXCHANGE BETWEEN CHINA AND THE REST OF THE WORLD

Looking back on the course of *Three Kingdoms* studies, we see that exchange between scholars in China and the rest of the world has played a decisive role in spurring research. First, for historical reasons, it has been more convenient for scholars of other countries to get hold of rare sources (such as some rare editions), and thus they can provide us with important references. Second, due to differences in the structure of knowledge and work environment, the approaches and methods by which scholars outside of China conduct research have their own unique strengths and can profitably be incorporated into Chinese scholarship. Third, since their social and cultural backgrounds are different from those of the Chinese, scholars outside of China inevitably have a somewhat different understanding of quite a few issues—this can teach us some useful lessons. For all these reasons we should adopt attitudes of sincerity and cordiality, open-mindedness and self-confidence in our mutual dealings with our colleagues throughout the world. We should exchange ideas as equals, learn from each other, adopt each other's strengths in order to offset our own weaknesses, and together promote academic development.

Let us take research on editions as an example. In 1968 when we still held the erroneous belief that all Ming editions derived from the Jiajing edition, the eminent Japanese scholar Tamaki Ogawa led the way by pointing out that quite a few Ming dynasty editions published after the Wanli period included the plotline concerning Hua Guansuo. This plotline had been completely absent from the Jiajing edition. Thus, it was obvious that these editions could not have originated from the Jiajing edition.[12] In 1976, the famous Australian scholar of Chinese descent Cunren Liu wrote an article raising objections to the prejudice that belittled the *Sanguo zhi zhuan* system of texts. He wrote that: "Although those editions of the *Sanguo zhi zhuan* that we can see today were produced in the Wanli and even the Tianqi periods, and thus long after *The Vernacular Romance of the Three Kingdoms* (1522), it is distinctly possible that the text on which they were based (no matter whether it was one ancestral text or many texts) existed before 1522."[13] During the 1980s the Australian scholar Anne E. McLaren, and the Japanese scholars Bunkyo Kin, Satoshi Nakagawa, Nozomi Ueda, and others did significant research on editions of *Three Kingdoms*, and came up with some excellent ideas.[14] In the 1990s the English scholar Andrew West published the monograph *A Study of Editions of "Romance of the Three Kingdoms"* in which he conducted what is to date the most comprehensive and detailed survey of all extant editions of *Three Kingdoms*.[15] His research methods were innovative, and his argument was quite compelling. These studies have been very helpful to Chinese scholars, and have generally received favorable comments from them. Conversely, our colleagues overseas praise the results achieved by Chinese scholars from the 1980s on in their research and ordering of editions. This kind of mutual exchange has been a strong impetus to further research on editions of *Three Kingdoms*.

In addition to this, in the area of research methodology work such as that of the Russian scholar Boris Riftin on the relationships between *Romance of the Three Kingdoms* and folk literature and that of the Japanese scholar Hidetaka Ootsuka, which explores the origins in vernacular literary works of characters and episodes depicted in *Three Kingdoms*, have been very instructive for us and offer worthwhile lessons.

Unfortunately, because avenues of communication are too few, up until now exchange between Chinese scholars and those from other parts of the world has been rare. There are still many gaps in such areas as mutual exchange of news, and our incorporation of each other's research results. In this new century we ought to strengthen cultural exchange between China and the rest of the world, and transform cooperation between scholars into innumerable great achievements in *Three Kingdoms* research.

A new century has already dawned. Looking forward to the future prospects of research on *Three Kingdoms* we are full of confidence. Let us make sincere efforts to further advance our research so that this great classic may shine ever more brightly.

NOTES

1. Moss Roberts, trans., *Three Kingdoms: A Historical Novel*, attributed to Luo Guanzhong (Berkeley and Los Angeles: University of California Press, 1991), 5.

2. Originally published in *Xiaoshuo Yuebao* 20, no. 10 (1929): 1548–78; later included in Zhenduo Zheng, *Zhongguo Wenxue Yanjiu*, vol. 1 (Beijing: Zuojia chubanshe, 1957), and *Zheng Zhenduo Wenji* (Beijing: Renmin wenxue chubanshe, 1988), 200.

3. Ying Zhang and Su Chen, "Youguan *San Guo Yanyi* chengshu niandai he banben yanbian wenti de jidian yiyi," in *Ming Qing xiaoshuo yanjiu* 5 (Zhongguo Wenlian chuban gongsi, 1987), 26–40; Xianghua Chen, *Zhuge Liang xingxiangshi yanjiu* (Hangzhou: Zhejiang guji chubanshe, 1990), 276–77; Zhaoxin Zhou, *San Guo yanyi kaoping* (Beijing: Beijing Daxue chubanshe, 1990), 304–6; Bojun Shen, "*Jiaoli ben San Guo Yanyi*, Qianyan" (Jiangsu: Jiangsu guji chubanshe, 1992), 4–7.

4. Manzi He, "Zai pingjia *San Guo Yanyi* de wenxue chengjiu yiqian," *San Guo Yanyi Xuekan* 1 (1985): 153–57.

5. Zhensheng Qiu, "Wangu yunxiao yi yu mao—Zhuge Liang yishu xingxiang de shengming li," *Wenxue Pinglun*, no. 1 (1985): 123–31; Xianghua Chen, *Zhuge Liang xingxiang yanjiu*.

6. Jun Huang, "Yu yu Tiangong shi bi gao—Zhuge Liang xingxiangshi waibu yanjiu qianyi," in Huiwu Li and Luo fei Tan eds. *San Guo Yanyi yu Jingzhou*, (Zhengzhou: Zhongzhou guji chubanshe, September 1993), 313–17.

7. Jifu Fu, "*San Guo* renwu shi leixinghua dianxing de guanghui fanben," *Shehui kexue zhanxian*, no. 4 (1989): 275–85; also in *San Guo yanyi yanjiu ji* (Sichuan: Sichuan sheng shehui kexue yuan chubanshe, 1993), 101–8.

8. Shangsheng Liu, *Zhongguo gudai xiaoshuo yishu shi* (Changsha: Hunan shifan daxue chubanshe, 1993), 112–21.

9. Bojun Shen, "*San Guo* renwu shu geng duo," *Sichuan Ribao*, June 23, 1984, 3.

10. Bojun Shen and Liangxiao Tan eds. *Sanguo yanyi cidian* (Chengdu: Bashu shushe, 1989).

11. Bojun Shen, "*San Guo Yanyi* jiujing xie le duoshao renwu," *Renmin Ribao* Overseas Edition, April 24, 1992; later collected in Shen, *San Guo Mantan* (Chengdu: Bashu shushe, 1995), 2–3, and in Shen, *San Guo Manhua* (Chengdu: Sichuan renmin chubanshe, 2000), 3–4.

12. Tamaki Ogawa, *Chugoku shosetsu shi kenkyu* (Tokyo: Iwanami Shoten, 1968.)

13. Cunren Liu, "Luo Guanzhong jiangshi xiaoshuo zhi zhenwei xingzhi," *Xianggang Zhongwen Daxue Zhongguo wenhua yanjiusuo xuebao* 8, no.1 (December 1976): 169–234; also collected in Shide Liu, ed., *Zhongguo gudai xiaoshuo yanjiu* (Shanghai: Shanghai guji chubanshe, 1983), 60.

14. Anne E. McLaren, "Chantefables and the Textual Evolution of the *San-Kuo-Chih yen-I*," *T'oung Pao* 71 (1985): 159–227; Bunkyo Kin, "On the Editions of *San Kuo Yen I* or *Stories of Three Kingdoms* Printed in Hokkien Province," *Shukan Toyogaku* 61 (May 1989): 43–64; Satoshi Nakagawa "A Study of Several Editions of *San-kuo yen-I*" *Shukan Toyogaku* 61 (May 1989): 65–84; Nozomi Ueda, "Sangoku Engi hanbon shiron," *Toyo Bunka* 71 (1990): 151–189. All the above essays have been translated into Chinese and collected in Zhaoxin Zhou, ed., *Sanguo yanyi congkao* (Beijing: Beijing University Press, 1995).

15. Christopher West (Wei An), *Sanguo yanyi banben kao* (Shanghai: Shanghai guji chubanshe, 1996.)

Bibliography

Arlington, L. C. *The Chinese Drama from Earliest Times until Now.* Shanghai: Benjamin Bloom, 1930).

Arlington, L. C., and Harold Acton. *Famous Chinese Plays.* New York: Russell and Russell, 1937.

Arthur, Chris. "The Telefaithful." *Contemporary Review* 268, no. 1563 (1996): 194–204.

Besio, Kimberly. "The Disposition of Defiance: Zhang Fei as a Comic Hero of Yuan *Zaju*." PhD diss., University of California, Berkeley, 1992.

———. "Enacting Loyalty: History and Theatricality in 'The Peach Orchard Pledge.'" *CHINOPERL Papers* 18 (1995): 61–81.

———. "Zhang Fei in Yuan Vernacular Literature: Legend, Heroism and History in the Reproduction of the Three Kingdoms Story Cycle." *Journal of Sung-Yuan Studies* 27 (1997): 63–98.

Bo, J. "TV Producer's Career Sees Dramatic Rise." *China Daily,* January 15, 2003.

Brewitt-Taylor, C. H., trans. *Romance of the Three Kingdoms.* By Lo Kuan-chung. Rutland, VT: Charles E. Tuttle, 1959.

Burnett, Mark Thornton, and Ramona Wray. *Shakespeare, Film, Fin de Siècle.* New York: St. Martin's Press, 2000.

Chen, Du 陳度. "Cao Cao yu Liu Bei jiujing shei shi yingxiong? 曹操與劉備究竟誰是英雄" *Dazhong dianshi* 2 (1995): 69.

Chen, Jack. *The Chinese Theatre.* London: Dennis Dobson, 1948.

Chen, Liang 陳亮. *Chen Liang ji* 陳亮集. Beijing: Zhonghua shuju, 1987.

Chen, Shou 陳壽. *Sanguo zhi* 三國志. Beijing: Zhonghua shuju, 1982.

———. *Sanguo zhi.* Changsha: Yuelu shushe, 1998.

Chen, Xianghua 陳翔華. *Zhuge Liang xingxiangshi yanjiu* 諸葛亮形象史研究. Hangzhou: Zhejiang guji chubanshe, 1990.

Chen, Yaxian 陳亞先. "Cao Cao yu Yang Xiu 曹操與楊修." Shanghai Jingju Company's August 2 revised manuscript, 1995 (revised from original 1987 version).

———. Interview by Elizabeth Wichmann-Walczak. Shanghai, November 15, 1995.

———. Interview by Elizabeth Wichmann-Walczak. Shanghai, March 15, 1996.

———. Telephone interview by Elizabeth Wichmann-Walczak. Honolulu and Shanghai, April 15, 1999.

Chen, Zhouchang 陳周昌. "*Sanguo zhi tongsu yanyi* xingcheng guocheng lunlue三國志通俗演義形成過程論略." In Editorial Section, *Sanguo yanyi yanjiu ji*, 306–25.

"China's Softly, Softly Bid to Woo Taipei." *Australian Financial Review*, December 4, 2001, 11.

"Chinese Society Has New Set of Role Models, New Kinds of Idols." *Xinhua News Agency*, January 16, 2003.

Cho, Yang-uk 조양욱. *Sam Guk Chi* 삼국지. Seoul: Chakka Chôngsin, 1997.

Choê, Myông 최명. "'Say No' to Three Kingdoms." [In Korean.] *Han'guk Daily* (*Han'guk ilbo* 한국일보), November 16, 2002.

Choi, Yông-hae 최영해. *Sam Guk Chi* 삼국지. Seoul: Chông'ûmsa, 1959.

Chông, Pi-sôk 정비석. *Sam Guk Chi* 삼국지. Seoul: Taehyôn Munhwasa, 1981.

Chông, Wôn-gi 정원기. *Sam Guk Chi for Manias* [In Korean.] Seoul: Ch'ôngyang, 2000.

Chow, C. "Still Fitting after All These Years." *Straits Times*, January 17, 2002.

Corrigan, Robert W., ed. *Sophocles: "Oedipus the King," "Philoctetes," "Electra," "Antigone" in Modern Translations*. 2nd ed. New York: Dell, 1968.

de Bary, W. Theodore, Wing-tsit Chan, and Burton Watson, comps. *Sources of Chinese Tradition*. New York: Columbia University Press, 1960.

Diesinger, Gunter. *Vom General zum Gott: Kuan Yu (gest. 220 n. Chr.) und seine "posthume Karriere."* Frankfurt : Haag und Herschen, 1984.

Dolby, William. "Yuan Drama." In *Chinese Theater*, edited by Colin Mackerras, 32–59. Honolulu: University of Hawaii Press, 1983.

Duara, Prasenjit. "Superscribing Symbols: The Myth of Guandi, Chinese God of War." *Journal of Asian Studies* 47 (1988): 778–95.

Eco, Umberto. *The Role of the Reader: Explorations in the Semiotics of Texts*. Bloomington: Indiana University Press, 1979.

Editorial Section of *Journal of Social Science Research* 社會科學研究業刊編部 and the Literature Institute of the Sichuan Academy of Social Science 四川省社會科學院文學研究所, ed. *Sanguo yanyi yanjiu ji* 三國演義研究集. Sichuan: Sichuan sheng shehui kexue yuan chubanshe, 1983.

Fan, Ye 范曄. *Hou Han shu* 後漢書. Changsha: Yuelu shushe, 1994.

Fang, Achilles. *The Chronicle of the Three Kingdoms (220–265): Chapters 69–79 from the Tzu Chih T'ung Chien of Ssu-ma Kuang*. 2 vols. Cambridge, MA: Harvard University Press, 1952, 1965.

Fang, Xuanling 房玄齡. *Jin shu* 晉書. Beijing: Zhonghua shuju, 1974.

Feng, Fanying 馮凡英. "Yibu meiyou chaoji mingxing de youxiu dianshiju 一部沒有超級名星的优秀電視劇." *Dazhong dianshi* 1 (1995): 60.

Feng, J. "TV Series 'The Romance of Three Kingdoms' Wins Acclaim." *Beijing Review*, March 27–April 2, 1995, 30.

Feng, Youlan 馮友蘭. *Zhongguo zhexueshi* 中國哲學史. Shanghai: Shangwu yinshuguan, 1935.

Feng, Yu 馮瑜. "Ping Cao Cao de san xiao 評曹操的三笑." *Dazhong dianshi* 3 (1995): 69–70.

Freud, Sigmund. *Civilization and Its Discontents.* and Company: New York: W.W. Norton, 1961.

Frye, Northrop. *Anatomy of Criticism*. New York: Atheneum, 1969.

Fu, Jifu 傅繼馥. "*Sanguo* renwu shi leixinghua dianxing de guanghui fanben 三國人物是類型化典型的光輝範本." *Shehui kexue zhanxian* 4 (1989): 275–85.

Gao, Wenbi 高文畢. "Dianshi Sanguo Yanyi shi yibu zui chenggong de gudina mingzhu gaibianju 電視三國演義是一部最成功的古典名著改變劇." *Dazhong dianshi* 4 (1995): 68.

———. "Zhizuo daxing dianshi lianju de kunnan 制作大型電視連續劇的困難." *Dazhong dianshi* 1 (1995): 60.

Gao, Yiming 高一鳴. Interview by Elizabeth Wichmann-Walczak. Beijing, December 3, 1995.

Gitlin, Todd. "Flat and Happy." *Wilson Quarterly* 17, no. 4 (1993): 47–49.

Gomery, Douglas. "As the Dial Turns." *Wilson Quarterly* 17, no. 4 (1993): 41–46.

Goodall, Peter. *High Culture, Popular Culture: The Long Debate*. St. Leonards, Australia: Allen & Unwin, 1995.

Gu, Yuqian 顧宇倩. "Yuan zaju Sanguo xi ticai tanyuan 元雜劇三國戲題材探源." *Yangzhou Daxue xuebao* 1 (1999): 28–31.

Guo, Yingde 郭英德. "Qian tan Yuan zaju Sanguo xi de yishu tezheng 淺談元雜劇三國戲的藝術特徵." In Editorial Section, *Sanguo yanyi yanjiu ji*, 129–39.

Hayes, James. "Specialists and Written Materials in the Village World." In Johnson, Nathan, and Rawski, *Popular Culture in Late Imperial China*, 75–111.

He, Manzi 何滿子. "Zai pingjia Sanguo Yanyi de wenxue chengjiu yiqian 在評價三國演義的文學成就以前." *Sanguo Yanyi Xuekan* 1 (1985): 153–57.

He, Shu 何澍. Interview by Elizabeth Wichmann-Walczak. Shanghai, November 30, 1995.

Hegel, Robert E. "Distinguishing Levels of Audiences for Ming-Ch'ing Vernacular Literature." In Johnson, Nathan, and Rawski, *Popular Culture in Late Imperial China*, 112–42.

Henry, Eric. "Chu-ko Liang in the Eyes of His Contemporaries." *Harvard Journal of Asiatic Studies* 52, no.2 (December 1992): 589–612.

Holub, Robert C. *Reception Theory: A Critical Introduction*. New York: Methuen, 1984.

Homer. *Iliad*. Translated by E.V. Rieu. Harmondsworth, England: Penguin, 1950.

Hong, Junhao. *The Internationalization of Television in China: The Evolution of Ideology, Society, and Media Reform since the Reform*. Westport, CT: Praeger, 1998.

Hsia, C. T. *The Classic Chinese Novel*. New York: Columbia University Press, 1968.

Hu, Dongsheng 胡冬生. Interview by Elizabeth Wichmann-Walczak. Beijing, November 28, 1995.

Hu,Yong 胡勇. "Xiyi dianshi lianxuju Sanguo Yanyi de zhuti 析疑電視連續劇三國演義的主題." *Dazhong dianshi* 5 (1995): 16.

Huang, Huajie黃華節. *Guan Yu de renge yu shenge* 關公的人格與神格. Taipei: Taibei shangwu yinshuguan, 1967.

Huang, Jun 黃鈞. "Yu yu Tiangong shi bi gao—Zhuge Liang xingxiangshi waibu yanjiu qianyi 欲與天公試比高—諸葛亮形象史外部研究淺議." In Li, Huiwu 李悔吾and Tan, Luofei 憚洛菲 ed. *Sanguo yanyi yu Jingzhou*, 313–17. Zhengzhou: Zhongzhou guji chubanshe, 1993.

Huayang guozhi 華陽國志. *Sibu congkan chubian* 四部叢刊初編. Vol. 65. Shanghai: Shangwu yinshuguan, 1929.

Idema, Wilt. *Chinese Vernacular Fiction: The Formative Period*. Leiden: E. J. Brill, 1974.

———. "The Founding of the Han Dynasty in Early Drama: The Autocratic Suppression of Popular Debunking." In *Thought and Law in Qin and Han China: Studies Presented to Anthony Hulsewe on the Occasion of His Eightieth Birthday*, edited by Wilt Idema and Erik Zurcher, 181–207. Leiden: E. J. Brill, 1990.

———. "The Remaking of an Unfilial Hero: Some Notes on the Earliest Dramatic Adaptations of 'The Story of Hsüeh Jen-Kuei.'" In *As the Twig is Bent . . . Essays in Honour of Frits Vos*, edited by Erika De Poorter, 83–111. Amsterdam: J. C. Gieben, 1990.

———. "Some Aspects of *Pai-yueh-t'ing*: Script and Performance." In *Proceedings of International Conference on Kuan Han-Ch'ing*, edited by Zeng Yongyi 曾永義. 3–23. Taipei: Xingzhengyuan wenhua jianshe weiyuanhui, 1994.

Ikegami, Eiko. "A Sociological Theory of Publics: Identity and Culture as Emergent Properties in Networks." *Social Research* 67, no. 4 (Winter 2000): 989–1029.

Innis, Harold Adams. *The Bias of Communication*. Toronto: University Press of Toronto, 1951.

Jauss, Hans Robert. *Toward an Aesthetic of Reception*. Translated by Timothy Bahti. Introduction by Paul de Man. Minneapolis: University of Minnesota Press, 1982.

Jiang, Yifan 蔣一凡. "San xiang Sanguo 三想三國." *Dazhong dianshi* 1 (1995): 70.

Johnson, David, Andrew J. Nathan , and Evelyn S. Rawski, eds. *Popular Culture in Late Imperial China*. Berkeley and Los Angeles: University of California Press, 1985.

Kalvodova, Sis Vladimir, and Joseph Vanis. *Chinese Theatre*. Translated by Iris Unwin. London: Spring Books, n.d.

Kang, Yông-tu 강영두. *Yônhap News* [in Korea], October 17, 2002.

Kim, Hong-sin 김홍신. *Sam Guk Chi*삼국지. Seoul: Daesan, 2000.

Kim, Tong-ni 김동리, Sun-wôn Hwang 황순원, and Yun-sôk Hô 허윤석. *Sam Guk Chi* 삼국지. Seoul: Pak'yôngsa, 1964.

Kim, Ûn-yông 김은영. *Sam Guk Chi* 삼국지. Seoul: Mun'unsa, 1955.

Kim, Won-jung 김원중. *The Correct Version of "The Romance of Three Kingdoms"* [in Korea]. Seoul: Sinwôn munhwasa, 1999.

Kin, Bunkyo 金文京. "On the Editions of *San Kuo Yen I* or *Stories of Three Kingdoms* Printed in Hokkien Province [In Japanese] 三國演義版本試探—建安諸本お中心に." *Shukan Toyogaku* 61 (May 1989): 43–64.

King, Gail Oman. *The Story of Hua Guansuo.* Tempe: Arizona State University Center for Chinese Studies, 1989.

Ko, Yu-sang고유상. *Sam Guk Chi* 삼국지. Seoul: Pakmun Sôkwan, 1917.

Krutch, Joseph Wood. "The Tragic Fallacy." In *European Theories of the Drama,* edited by Barrett Clark, 520–21. New York: Crown, 1965.

Lau, D. C. *Confucius's Analects.* Hong Kong: Chinese University Press, 1983.

———. *Mencius.* Hong Kong: Chinese University Press, 1984.

Let's Learn English through the Comic Book: Three Kingdoms 만화를 보면서 배우는 영어 삼국지. Seoul: Ijibuk, 2002.

Li, Chunxiang 李春祥. "Yuandai de Sanguo xi ji qi dui *Sanguo yanyi* de yingxiang 元代的三國戲及其對三國演義的影響." In Editorial Section, *Sanguo yanyi yanjiu ji,* 343–60.

Li, Hua. *Chinese Woodcuts.* Beijing: Foreign Languages Press, 1995.

Li, Zhongcheng 黎中城.. Interview by Elizabeth Wichmann-Walczak. Shanghai, December 13, 1995.

———. Interviews by Elizabeth Wichmann-Walczak. Shanghai, April 3 and May 8, 1996.

Lin, Yutang. *My Country and My People.* New York: Halcyon House, 1938.

Liu, Cunren 劉存仁. "Luo Guanzhong jiangshi xiaoshuo zhi zhenwei xingzhi 羅貫中講史小說之真偽性質." *Xianggang Zhongwen Daxue Zhongguo wenhua yanjiusuo xuebao.* 8, no. 1 (December 1976): 169–234.

Liu, Ling 劉玲. "Yingxiong renwu quefa yingxiong qizhi 英雄人物缺乏英雄氣質." *Dazhong dianshi* 3 (1995): 70.

Liu, Shangsheng 劉上生. *Zhongguo gudai xiaoshuo yishu shi* 中國古代小說藝術史. Changsha: Hunan shifan daxue chubanshe, 1993.

Liu, Shide 劉世德, ed. *Zhongguo gudai xiaoshuo yanjiu* 中國古代小說研究. Shanghai: Shanghai guji chubanshe, 1983.

Liu, Xinxin 劉欣欣. "Zuihao you zimu 最好有字幕." *Dazhong dianshi* 3 (1995): 69.

Liu, Yiguo 劉益國. "Tan *Sanguo zhi tongsu yanyi* zhong Zhuge Liang xingxiang de xingcheng he suzao 談三國志通俗演義中諸葛亮形象的形成和形成和塑造." In Editorial Section, *Sanguo yanyi yanjiu ji,* 197–210.

Lo, Andrew Hingbun. "*San-kuo-chih Yen-I* and *Shui-hu chuan* in the Context of Historiography: An Interpretative Study." PhD diss. Princeton, 1981.

Lu, Bi 盧弼. *Sanguo zhi jijie* 三國志集解. 1957. Reprint, Beijing: Zhonghua shuju, 1982.

Lu, Xun 魯迅. *Zhongguo xiaoshuo shi lue* 中國小說史略. Hong Kong: Sanlian Shuju, 1958.

Luo, Guanzhong 羅貫中. *Sanguo yanyi* 三國演義. Beijing: Zuojia chubanshe, 1953.

———. *Sanguo Yanyi.* Hong Kong: Xianggang Youlian chuban youxian gongsi, 1969.

———. *Sanguo zhi tongsu yanyi* 三國志通俗演義. Shanghai: Shanghai guji chubanshe, 1980.

———. *Sanguo zhi yanyi* 三國志演義. Hong Kong: Shangwu yinshuguan, 1962.

Ma, Ke 馬科. Interviews by Elizabeth Wichmann-Walczak. Shanghai, November 3, 1995; Beijing, December 2 and 6, 1995.

———. Telephone interview by Elizabeth Wichmann-Walczak. Honolulu and Shanghai, November 15, 1997.

McLaren, Anne E. "Chantefables and the Textual Evolution of the *San-Kuo-Chih Yen-I*." *T'oung Pao* 71 (1985): 159–227.

———. *Chinese Popular Culture and Ming Chantefables*. Leiden: E. J. Brill, 1998.

———. "Ming Audiences and Vernacular Hermeneutics: The Uses of *The Romance of the Three Kingdoms*." *T'oung Pao* 81 (1995): 51–80.

McLuhan, Marshall. *Gutenberg Galaxy*. Toronto: University of Toronto Press, 1962.

Mukerji, Chandra, and Michael Schudson. "Popular Culture." *Annual Review of Sociology* 12 (1986): 47–66.

Nakagawa, Satoshi 中川諭. "A Study of Several Editions of *San-kuo yen-I* 三國演義版本の研究." *Shukan Toyogaku* 61 (May 1989): 65–84.

Neuman, W. Russell. "Television and American Culture: The Mass Medium and the Pluralist Audience." *Public Opinion Quarterly* 46 (1982): 471–487.

Ogawa, Tamaki 小川環樹. *Chugoku shosetsu shi no kenkyu* 中國小説史の研究. Tokyo: Iwanami Shoten, 1968.

———. "*Sanguo yanyi de yanbian* 三國演義的演變." Translated by Hu Tianmin 胡天民. *Sanguo yanyi xuekan* 1 (1985): 323–34.

Ong, Lijun 翁麗君. Interview by Elizabeth Wichmann-Walczak. Beijing, November 26, 1995.

Pak, Kôn-hûi 박건희. *Sam Guk Chi* 삼국지. Seoul: Chosôn Sôkwan, 1913.

Pak, Kyông-min 박경민. *Digital Sam Guk Chi* [In Korean.] Seoul: Asea Munhwasa, 2000.

Pak, Yông 박영. *Sam Guk Chi* 삼국지. Seoul: Taehyôn, 2000.

Pak, Yông-Kyu 박영규. *After the Three Kingdoms*. [In Korean.] Seoul: Tûlnyôk, 1999.

———. *Three Kingdoms* 삼국지. Seoul: Min'ûmsa, 2002.

Pan, Lüsheng 潘魯生, and Tang Jialu 唐家路. *Nianhua* 年畫. Shanghai: Shanghai renmin yishu chubanshe chubanxing, n.d.

Pang, Ki-hwan 방기환. *Sam Guk Chi* 삼국지. Seoul: Samhûisa, 1977.

Paolucci, Anne, and Henry Paolucci, eds. *Hegel on Tragedy*. New York: Anchor Books, 1962.

Phan, Anh-Thu. "China Seen as Market and Maker of Games." *South China Morning Post*, January 18, 2002, 12.

———. "Developer to Put Growth Plans into Play; Firm Prepares for Move into Lucrative Online Market Showcasing Role-Playing Games with Chinese Historical Themes." *South China Morning Post*, January 18, 2002, 17.

Plaks, Andrew H. *The Four Masterworks of the Ming Novel*. Princeton, NJ: Princeton University Press, 1987.

Qian, Mu 錢穆. *Zhongguo zhishifenzi* 中國知識分子. Hong Kong: Zhongguo wenti chubanshe, 1951.

Qian, Yuping 錢玉萍. *Zhongguo gudian wenxue* 中國古典文學. Beijing: Beijing Education College Press, 1987.

Qiu, Zhensheng 邱振聲. *Sanguo yanyi zongheng tan* 三國演義縱橫談. Beijing: Beijing Daxue chubanshe, 1995.

———. "Wangu yunxiao yi yu mao—Zhuge Liang yishu xingxiang de shengming li 萬古雲霄一羽毛—諸葛亮藝術形象的生命力." *Wenxue Pinglun* 1 (1985): 123–131.

Qiu, Zhensheng and Liu Mingtao 劉名濤. "Wangu yunxiao yi yu mao 萬古雲霄一羽毛." In *Sanguo yanyi lunwen ji* 三国演义论文集, edited by Henan Sheng shehui kexue yuan wenxue yanjiu suo, 101–18, Zhengzhou: Zhongzhou guji chubanshe, 1985.

Ren, Sha 任沙. "Guodu fancha zaocheng shizhen 過度反差造成失真." *Dazhong dianshi* 2 (1995):71.

Ricco, Barry D. "Popular Culture and High Culture: Dwight MacDonald, His Critics and the Ideal of Cultural Hierarchy in Modern America." *Journal of American Culture* 16, no. 4 (1993): 7–18.

Riftin, Boris (Li Fuqing 李福清). *Sanguo yanyi yu minjian wenxue chuantong* 三國演義與民間文學傳統. Shanghai: Shanghai guji chubanshe, 1997.

Roberts, Moss, trans. *Three Kingdoms: A Historical Novel.* Berkeley and Los Angeles: University of California Press; and Beijing: Foreign Language Press, 1991.

———. *Three Kingdoms, A Historical Novel.* Attributed to Luo Guanzhong; Abridged ed. Berkeley and Los Angeles: University of California Press; Beijing: Foreign Languages Press, 1999.

Rong, Fan 榮繁. "Cao Cao, yige zhenshi de fuza renwu 曹操, 一個真實的複雜人物." *Dazhong dianshi* 2 (1995): 68.

Roy, David T. "How to Read the *Romance of the Three Kingdoms*." In *How to Read the Chinese Novel* edited by David L. Rolston, 152–95. Princeton, NJ: Princeton University Press, 1990.

Ruan, Yuanyuan 阮圓圓. "Rang lishi zoujin women 讓歷史走近我們." *Dazhong dianshi* 6 (1995): 20.

Rudova, Maria. *Chinese Popular Prints.* Leningrad: Aurora Publishers, 1988.

Sam Guk Chi Dictionary (Sam Guk Chi sajôn 삼국지 사전). Seoul: Pôm'usa, 2000.

Sanguozhi pinghua 三國志平話. Jian'an: 1321–23. Facsimile reprinted in *Quanxiang pinghua wuzhong* 全相平話五種. Shanghai: Gudian wenxue chubanshe, 1955.

Schimmelpfennig, Michael. "*The Three Kingdoms:* A Historical Novel." *China Review International* 8, no. 1 (2001): 215–218.

Sewall, Richard. *The Vision of Tragedy.* New Haven, CT: Yale University Press, 1959.

Shang, Changrong 尚長榮. Interviews by Elizabeth Wichmann-Walczak. Shanghai, November 8 and 13, 1995; Beijing, November 30 and December 3, 1995.

———. Interview by Elizabeth Wichmann-Walczak. Shanghai, May 2, 1996.

———. Telephone interview by Elizabeth Wichmann-Walczak. Honolulu and Shanghai, May 15, 1997.

———. Telephone interviews by Elizabeth Wichmann-Walczak. Honolulu and Shanghai, December 14 and June 6, 1998.

————. Telephone interview by Elizabeth Wichmann-Walczak. Honolulu and Shanghai, February 1 and June 2, 1999.

Shanghai Jingju Yuan (Shanghai Jingju Company 上海京劇院). "Jingju Zou Xiang Qingnian: Shanghai Jingju Yuan Xunhui Zhanyan 京劇走向青年：上海京劇院巡迴展演" (Jingju moves toward the youth: Shanghai Jingju Company's Touring Exhibition Performances). *Beijing Zhanyan Shuoming Shu* 北京展演說明書 Performance program/playbill for Beijing tour, November 1995.

Shen, Bojun 沈伯俊. *Jiaoli ben Sanguo Yanyi* 校理本三國演義. Jiangsu: Jiangsu guji chubanshe, 1992.

————. *Sanguo Manhua* 三國漫話. Chengdu: Sichuan renmin chubanshe, 2000.

————. *Sanguo Mantan* 三國漫談. Chengdu: Bashu shushe, 1995.

————. "*Sanguo* renwu shu geng duo 三國人物數更多." *Sichuan Ribao*, June 23, 1984, 3.

————. "*Sanguo yanyi* jiujing xie le duoshao renwu 三國演義究竟寫了多少人物." *Renmin Ribao*, Overseas Edition, April 24, 1992.

————, and Tan Liangxiao 譚良嘯, eds. *Sanguo yanyi cidian* 三國演義詞典. Chengdu: Bashu shushe, 1989.

Sheng, He. "Regulating Media Violence." *China Daily*, February 22, 2002.

Silverstone, Roger. *The Message of Television: Myth and Narrative in Contemporary Culture.* London: Heinemann Educational, 1981.

Sima, Guang 司馬光. *Zizhi tongjian* 資治通鑒. Beijing: Zhonghua shuju, 1956.

Takahashi, Shigeki 高橋繁樹. "Shokatsu ryoo *Hakuboo shuuten* no kosatsu—Sankoku Heiwa to Sankoku Zatsugeki '諸葛亮博望燒屯' の考察三國平話と三國雜劇." *Chugoku koten kenkyu* 20 (1975): 158–71.

Tan, Liangxiao 譚良嘯. "Zhuge Liang fushi lun kao 諸葛亮服飾論考." *Shehui kexue yanjiu* 5 (1994): 93–97.

Tanaka, Issei. "The Social and Historical Context of Ming-Ch'ing Local Drama." In Johnson, Nathan, and Rawski, *Popular Culture in Late Imperial China*, 143–60.

Tillman, Hoyt Cleveland. *Confucian Discourse and Chu Hsi's Ascendancy.* Honolulu: University of Hawaii Press, 1992.

————. "One Significant Rise in Chu-ko Liang's Popularity: An Impact of the 1127 Jurchen Conquest." *Chinese Studies (Hanxue yanjiu)* 14, no. 2 (December 1996): 1–34.

————. "Reassessing Du Fu's Line on Zhuge Liang." *Monumenta Serica: Journal of Oriental Studies* 50 (2002): 295–313.

————. (Tian Hao 田浩). "Shixue yu wenhua sixiang: Sima Guang dui Zhuge Liang gushi de chongjian 史學與文化思想：司馬光對諸葛亮故事的重建." *Lishi Yuyan Yanjiusuo jikan* (Bulletin of the Institute of History and Philology, Academia Sinica) 73, no. 1 (March 2002): 165–98.

————. "Zhongguo lishi yishi zhong de Zhuge Liang 中國歷史意識中的諸葛亮." In *Zhou Qin Han Tang kaogu yu wenhua guoji xueshu huiyi lunwenji* 周秦漢唐考古與文化國際學術論文集, 133–46. Xi'an: Xibeidaxue xuebao bianjibu, 1988.

Tu, Yaming 涂亞明. "Dianshi lianxu ju Sanguo Yanyi zhiwai de gushi 電視連續劇三國演義之外的故事." *Dazhong dianshi* 8 (1994): 4–7.

Ueda, Nozomi 上田望. "*Sangoku Engi* hanbon shiron 三國演義版本試論." *Toyo bunka* 71 (1990): 151–189.

Van Den Bulck, Hilde. "Public Service Television and National Identity as a Project of Modernity: The Example of Flemish." *Media, Culture & Society* 23 (2001): 53–69.

Vygotskii, Lev Semenovich. *Thought and Language.* Cambridge, MA: MIT Press, 1962.

Wang, Bomin 王伯敏. *Zhongguo banhuashi* 中國版畫史. Shanghai: Shanghai renmin meishu chubanshe, 1981.

Wang, Bomin and Bo Songnian 薄松年. *Chinese New Year Prints.* Beijing: Cultural Relics Publishing House, 1995.

Wang, Fang 王芳. "Shi nian jian xin 十年艱辛." *Dazhong dianshi* 11 (1995): 4–6 and 12 (1995): 18–21.

Wang, Jilie, 王季烈 ed., *Guben Yuan Ming zaju* 孤本元明雜劇. Shanghai: Shangwu Yinshuguan, 1938.

Wang, Ling 王玲. *Zhongguo Wenxue Mingzhu* 中國文學名著. Tianjing: Tianjing People's Press, 1991.

Wang, Luning 王魯寧. *Zhongguo gudian xiaoshuo zai haiwai* 中國古典小說在海外. Beijing: Kelin Press, 1988.

Ward, Barbara E. "Not Merely Players: Drama, Art and Ritual in Traditional China." *Man,* n.s., vol. 14, no.1 (1979), 18–39.

———. "Regional Operas and Their Audiences." In Johnson, Nathan, and Rawski, *Popular Culture in Late Imperial China,* 161–87.

West, Christopher (Wei An 魏安). *Sanguo yanyi banben kao* 三國演義版本考. Shanghai: Shanghai guji, 1996.

West, Stephen. "Text and Ideology: Ming Editors and Northern Drama." In *Ming Qing xiqu guoji yantao hui lunwen ji* 明清戲曲國際研討會論文集, Hua, Wei 華瑋 and Wang, Ailing 王璦玲, 237–83. Taipei: Zhongyang yanjiuyuan, 1998.

Who's Who in Sam Guk Chi (Sam Guk Chi inmul sajŏn 삼국지 인물 사전). Seoul: Tŭlnyŏk, 2000.

Wichmann, Elizabeth. *Listening to Theater: The Aural Dimension of Beijing Opera.* Honolulu: University of Hawaii Press, 1991.

———. "Tradition and Innovation in Contemporary Beijing Opera Performance." *Drama Review* 34, no. 1. (Spring 1990): 146–78.

———. "'Reform' at the Shanghai Jingju Company and Its Impact on Creative Authority and Repertory." *Drama Review* 44, no. 4 (Winter 2000.): 96–119.

Willet, John. *The Theatre of Bertolt Brecht: A Study from Eight Aspects.* New York: New Directions, 1959.

Woiwode, Larry. "Television: The Cyclops That Eats Books." *USA Today,* (March 1, 1993, 84 (2).

Xiao, Xiong 肖雄. "Tan dianshi lianxu ju *Sangguo yanyi* de wushu biaoyan 談電視連續劇三國演義的武術表演." *Dazhong dianshi* 1 (1995): 62.

Xu, Qinjun 徐沁君, ed. *Xinjiao Yuankan zaju sanshizhong* 新校元刊雜劇三十種. Beijing: Zhonghua shuju, 1980.

Yan, Yan 嚴衍. *Zizhi tongjian bu* 資治通鑒補. China: Sheng shi si bu lou, 1876.

Yang, Chu-dong 양주동. *Sam Guk Chi* 삼국지. Seoul: Chinsun Sôkwan, 1976.

Yang, Hsien-yi, and Gladys Yang, trans. *A Brief History of Chinese Fiction* by Lu Xun. Westport, CT: Hyperion, 1973.

Yang, Jialuo 楊家駱, ed. *Quan Yuan zaju sanbian* 全元雜劇三編. Taipei: Shijie shuju, 1973.

Yang, Jianying 揚劍英. "Zuihao neng shiyong geng tongsu yidong de yuyan 最好能使用通俗易懂的語言." *Dazhong dianshi* 1 (1995): 61.

Yang, Winston L.Y. "The Literary Transformation of Historical Figures in the *San-kuo chih yen-i*: A Study of the Use of the *San-kuo chih* as a Source of the *San-kuo chih yen-i*." In *Critical Essays on Chinese Fiction*, edited by Winston L.Y. Yang and Curtis P. Adkins, 45–84. Hong Kong: Chinese University Press, 1980.

Yang, Zhifang 楊志芳. "Gudian zuopin de younan 古典作品的幽難." *Dazhong dianshi* 3 (1995): 70.

Ye, Weisi 葉維四, and Xin Mao 冒炘. *Sanguo yanyi chuangzuo lun* 三國演義創作論. Jiangsu: Jiangsu renmin chubanshe, 1984.

Yi, Chu-wan 이주완. *Sam Guk Chi* 삼국지. Seoul: Yôngp'ung Sôkwan, 1918.

Yi, Hang-kyu 이항규. *One Volume Sam Guk Chi* [In Korean.] Seoul: Tonghae, 2000.

Yi, Hûi-jae 이희재. *Manhwa Sam Guk Chi* 만화 삼국지 *The Comic Book: Three Kingdoms*. Seoul: Aiseum, 2002.

Yi, In-kwang 이인광. *Sam Guk Chi* 삼국지. Seoul: Pakmun Sôkwan, 1926.

Yi, Kye-sông 이계성. *Sam Guk Chi* 삼국지. Seoul: Sôul Munhwasa, 1999.

Yi, Man-su 이만수. *Let's Learn One Thousand Chinese Characters in "Three Kingdoms".* [In Korean.] Seoul: Uriduri, 2004.

Yi, Mun-yôl 이문열. *The Romance of Three Kingdoms.* [In Korean.] Seoul: Minûmsa, 1999.

———. *Three Kingdoms* [In Korean.] Seoul: Min'ûmsa, 2002.

———. "*Three Kingdoms* Is Worth Reading" [In Korean.] *Han'guk ilbo* (*Han'guk Daily*), November 22, 2002.

Yi, Sông-hak 이성학. *Sam Guk Chi* 삼국지. Seoul: Sônjin Munhwasa, 1958.

Yuan, Hong 袁宏. *Hou Han ji jiaozhu* 後漢紀校注. Edited by Zhou Tianyou 周天游. Tianjin: Tianjin guji chubanshe, 1987.

Zhang, Ying 張穎, and Su Chen 陳速. "Youguan *Sanguo yanyi* chengshu niandai he banben yanbian wenti de jidian yiyi 有關三國演義成書年代和版本演變問題的幾點異議." In *Ming Qing xiaoshuo yanjiu* 5, 26–40. Beijing: Zhongguo Wenlian chuban gongsi, 1987.

Zhang, Zhenjun 張振軍. *Chuantong xiaoshuo yu Zhongguo wenhua* 傳統小說與中國文化. Guangxi: Guangxi shifan daxue chubanshe, 1996.

Zhao, Fanglin 趙方林. "Bao Guo'an banyan Cao Cao de xu rusheng 鮑國安扮演曹操的栩如生." *Dazhong dianshi* 3 (1995): 69.

Zhao, Guanpeng 趙關鵬. "Tang Guoqiang de jiechu biaoyan 唐國強的杰出表演." *Dazhong dianshi* 2 (1995): 69.

Zhao, Haiying 趙海鷹. "Leisheng da, yudian xiao: Sanguo Yanyi zhong de renwu 雷聲大，雨點小：電視劇三國演義中的人物." *Dazhong dianshi* 1 (1995): 61.

Zheng, Qian 鄭騫, ed. *Jiaoding Yuankan zaju sanshizhong* 校訂元刊雜劇三十種. Taipei: Shijie Shuju, 1962.

Zheng, Zhenduo 鄭振鐸. "*Sanguo yanyi de yanhua*三國演義的演化." *Xiaoshuo yuebao* 20, no. 10 (October 1929.): 1548–78.

———. *Zhongguo Wenxue Yanjiu* 中國文學研究. Vol. 1. Beijing: Zuojia chubanshe, 1957.

Zheng Zhenduo Wenji 鄭振鐸文集. Beijing: Renmin wenxue chubanshe, 1988.

Zhong, H. "Battle of the Books." *China Daily*, July 19, 2002.

Zhongguo Xiju Jia Xiehui 中國戲劇家協會 (Chinese Theater Artists Association). "Cao Cao yu Yang Xiu de biaoyan yishu 曹操與楊修 的表演" [Cao Cao and Yang Xiu's Performance Art.] *Beijing Zuotan Hui* 北京座談會. A symposium held December 7, 1995. Citations are from notes taken by Elizabeth Wichmann-Walczak.

Zhou, Zhaoxin 周兆新, ed. *Sanguo yanyi congkao* 三國演義叢考. Beijing: Beijing University Press, 1995.

———. *Sanguo yanyi kaoping* 三國演義考評. Beijing: Beijing Daxue chubanshe, 1990.

———. "Yuan Ming shidai Sanguo gushi de duo zhong xingtai 元明時代三國故事的多種形態." In Zhaoxin Zhou, *Sanguo yanyi congkao*, 301–46.

Zhu, Dan 朱刑. "Jiegou jianjie xingge shengdong 結構簡潔性格生動." *Dazhong dianshi* 1 (1995): 60.

———. "Shi wei xiang yu buxiang zhijian 試為象與不象之間." *Dazhong dianshi* 4 (1995): 69.

Zhu, L. "Real Life Stories Mirror Social Life." *China Daily*, 11 January 2002.

Zhu, Xi 朱熹. *Yupi Zizhi tongjian gangmu* 御批資治通鑒綱目. *Yingyin Wenyuange Siku quan shu* 影印文淵閣四庫全書. Vols. 689–691. Taipei: Taiwan shangwu yinshuguan, 1983.

———. *Zhuzi wenji* 朱子文集. Taipei: Yunchen wenhua chubanshe, 2000.

Zhu, Xiawen. 朱霞雯. "Xingshen jiebei: Lun Bao Guo'an banyan de Cao Cao 形神皆備:論鮑國安扮演的曹操." *Dazhong dianshi* 1 (1995): 70.

Zhui baiqiu 綴白裘. Beijing: Zhonghua Shuju, 1955.

Zuo, Hanzhong 左漢中, ed. *Minjian jianzhi mubanhua* 民間剪紙木板畫. Changsha: Hunan meishu chubanshe 1995.

Contributors

Kimberly Besio, associate professor of East Asian Studies (Chinese), Colby College, is a graduate of the University of Hawaii at Manoa, and received her MA and PhD from the University of California at Berkeley. Her research interests center on traditional Chinese fiction and drama, and gender construction in premodern China. She has published articles related to these topics in *Ming Studies, CHINO-PERL, Journal of Sung-Yuan Studies,* and *Journal of the Economic and Social History of the Orient.*

Dominic Cheung, alias Chang Ts'o, is professor and chair of the Department of East Asian Languages and Cultures at the University of Southern California. His English publications include *Feng Chih: A Critical Study* (Boston: Twayne Publishers, 1979), *The Isle Full of Noises: Modern Chinese Poetry from Taiwan* (New York: Columbia University Press, 1987), *Exiles and Native Sons: Modern Short Stories from Taiwan,* coedited with Michelle Yeh (Taipei: National Institute for Compilation and Translation, 1992), and *Drifting,* a volume of selected poems, (Los Angeles: Green Integer, 2000). A well-known Chinese poet, he has also published 14 volumes of modern poetry in Chinese.

George A. Hayden received his BA degree from Pomona College, and his MA and PhD in Chinese language and literature from Stanford University. His publications include *Crime and Punishment in Medieval Chinese Drama: Three Judge Pao Plays* and articles on *Shui hu zhuan* and the rhymes and pronunciation of Ming drama. He has taught Chinese language and literature and East Asian culture at Pomona College and the University of Kansas, and at the University of Southern California since 1973.

Junhao Hong is an associate professor in the Department of Communication at the State University of New York at Buffalo. He received his PhD in Radio, Film, and Television from the University of Texas, Austin. His research interests include international and intercultural communication, media and society, and new communication technology.

Jinhee Kim teaches Korean and comparative literature at the University of Southern California, Los Angeles. She received her PhD in comparative literature from Indiana University. Her principal research interests, which initially focused on modern Korean literature and literary theories culminated in her PhD dissertation, "Disembodying the Other: Studies of East-West Relations and Modern Korean Drama." The range of her academic interests has extended to Korean American literature and Korean cinema. She has published numerous articles in each field. She is the author of *Korean Drama under Japanese Occupation: Plays by Ch'i-jin Yu and Man-sik Ch'ae* (2004) and *Plays of Colonial Korea: Se-Dôk Ham* (forthcoming in 2005). She is currently working on a manuscript entitled *Voice from Afar: Critical Essays of Korean American Literature*. A community activist, she is serving as the executive director of the Los Angeles Korean International Film Festival (www. lakiff.com), which she founded in 2003.

Catherine Pagani received her PhD in art history from the University of Toronto, and teaches art history at the University of Alabama. Specializing in East Asian art history, Professor Pagani has published on subjects that include opium paraphernalia, Japanese woodblock prints, and rural Chinese textiles. Her *Eastern Magnificence and European Ingenuity: Clocks of Late Imperial China* was published by the University of Michigan Press.

Moss Roberts is professor of Chinese at New York University. He is the translator of the classical novel *Three Kingdoms* (*Sanguo yanyi*), copublished by University of California Press and China's Foreign Languages Press. His translation of *Three Kingdoms* in fact inspired the idea of an international colloquium on Three Kingdoms culture, held in Sichuan. He is also the editor and translator of *Chinese Fairy Tales and Fantasies* (New York: Parthenon, 1979) and translator of *Dao De Jing: The Book of the Way* (Berkeley: University of California Press, 2001)

Bojun Shen is a graduate of the Department of Foreign Languages, Sichuan University. He joined the Research Institute of Literature of Sichuan Social Sciences Institute after finishing first in the Institute's competitive recruiting examination. He is now director of the Research Institute of Literature. Shen is also secretary general and deputy director of the standing committee of the *Sanguo yanyi* (*Three Kingdoms*) Association of China, and director of the Three Kingdoms Cultural Studies Institute of Sichuan. He has published numerous book length studies on the novel *Sanguo yanyi*, and is recognized as a leading authority on the study of *Sanguo yanyi*.

Hoyt Cleveland Tillman received his PhD from Harvard University and is Professor of history at Arizona State University. He is the author of *Confucian Discourse and Chu Hsi's Ascendancy* (Cambridge, MA: Harvard University Press, 1992); *Utilitarian Confucianism: Ch'en Liang's Challenge to Chu Hsi* (Cambridge, MA: Harvard University Press, 1982); *Ch'en Liang on Public Interest and the Law* (Honolulu: University of Hawaii Press, 1994); *Zhu Xi de siwei shijie* (Chu Hsi's World of Thought) (Taipei and Xi'an: yunchew wenhua 2002); coeditor with Stephen H. West of *China under Jurchen Rule: Essays on Chin Intellectual and Cultural History* (Albany: State University of New York Press, 1995); and author of over forty articles in referred journal and books.

Constantine Tung received his PhD from Claremont Graduate University. He has taught at the State University of New York at Buffalo, Pomona College, and the University of California at Santa Barbara. His research interests have been in modern and contemporary Chinese drama and war fiction, and he has published articles in *Modern Drama, Comparative Drama, Educational Theatre Journal, Journal of Chinese Studies,* and others. He was the chief organizer on the U.S. side of the conference, "The Historical, Fictional, Theatrical and Artistic Three Kingdoms: A Sino-American Colloquium," which produced this volume of essays.

Elizabeth Wichmann-Walczak is professor of Asian theater at the University of Hawaii at Manoa, where she writes on the aesthetics of *jingju* and their evolution, and translates, produces, and directs English-language *jingju* productions. She is the first non-Chinese to perform *jingju* in the People's Republic of China, and holds numerous Chinese awards for *jingju* research, creation, and performance. She is also the first honorary and the first non-Chinese member of the National Xiqu Institute, and of the Jiangsu and Shanghai branches of the Chinese Theater Artists Association.

Jiyuan Yu, associate professor of philosophy, teaches Greek philosophy and Chinese philosophy at the State University of New York at Buffalo and was a research fellow of philosophy at Oxford University. He was appointed Fellow at the National Humanities Center at the Chapel Hill-Durham-Raleigh research triangle in North Carolina for the year of 2002–3. He is the coauthor (with Nicholas Bunnin) of *The Blackwell Dictionary of Western Philosophy* (Malden, MA: Blackwell, 2004), coeditor (with Jorge Garcia) of *Rationality and Happiness: From the Ancient to the Early Medievals* (Rochester, NY: University of Rochester Press, 2003), and guest editor of *Ethics in Greek Philosophy and Chinese Philosophy* for a special issue of the *Journal of Chinese Philosophy* (September 2002).

Index